The Man behind the Beard

The Man behind the Beard

*Deneys Schreiner,
a South African Liberal Life*

Graham Dominy

UNIVERSITY OF KWAZULU-NATAL PRESS

Published in 2020 by University of KwaZulu-Natal Press
Private Bag X01
Scottsville, 3201
Pietermaritzburg
South Africa
Email: books@ukzn.ac.za
Website: www.ukznpress.co.za

© 2020 Graham Dominy

All rights reserved. No part of this publication may be reproduced or transmitted in any form or by electrical or mechanical means, including information storage and retrieval systems, without prior permission in writing from the publishers.

ISBN: 978 1 86914 444 9
e-ISBN 978 1 86914 445 6

Managing Editor: Elana Bregin
Editor: Alison Lockhart
Layout: Patricia Comrie
Proofreader: Catherine Munro
Indexer: Judith Shier
Cover origination: Kita Stevens
Cover design: MDesign

Typeset in 11pt Garamond

Printed and bound by Creda Communications, Cape Town

For Else Schreiner (1922–2018), the inspiration for this book.
In Memoriam

Old man with the white beard and twinkling eyes
Do you walk with me in spirit
Or only in the faded prints of old photographs
and the stories that we tell and retell and reinvent?
Now that your burned bones have sunk to the seafloor
Settled into the buried urn in the family plot
Is your mind at rest too
Or does it pace at night on the long legs of infinite existence?
— Barbara Schreiner, 'Death' in *Three-Peace*

Contents

Photo insert between pages 108 and 109

Foreword by Blade Nzimande	ix
Preface	xv
Acknowledgements	xix

Introduction: Almost to the Top of the 'Greasy Pole'		1
1	Beginnings	8
2	From Boyhood to Battle via Wits (1923–42)	23
3	'Up North': The Army and the Shaping of His Character (1943–5)	34
4	Science and Romance: The Cambridge Years (1945–51)	50
5	Research on a Cold War Campus: Pennsylvania State College (1951–2)	65
6	Launch into Liberalism and Academia: Johannesburg (1953–9)	76
7	Science Faculty and Family: Pietermaritzburg (1959–75)	88
8	Academy and Activism (1959–75)	109
9	Pietermaritzburg Vice Principal: Challenges and Tragedy (1976–87)	124
10	Vice Principal: Protests and Political Engagement (1976–80)	142

11 'Toughest One Yet for Prof Schreiner': The Buthelezi Commission (1980–2)	153
12 Aftermath of the Buthelezi Commission Report: Deneys's Predictions Fulfilled (1982–7)	172
13 Jennifer's Trial and Retirement Years (1987–2008)	183
Conclusion: Drawing the Strands Together	196
Select Bibliography	200
Index	210

Foreword

I think it would be proper for all those who knew or worked with Deneys Schreiner, and his dear wife Else, to thank Graham Dominy for this biography. In this book, Graham is doing what I have personally known him for, as a friend to the Schreiners, a historian and archivist, but most importantly, as an activist for a democratic South Africa. Not only should the story of Deneys be told because he belonged to the illustrious Schreiner family of social activists, but also because of his own role at critical periods in the history of our country and his contribution to the inauguration of a democratic South Africa.

An insightful historical account of the life and times of Deneys Schreiner, *The Man behind the Beard* offers far more than the title suggests. In his introduction, Graham points out: 'Deneys lived in a world of connections, academic and personal, national and international' and it is these connections he explores in fine detail here.

Graham first met Deneys in 1972 as a first-year student at the University of Natal, Pietermaritzburg. Deneys, a Cambridge-trained research scientist with teaching experience in the United States, was working as a professor in chemistry and ended his academic career as vice principal at the Pietermaritzburg campus of the University of Natal.

I was born and grew up in KwaDambuza, Pietermaritzburg. I received my secondary education at Georgetown High School in Edendale, also in Pietermaritzburg. My roots and life in the city furnished the basis for my connection with the Schreiners, which was deepened in my work with Deneys's eldest daughter, Jennifer, fondly known as Jenny. I served with Jenny as a member and leader of the South African Communist Party (SACP) and the African National Congress (ANC) for decades.

As Graham suggests, Pietermaritzburg was unusual during apartheid in that the oppressive regime's Group Areas Act (which enforced spatial racial segregation and curtailed freedom of movement and contact between different races) was not enforced fully in the city. Why? Edendale, the large township in the area, was established in 1851 as a mission station. This facilitated the movement of missionaries and thus connections between people of all races in the area. African intellectuals, whom many looked up to, played a crucial, engaging role in these connections. Among them were Henry Selby Msimang and Archibald 'Archie' Jacob Gumede.

Msimang was a founding member of the ANC, editor of *Morumioa-Inxusa-Messenger*, and key labour movement organiser, among other numerous roles he played during his lifetime. Gumede, son of Josiah Tshangana Gumede (ANC president from 1927 to 1930), was a high-profile ANC activist in his own right. He worked closely with Harry Gwala, affectionately known as the 'Lion of the Midlands', a senior stalwart of the SACP and the ANC. He also met and became closely associated with Moses Mabhida, SACP general secretary from 1979 to 1986, and Albert Luthuli, ANC president from 1952 to 1967.

Graham traces three generations of the Schreiners before Deneys, starting in the 1800s with Gottlob Schreiner, son of a well-established German cobbler. Deneys belonged to the fourth generation after Gottlob. The book ends with the fifth generation of Schreiners.

Trained as a missionary, Gottlob Schreiner went from Germany to the United Kingdom (UK). He received further training and married Rebecca Lyndall in the UK before leaving for South Africa. The second generation of the Schreiners includes William Philip (WP) Schreiner. Born to Gottlob and Rebecca, WP became part of the colonial administrative bloc in South Africa. He became the prime minister of the Cape Colony, senator in the first parliament of the Union of South Africa and, during the First World War, high commissioner to the UK.

This brings us to one of the crucial points in Graham's book. He draws our attention to what could be a profound analytical description of colonial expansion. The Zulu king, Cetshwayo kaMpande, is attributed to have said: 'First came the traders, then the missionaries, then the red soldier.' This aphorism calls for more research on the role played by all forms of social organisation, including the religious sector, particularly what the book refers to as the 'spiritual wing of imperialism', in pushing colonialism, apartheid and imperialism, and thus the economic exploitation of one human being or group by another.

Gottlob and WP Schreiner were, however, not conservatives. In their own ways they challenged various aspects of the colonial system from within. What could be characterised as a tendency of rebellion against the system often led to their being isolated in their respective roles. Their actions frequently contradicted the system and those of its conservative loyalists. Gottlob and WP thus developed a different world view from most white people around them. The overall trajectory this articulated formed the basis of a liberal line of development in the history of the Schreiners. This increasingly brought the Schreiners into conflict with the colonial and apartheid regimes and conservatives. For instance, WP, a lawyer, led the defence team in the trial of Dinizulu kaCetshwayo, 'son of the last independent Zulu king'. This was 'on spurious treason charges for allegedly encouraging the Bambatha rebellion' – one of the most courageous anti-colonial struggles fought by the African people.

After WP came the generation of Deneys and, of course, Deneys himself, the heart of the book. Deneys expanded what I characterise above as the Schreiners' tendency to rebel against the colonial and apartheid order, which became a greater struggle against the system. His was a strong and far-reaching disagreement with the colonial and apartheid regime, campaigning for desegregation within the framework of a liberal world view. Deneys grew his beard in opposition to segregation and in pushing the struggle for a common voters' roll.

While Deneys was pushing the struggle for a common voters' roll, other liberals argued for the so-called qualified franchise. The latter was defeated in the negotiations that took place in the 1990s, largely as a result of decades of liberation struggle fought mainly by forces led by the ANC, SACP, progressive trade union and civic movements and other progressive sections of South African society from different walks of life.

Deneys's daughter Jenny deepened the struggle by introducing a far more radical opposition to the apartheid regime. Rather than liberalism, which the Schreiners saw as the guide to their thinking and conduct, she chose a different path – the pursuit of a revolutionary national and Marxist-Leninist opposition to the regime of colonial and apartheid rule and, of course, to imperialism. She joined the ANC and the SACP and then the military wing, Umkhonto weSizwe, to pursue the armed struggle. She was arrested and imprisoned in 1987.

Jenny's revolutionary path brought the ideological struggle into the Schreiner home, resulting in a battle of ideas with liberalism. Her detention disrupted Deneys's 'gracious slide into a comfortable retirement'. Together with his wife Else, a founding member of the Black Sash and activist in her own right, Deneys, as Graham notes, 'engaged in an all-out campaign to get justice for their daughter and her comrades, a campaign that lasted until 1991, more than a year after Nelson Mandela walked out of the Victor Verster Prison, a free man at last'.

Deneys shaved off his beard only after South Africa held its first democratic general elections on 27 April 1994. He died on the same date in 2008.

Graham's book covers not only the history of the Schreiners, but also the corresponding history of South Africa and key developments in the other countries they lived in. For example, there were edicts during the anti-communist McCarthy-era in the United States when Deneys was there, which required that he swear allegiance to the United States. He 'subtly defied' them.

I first came to know Prof Schreiner as my vice principal in 1980, when, after permission from the Bantu Education Minister, Piet Koornhof, I registered at the then University of Natal's Pietermaritzburg campus for an Honours degree. My study programme was not offered at the University of Zululand, where I had done my undergraduate degree, hence the (always hesitant) granting of an exemption for me to enrol in a university reserved for whites at the time. The University of Natal's Pietermaritzburg campus was about 11 kilometres from my Dambuza home. The year 1980 was a year of the resurgence of mass community struggles that were to culminate in the launch of the United Democratic Front (UDF) in 1983.

Prof Schreiner made us all feel welcome at the institution, especially as black students in a white university at the height of apartheid. We were not allowed to stay in the residences (which he deliberately defied) nor to access some of the facilities in the vicinity of the institution. His overt stance against apartheid made him a father figure to all in the institution in many ways.

In Pietermaritzburg, the early 1980s were the beginnings of the apartheid-sponsored violence in communities like Edendale and Imbali, violence that was falsely projected as black-on-black violence between UDF and Inkatha, so as to hide the hand of the apartheid regime. It was also the period, as Graham correctly points out, in which the apartheid regime was imposing the Tricameral Parliament. I remember Prof Schreiner leading some of the protests by university academics (in full academic regalia) against apartheid repression. And in those protests it was not only his academic cap (which looked very unusual to me at the time) that was distinct, but also, more particularly, his beard! That beard was there still there when I graduated for my Honours and Master's degrees, in 1981 and 1983, respectively.

As Deneys was leading those marches and seeking alternatives to the apartheid system of governance, Else was deeply involved with the Black Sash, which, from the early 1980s, was exposing the involvement of the apartheid government in the violence and helping victims. Dambuza, my home town, was one of the first areas targeted for forcible imposition of Inkatha at Edendale, also as part of an attempt by the apartheid regime to forcibly incorporate Edendale into the KwaZulu Bantustan. Graham is correct to point out that the apartheid project had partly remained incomplete in terms of segregation in parts of Pietermaritzburg. Edendale was one of very few areas where Africans had freehold land titles, outside of the KwaZulu Bantustans.

I met the Schreiners as a family in the early 2000s when both Else and Deneys, to paraphrase the latter, pretended to be retired! My wife, Phumelele, and I were also part of the celebration of their 50th wedding anniversary. Over one of the many lunches and family gatherings, including Deneys and Else's visit to my wife's rural homestead in Babanango, we touched on a matter of a very bright schoolboy from Dambuza. Deneys, of his own accord, reached out to his contacts and found a scholarship for this young man, Ayanda Mkhize, to attend school at Kearsney College. A boy from Dambuza at Kearsney was really unprecedented!

The book is an informative biography and provokes engagement with parts of its account of history. I honestly believe that it lays a very strong foundation for a sequel – a joint biography of the inseparable 'twins', Deneys and Else, as their story of service and commitment is inseparable.

Dr Bonginkosi Emmanuel Nzimande
(fondly known as 'Blade')

Preface

When Else Schreiner asked me if I would be interested in writing a biography of her late husband, Deneys, I was deeply touched and greatly honoured. This task had first fallen to well-known writer and journalist David Robbins, who had been an important commentator and analyst of the work of the Buthelezi Commission. Unfortunately, David was not in a position to complete the task, but he has afforded me every co-operation and there are traces of his work and inspiration in some of the earlier chapters in this work. However, there are undoubtedly shades of difference between the picture of Deneys Schreiner that emerges from these pages and any picture that may have emerged from David's pages, had he been able to write the biography.

I first met Deneys Schreiner in 1972, when I was a first-year student on the Pietermaritzburg campus of what was then the University of Natal. He was an imposing figure, with his famous beard and twinkling eyes. I stayed on in Pietermaritzburg after graduating and gradually grew accustomed to addressing almost all my former lecturers and professors by their first names. However, Deneys Schreiner remained 'Prof' to me until his dying day, despite my family's close connections with the whole Schreiner family. It has required a considerable mental adjustment to relabel him as 'Deneys' for the purposes of this biography.

According to the noted British Marxist historian Christopher Hill: 'History has to be rewritten in every generation, because although the past does not change, the present does; each generation asks new questions of the past, and finds new areas of sympathy as it re-lives different aspects of the experiences of its predecessors.'[1]

Deneys Schreiner died on Freedom Day, 27 April 2008, and it is time to ask new questions of his life. Many memoirs and biographies have been written by or about leading figures in the struggle against apartheid. This work highlights the life of a man who did not seek the limelight, but whose contribution was remarkable and multifaceted. He showed personal courage, as well as intellectual rigour and moral leadership. Despite his early decision to study the sciences, rather than the law, he participated in and led many of the investigations into developing alternatives to apartheid from the early 1960s to the early 1990s.

This alone makes his contribution to public life worthy of study. The current dominant historical narrative posits a set of binary opposites: segregation versus integration; repression versus passive, then active, resistance and, finally, the glorious and triumphal birth of democracy in 1994 (with, of course, a huge legacy of socio-economic problems still to be addressed). Deneys was a liberal whose chosen political path was one of non-violence, but his daughter Jennifer chose the path of armed resistance and the ideology of Marxism. This set up a dynamic in the family that may have been emotionally draining, but was ultimately resolved with respect and good humour.

This provides a second reason for the importance of writing a life of Deneys Schreiner; namely, the need to explore the tensions between constitutional and non-violent opposition to apartheid and armed and violent resistance. This is particularly significant when these dynamics and tensions played out in one family and across two generations. This brings Hill's point above about each generation needing to rewrite history vividly to life.

One of the problems in writing about the Schreiner family over generations is the repetition of first names. The name 'Deneys'

---

1. Christopher Hill, *The World Turned Upside Down: Radical Ideas during the English Revolution* (London: Penguin, 1991), p.15.

has been used for at least four generations and the nicknames 'Neys' and 'Neysie' are also unhelpful because they are applied all the way down the male line and are recycled in new generations of youngsters. Partly for this reason, but also because historians and legal commentators have described other Schreiners by their initials, I have chosen to use initials as well, especially for the older generations. William Philip Schreiner, premier of the Cape Colony, is referred to as WP. His son Oliver Deneys, the prominent judge on the Appellate Division of the Supreme Court, is referred to as OD, which is the usage of Professor Ellison Kahn and Justice Edwin Cameron in their writings. Indeed, within the Schreiner family itself, WP and OD are usually referred to as such. OD was the father of the Deneys of this narrative, who is often referred to in the family correspondence as 'Neys' or 'Neysie', depending on his age, but, to reduce confusion, I stick to Deneys.

Deneys had two daughters, Jennifer (whom I refer to as Jenny as well as Jennifer) and Barbara, and two sons, Oliver, who predeceased him, and another Deneys, who has a son, also called Deneys. They are also referred to in the family as Neys and Neysie. I try to reserve those terms for these two Schreiners, unless in direct quotations from family correspondence when referring to the older generations.

The chapter headings include the years covered in each chapter and there are obvious overlaps. However, these serve as broad guidelines, rather than precise indications of exact events and, therefore, months have not been included. The first six chapters are chronological, but when examining Deneys's life and work in Pietermaritzburg, the themes and issues are too broad and complex for a simple chronological structure to be manageable, let alone intelligible. Accordingly, both chapters 7 and 8 cover the period from 1959 to 1975, but the contents reflect different themes. Chapter 7 deals with his academic life in the science faculty and his family life. Chapter 8 examines the broader influence of apartheid on the university and the province of Natal and the early efforts at resistance and visualising alternatives to apartheid.

In Chapter 9 the internal university challenges Deneys dealt with as vice principal between 1976 and 1987 are discussed. This is done in conjunction with more personal matters, including the death of his son Oliver, which had a devastating impact on Deneys and the family. Chapter 10 focuses on the broader political challenges and manoeuvring during his first four years as vice principal (1976–80). Chapter 11 discusses the Buthelezi Commission and Deneys's major political interventions between 1980 and 1982. While this might seem out of place chronologically, the position of the Buthelezi Commission in South African history has been neglected, despite its having influenced later constitutional discussions, both regionally and nationally. This underpins the positioning of this chapter as a logical extension to earlier constitutional endeavours. The later constitutional discussions, both regional and national, are dealt with in relation to Jennifer's activities and trial.

Chapter 12 moves the focus back to the effect that the anti-apartheid struggle had on the family between 1982 and 1987 and, in particular, Jennifer's role in Umkhonto weSizwe and her arrest and detention under the Terrorism Act. Chapter 13 includes a discussion of Jennifer's trial and sketches Deneys's and Else's activities during their retirement years. The importance of the Tembaletu Trust is highlighted. The various strands of his life are gathered together in the conclusion.

Sadly, Else Schreiner died in 2018, but mercifully she was able to see a printed first draft of this biography while she was still well enough to read it.

Acknowledgements

Writing a work of biography requires a writer to rely on many people and institutions for a tremendous amount of help. All those who gave their time, knowledge and memories in interviews, or who answered emailed questions, are listed in the bibliography and I am grateful to them all. However, many other people and institutions provided critical information and other assistance. If there are any omissions in my words of gratitude, I can only apologise.

At the University of KwaZulu-Natal, Pietermaritzburg, where Deneys Schreiner spent the greater part of his working life, I am most grateful to Nazim Gani and the staff at the Alan Paton Centre. The staff at the University Archives were also most helpful and accommodating. My thanks also to the two anonymous peer reviewers, who recommended the book's publication, and to Debra Primo, Kholeka Mabeta, Elana Bregin and Alison Lockhart of UKZN Press, who accepted and shepherded this work through the production process.

I must also acknowledge the staff of the main library and the special collections of the University of South Africa, Pretoria, where I am a research fellow. It is one of the finest academic libraries in South Africa and the staff have answered my enquiries with patience and knowledge. My former colleagues at the National Archives of South Africa in Pretoria and at the Pietermaritzburg Repository of the Provincial Archives of KwaZulu-Natal were always supportive and I am very grateful to them for their assistance. The Department of Defence Documentation Centre in Pretoria (the nation's military archives) was also very obliging. Internationally, my thanks are due to the staff of the archives and libraries of Pennsylvania State University in the United States of America for their prompt assistance.

The Schreiner family have been very open with me and I am most grateful to Barbara Schreiner for giving me access to OD Schreiner's correspondence files, without which this biography could not have been written. I am also profoundly grateful to the late Else Schreiner and to Jenny Schreiner for sharing Deneys's private correspondence with me. Deneys (Neys), Heather and Lyndall Schreiner were also very supportive. David Robbins shared his notes and thoughts with me, which gave me a kick-start into the biography. Gail Robbins has also been very helpful. Douglas and Colleen Irvine shared their memories and John Laband not only provided me with his reminiscences, but also provided invaluable sleuthing of sources that were difficult for me to trace when I was in Muscat, Oman. Bill Guest, author of the magisterial three-volume history of the University of Natal, gave me his time, insights and pointers. Richard Steyn, the editor of the *Natal Witness* during the turbulent late 1970s and the 1980s, was also helpful.

Closer to home, I thank my son James Dominy, and his wife Amanda, for unfailingly and gracefully enduring my constant bleats for help with technological problems. Above all, I thank Anne, my constant companion and 'first critic' for over forty years, not only for her love, but also for assistance with editing, proofreading and for her incisive suggestions and advice.

Finally, despite all the assistance from others, it is important to say that I alone am responsible for any errors and omissions.

Introduction

Almost to the Top of the 'Greasy Pole'

For those who measure success in terms of money, power and prestige, the Schreiner family has had but one member who, to use Benjamin Disraeli's phrase, 'climbed to the top of the greasy pole'.[1] This was William Philip (WP) Schreiner, prime minister of the Cape Colony, senator in the first parliament of the Union of South Africa and South African high commissioner (ambassador) in London throughout the First World War.

But these titles matter less in a family such as the Schreiners than the principles that guide their lives. WP's sister, Olive Schreiner, wrote the classic *The Story of an African Farm*, first published in 1883, an account of frontier life, colonialism, nascent feminism and mysticism. Her reputation may be luminous, but her life was hard, both physically and emotionally. Her writings explore what we would now call human rights and she was an early exponent of women's rights in the South African context, but her espousal of peace rather than war during the Anglo-Boer War led to her isolation during her last years in the small Karoo village of Hanover, then under British military occupation.

WP Schreiner had been attorney general of the Cape under Cecil Rhodes, but resigned after the debacle of the failed invasion of the Transvaal, known as the Jameson Raid, at the beginning of 1896. He returned to power as prime minister of the Cape shortly before the Anglo-Boer War broke out, but clashed with the warmongering high commissioner, Sir Alfred Milner. He was manoeuvred out of power by Milner in 1900. Shortly after his return to politics in 1908,

WP chose to represent the Zulu prince Dinuzulu kaCetshwayo in his treason trial in Greytown, rather than espouse the cause of federalism at the national convention in Durban.

WP's son, Oliver Deneys (OD) Schreiner, was one of the country's most eminent jurists, but he was twice rejected for the post of chief justice by the Afrikaner nationalist government because of his principled stand against the removal of coloured people from the common voters' roll and the betrayal by the nationalists of one of the entrenched clauses in the Constitution of the Union of South Africa.

The family's most prominent current public figure, Jennifer (Jenny), daughter of Deneys and Else, endured detention and a political show trial in the dying days of apartheid. So from the nineteenth to the twenty-first centuries, the family has lived out its convictions and tempered ambition with principles.

The history of the Schreiner family invites comparison with the Huxley family. The Huxleys, over several generations, combined great intellect with great service in the sciences and the humanities.[2] It began with Thomas Henry Huxley, known as 'Darwin's Bulldog' because of his emphatic and trenchant support for the theory of evolution. His son Leonard married Julia Arnold, niece of the poet Matthew Arnold, and granddaughter of Thomas Arnold, headmaster of Rugby School. Two of their sons, Julian and Aldous, also achieved great distinction; Julian as a biologist and in later life as the first director general of UNESCO (United Nations Education Scientific and Cultural Organisation). Aldous became a writer, novelist and philosopher, producing eleven novels, the most influential of which were *Chrome Yellow* (1921), *Brave New World* (1932) and *Eyeless in Gaza* (1936).

Neither Julian, nor Aldous, was ever awarded a Nobel Prize, but their half-brother, Andrew, won the Nobel Prize for Physiology (Medicine) in 1963. Another Huxley, Elspeth, wife of Gervas, also a grandson of TH Huxley and cousin of Julian and Aldous, wrote extensively on her experiences in Kenya, her best-known work being *The Flame Trees of Thika: Memories of an African*

Childhood (1959). The Huxleys have been described by Noel Annan as members of an interconnected web of British families, an 'intellectual aristocracy'.[3]

Is it appropriate to call the Schreiners a part of a South African intellectual aristocracy? They are certainly a family whose members have distinguished themselves in law, literature, politics and science for well over a century. This book explores where Deneys Schreiner fits into the pattern and what an appropriate description of his role, individually or dynastically, would be. Unquestionably, Deneys lived in a world of connections, academic and personal, national and international. As a young scientist at the Bernard Price Institute at the University of the Witwatersrand, he worked under Sir Basil Schonland, the founder of the Council for Scientific and Industrial Research (CSIR). The Schreiners were close friends with Phillip Tobias, one of South Africa's leading paleo-anthropologists. Deneys's connections among the business elites in Johannesburg enabled him to secure generous support for his constitutional initiatives, as well as support for the University of Natal. Having studied at Cambridge and taught in the United States, he moved easily in the Anglo-American academic world.

George Deneys Lyndall Schreiner, to give him his full name, OD's second son and youngest child, was no exception in the family. A distinguished scientist and an able and seasoned university administrator, he stood by his principles in war and peace. He served in the South African Army in North Africa and Italy during the Second World War. As a young visiting academic in 1950s, McCarthy-era America, he subtly defied edicts to swear allegiance to the United States of America. Deneys's flourishing career ended as vice principal of the University of Natal in Pietermaritzburg, but not of the whole university, which also had an even larger campus, plus the medical school, in Durban. Apparently too many members of the academy thought he was too principled, too outspoken and therefore, too controversial, for the very top job.

Deneys was a political liberal, but not a woolly-headed one. He brought his rigorously trained scientific mind to bear on the political problems of the day. He was a founding member of the South African Liberal Party and, in 1960, took part in the Natal Convention, a failed effort to sketch out an alternative political future in the province to that being imposed by the apartheid policies of the National Party. In the 1970s, the viciousness, destructiveness and absurdity of apartheid was becoming more and more pervasive and corrosive and, as vice principal, he prompted, organised and sustained an academic investigation into constitutional options for the province, which resulted in a major publication.[4] However, it was ignored by the National Party government.

Nevertheless, in 1982, the chief minister of the KwaZulu homeland authority, Prince Mangosuthu Gatsha Buthelezi, picked Deneys to head a commission to develop constitutional alternatives for KwaZulu and the white-ruled province of Natal. Many people could have chaired this: after all, there were dozens of capable lawyers and, very likely, several distinguished judges, available. However, as discussed in Chapter 11, Buthelezi chose the grandson of the man who had defended his maternal grandfather in 1909, to the detriment of his own political career; a man with impeccable liberal credentials.

This was during the time when the apartheid government of PW Botha was crafting the tricameral parliamentary system that was designed to give a veneer of vaguely multiracial representivity to the increasingly securocratic and brutal late-apartheid regime. Deneys was caught in the crossfire, between the hostility of Botha and the increasing tensions between Buthelezi's Inkatha, a Zulu nationalist movement, and the emerging broad-based popular resistance movements (which could not and would not participate in the commission). However, neither side ever questioned his integrity.

Family was integral to Deneys's life and his wife, Else Kops, not only supported him in her role as the wife of a senior academic and university administrator, but also pursued her own political and activist career, including a run for public office in the Natal Provincial Council in 1979 as a Progressive Party candidate. Else was also president of the National Council of Women and between the two of them they developed national and international networks that provided them with invaluable support in later times of crisis.

They had four children: Oliver, their eldest son, studied science and law, uniting the careers of his father and grandfather; Deneys, their second son, became an engineer and has also had a distinguished career in his profession and in academia. Deneys was followed by Jennifer who first studied the natural sciences, then the social sciences, and then stepped from the academic milieu into serious political activism and armed resistance to apartheid. Barbara, the youngest, studied drama for her BA degree, but her postgraduate focus in environmental studies led her to specialise in the fields of water research and management. These varied paths were made possible because of the broad and questioning environment in which the children had grown up.

Deneys's years as vice principal were bracketed by tragedy and challenge. His eldest son, Oliver, studying on an Elsie Ballot scholarship at Cambridge, was killed in a hit-and-run road accident in Cambridge in 1978 (leaving a young wife and tiny baby). During 1987, Deneys's last year as vice principal, his eldest daughter, Jenny, was detained in terms of the Internal Security Act. There was no gracious slide into a comfortable retirement. Deneys and Else were engaged in an all-out campaign to get justice for their daughter and her comrades, a campaign that lasted until 1991, more than a year after Nelson Mandela walked out of the Victor Verster Prison, a free man at last.

The focus on Jenny's detention and trial had important implications. In the late 1980s and very early 1990s, another constitutional exercise began, this time focused on the city of Pietermaritzburg and its environs. Given the changing political environment, with the release of Mandela in February 1990, and the unbanning of the African National Congress (ANC) and other liberation movements, this exercise stood a real chance of providing tangible results and, indeed, it did. Deneys stimulated and prompted the efforts towards transformation in Pietermaritzburg. However, he was locked into the grinding, drawn-out trauma of Jenny's detention and trial. A strange echo of his grandfather's career, but with a daughter, instead of a prince, being involved in a show trial. Nevertheless, Deneys made a significant contribution to the transformation debate, especially to discussions on education and, arising from this, was able to establish the Tembeletu Educational Trust and provide adult and out-of-school learning opportunities for thousands of marginalised people from around the greater Pietermaritzburg area.

This biography explores the life of a man who was guided by principles rather than by ambition and commitment outweighed expedience in his calculations. Deneys's life was that of a leader by influence and example, not by direction or dictation. His influence was international, but the roots were South African and grew particularly strongly in Natal and at the University of Natal. However, this is not a history of the University of Natal, that task has been undertaken by Professor Bill Guest and the final volume of his three-volume history appeared in 2018.[5] This book is an account of the life of a man who was a scientist, an academic, an administrator, a political adviser, a sportsman, a patron of the arts, a husband, a father and a fisherman. All these qualities were given a public front by his beard, which has a story of its own.

Notes
1. Harold Wilson, *A Prime Minister on Prime Ministers* (London: Book Club Associates, 1977), p.98. Benjamin Disraeli (1804–1881) was a British statesman, writer and prime minister.
2. See Ronald W Clark, *The Huxleys* (London, Heinemann, 1968).
3. William Whyte, 'The Intellectual Aristocracy Revisited', *Journal of Victorian Culture* 10, 1 (2005), pp.15–45.
4. John Benyon (ed.), *Constitutional Change in South Africa: Proceedings of a Conference on Constitutional Models and Constitutional Change in South Africa* (held at University of Natal, Pietermaritzburg, 14–16 February 1978) (Pietermaritzburg, University of Natal Press, 1978).
5. Bill Guest, *Stella Aurorae: The History of a South African University, Volume 1, Natal University College (1909–1949)* (Pietermaritzburg: Natal Society Foundation, 2015); *Stella Aurorae: The History of a South African University,*

Volume 2, the University of Natal (1949–1976) (Pietermaritzburg: Natal Society Foundation, 2017); *Stella Aurorae: The History of a South African University, Volume 3, the University of Natal (1976–2003)* (Pietermaritzburg: Natal Society Foundation, 2018).

1

Beginnings

In 1959, Deneys Schreiner came to Pietermaritzburg to teach chemistry at the University of Natal. He would remain there for the rest of his academic career and, indeed, for the rest of his life. He found a home on Town Hill, at the end of Wendover Road, overlooking the city centre in the valley below. He was deeply impressed by an enormous tree in the well-wooded garden that tumbled down a steep hillside. The largest of all the trees – now a gnarled four-metre-high stump – had, on first sight, inspired Deneys to send a telegram to his wife, Else, who was still in Johannesburg with the children: 'I am about to buy a tree; and, oh yes, there is also a house.'[1]

'Highwood', the Schreiner home until Else's death in 2018, is a double-storey, double verandah, red brick building, a fine example of Pietermaritzburg's Victorian architectural heritage. It was built in 1898 and dates from the days when the city was at its apogee, when settler notables held sway and their colonial regime skimmed taxes and carrying charges off the growing traffic between Durban and the gold-rich Witwatersrand in what was then the Transvaal. The driveway is lined with dense azalea bushes, vegetation as characteristic of the old capital city of Natal as its red brick Victorian architecture. The house looks out over Pietermaritzburg's orderly Voortrekker-designed central grid, with prominent, imposing Victorian public buildings: the tower of the City Hall, the dome of the old Colonial Building and the double-domed Post Office, being the grandest and most visible from the upper verandah. On the next ridge to the east, the Scottsville ridge, is the Pietermaritzburg campus of the University of Natal, now the University of KwaZulu-Natal.

In 1959, white, largely English-speaking Natal society was undergoing one of its periodic existential crises. Pietermaritzburg was a hierarchical city, with certain families (the so-called ONFs – Old Natal Families), with real or imagined colonial lineages presiding over the dominant cultural institutions. There was the Victoria Club, aping the gentlemen's clubs of Pall Mall in London. There was the Royal Agricultural Society, which ran the annual Royal Show on the showgrounds at the bottom of Town Hill. The local citizen force regiment was still clinging to its designation as the 'Royal' Natal Carbineers. The city was the seat of the Anglican bishop of Natal, but had two rival cathedrals dating back to the nineteenth-century Colenso schism that pitted the bishops of Natal and Cape Town against each other and reverberated all the way back to London and Canterbury. The cultural atmosphere (or lack of culture), the ambiguities and the absurdities of the time were mercilessly and hilariously lampooned by Tom Sharpe in his first novel, *Riotous Assembly*, which was banned in apartheid South Africa for many years.[2]

The Afrikaner nationalist government had been in power for eleven years and Prime Minister Hendrik Verwoerd was hell-bent on declaring a republic and taking South Africa out of the Commonwealth. The coloured voters of the Cape Province had been removed from the common voters' roll in 1956 and the rigid ideology of apartheid was emerging from the practice of crude segregation. The major white political party in Natal at the time was the United Party, once the mighty party of General Jan Smuts, but in Natal it was an inward-looking, reactionary organisation, clinging to the sources of patronage available through its control of the Natal Provincial Council.

African nationalism was stirring nationwide and Natal was the home province of the founder of the African National Congress (ANC), John Dube, as well as of the contemporary, house-arrested leader, Chief Albert Luthuli. One of the leading figures in the

Treason Trial that began in 1956, Archie Gumede, was from Pietermaritzburg. Natal also had the largest Indian community (both Hindu and Muslim) in the country. Mohandas Gandhi had spent a life-defining cold night on the Pietermaritzburg station platform in 1893, after being evicted from a first-class railway carriage because of his colour.[3] Natal's Jewish community was the one of smallest in South Africa.

Pietermaritzburg was also virtually unique among cities in apartheid South Africa in that the Group Areas Act that enforced spatial racial segregation, and hence provided the framework for regulating the movement of people and contact between the races, was not fully enforced or enforceable in the city. A major reason for this was that the large township of Edendale, no more than five or six kilometres up the Msunduze Valley from the city centre, had been established as a mission station in 1851.[4] This gave it a peculiar status in terms of the Group Areas Act. There was a strong, educated and urbanised African community, known as the *amaKholwa*, who were descended from Christian converts in the nineteenth century and who had been established there for generations. They provided intellectual leadership for African organisations for most of the twentieth century. Among the most prominent were Archie Gumede and Selby Msimang, both friends of the Schreiners, who were descendants of *amaKholwa*. Indians, coloureds and a few whites also lived in Edendale until the government managed to force them out.[5]

What the bureaucrats of Pretoria could not do was prevent whites visiting Edendale freely without having to apply for government permits in terms of the Group Areas Act. This provided a window of opportunity for the University of Natal, as students and lecturers were able to travel freely into Edendale, meet with residents and provide educational, social and health services. However, during the late 1980s, rising tensions in the greater Pietermaritzburg area between Inkatha and groups aligned with the United Democratic Front (UDF), made Edendale less safe.

Coming to a university post, Deneys was at a half-remove from the local party-political whirl and also something of an outsider. His family lineage was as grand, if not grander, than that of any of the ONFs. The Schreiners could hold their own against the Hathorns, the Shepstones and the Smythes in the pantheon of distinguished families. Deneys's sociability (which sometimes masked his shyness) made him and Else into popular guests and hosts. His war service was a binding factor with men of his generation, yet he did not join ex-servicemen's organisations such as the MOTHS (Memorable Order of Tin Hats).

Many of Deneys's defining characteristics can be discerned from the atmosphere of 'Highwood': a lightly worn assumption of distinction, leadership and intellectualism. On the bookshelves are books by or about various Schreiners, particularly Olive Schreiner. One of the rarest is a slim paperback titled *The Missionary Letters of Gottlob Schreiner*, Olive's father and the first Schreiner to settle in South Africa.[6] This serves as an introduction to the history of the family.

Gottlob was born in the village of Fellbach, near Stuttgart, in what was then the German kingdom of Württemberg. The son of a well-established cobbler, Gottlob trained at the Basel Missionary Seminary to become a Lutheran missionary in 'heathen' parts of the world. As Germany was still a scattering of kingdoms and principalities with no empire, many missionaries were sent to British colonies. Gottlob went to London to complete his missionary training, initially with the Anglican Church Missionary Society. However, he soon left, as a result of complaints temporal and ecclesiastical: the school was not heated, he was not allowed to smoke and he objected to the episcopal hierarchy that ruled the Church of England.[7] Gottlob then linked up with the more evangelical and non-conformist London Missionary Society (LMS).[8]

He was ordained as a missionary by the Reverend FKA Steinkopf, pastor of the German community in London, on 27 June 1837. This was barely a week after the very young Queen Victoria ascended the throne of Great Britain and Ireland.[9] It was while he was in London, that Gottlob met and fell in love with Rebecca Lyndall, who was also a devout evangelical Christian, as well as being a brilliant, well-read and well-educated young woman. Gottlob wrote to his friends and mentors in the seminary in Basel: 'My betrothed I need not praise, and it is enough if I say that I feel ashamed at the great grace of God in having given me someone whom I look upon as above me in every respect and gift.'[10] Both Gottlob and Rebecca wished to 'preach the Gospel to the pagans'. They were married in the Savoy Chapel on 7 November 1837 by a leading figure in the LMS, the Reverend John Campbell, with Jan Tshatshu, a Xhosa convert as a witness.[11] The wedding was hardly a month before Gottlob set sail for Cape Town to begin his missionary endeavours in South Africa.[12] Gottlob wrote in oratorical tones to his seminary brethren in Basel, ascribing the safety of the voyage to the Cape to 'the gracious guidance of God over the depth of sea, staying at the Cape, rolling again upon the mighty waters to Algoa Bay, and then my beginning of the proclamation of a crucified Saviour in a language shortly before unknown'.[13]

South Africa then was a place of tumultuous changes. Powerful African chiefdoms and kingdoms challenged spreading white settler and colonial powers. The Great Trek of the Afrikaners was underway and the Battle of Blood River (Ncome) had not yet been fought. The process was best described by Zulu king, Cetshwayo kaMpande, in an aphorism that captures the practice of imperialism better than Karl Marx ever did: 'First came the traders, then the missionaries, then the red soldier.'[14]

As a missionary, Gottlob was a member of the spiritual wing of imperialism, the second wave, according to Cetshwayo's characterisation. However, his granddaughter Lyndall Gregg described him as a 'most tender-hearted man' whose gentleness and quiet grace was immortalised by Olive Schreiner in the character of old Otto, the German overseer in *The Story of an African Farm*.[15]

Gottlob was not a natural fit as a missionary; he clashed with other missionaries and was transferred from mission station to mission station. After temporary assignments at Bethelsdorp and in the Kat River settlement on the eastern frontier of the Cape Colony, he was posted to Philippolis in Griqua territory to the north of the Orange River. Both Gottlob and Rebecca suffered from ill-health and medical care was rudimentary and intermittent. In 1839 he wrote from Philippolis to the authorities in London:

> As a family trials and mercies have been our lot. My health is not very good lately, but have great reason to praise the Lord that though often performed in great weakness, I have not been prevented from fulfilling my duties. My dear partner has been afflicted, but through the blessings of God on the kind attendance of Dr Philips, surgeon C.M.S., who has been with us, she is again pretty well. Our little girl is healthy and a comfort to us in this wilderness.[16]

Gottlob eventually left the LMS and, practising as a Wesleyan (no major move for somebody brought up as a Lutheran), he was sent to Wittenbergen, near Aliwal North, in 1854. By then he and Rebecca had produced eight children, two of whom had died. A third child died after the trek to their new mission station, but in the following year Olive was born, and two years later, William Philip (WP).

Gottlob's relationship with the missionary society remained strained and he was sent to the training institute at Healdtown (the alma mater of Nelson Mandela in the late 1930s), but failed there as well. He then went into business, but this was not a success and the family was reduced to poverty. He returned to the Kat River Valley, where he died on 26 August 1876.[17]

Olive Schreiner did not have advanced formal schooling, but she had a home tutor, who supplemented the lessons from her well-read and well-educated mother. Rebecca had long been active in teaching children at the various mission stations where Gottlob had ministered. Olive read insatiably and enjoyed her early teenage years spent in Cradock, where her brother Theodore (Theo) was a local teacher and where there was a good library. She became a governess at the age of nineteen and began working on *The Story of an African Farm*, which she published under the masculine nom de plume 'Ralph Irons'. She wrote most of the book while working as a governess for the Fouché family on the farm Klein Gannahoek in the Cradock district.[18]

This became a major success and she was able to travel to Britain and to continental Europe. Olive met leading intellectuals of the era, such as Havelock Ellis, and statesmen, such as William Gladstone. In 1894, she married Samuel Cronwright, a Cape farmer who shared many of her political views and was also disillusioned with Cecil John Rhodes. Rudyard Kipling, author of *The Jungle Book* and the inspirational masculine poem 'If', sent Olive a collection of his books as a wedding present, an action that has been described as 'an interesting tribute from the great Imperialist Poet to the great Democratic Feminist, who hated all wars'.[19]

Olive gave birth to a baby girl in 1895, but the infant died within a day. Sadly, several other pregnancies ended in miscarriages. She suffered from asthma for much of her adult life and died from complications related to the disease in December 1920, some eighteen months after the death of her brother WP.

Despite the family's straitened circumstances, WP Schreiner was able to get a first-class education. He began his schooling in the remote Eastern Cape town of Bedford, near Healdtown, where his elder brother Theo was teaching. WP had many young South Africans who were to make their mark on the history of the country as his classmates. One was William Solomon, nephew of merchant and politician Saul Solomon and a future chief justice of the Union of South Africa. There was also young Emilie Solomon, sister to William, who many years later became head of the Congregational Church in South Africa. Then there was James Rose-Innes, later a politician and William Solomon's predecessor as chief justice of South Africa. WP's fees were paid by Theo, who also helped him, after he matriculated, to attend the South African College in Cape Town, then perhaps the foremost school in South Africa.

The South African College was a hybrid institution, not quite a full university, but already on the way to becoming the progenitor of the University of Cape Town. After being awarded his first degree by the University of Good Hope (the antecedent of the University of South Africa), WP went to England for legal and postgraduate studies in London and at Downing College, Cambridge. On his return to South Africa, he began his legal career at the Cape bar and acted as a legal adviser to the British governor of the Cape Colony. From this position, it was a natural step into politics and WP was elected to the Cape parliament in 1893.[20]

His political rise was rapid, he became attorney general almost immediately and served in the Cecil Rhodes ministry, resigning in disgust in 1896, after the Jameson Raid. He was re-elected in 1898 and appointed colonial premier or prime minister. In 1884, WP had married Frances Hester Reitz, a sister of Francis William Reitz, the president of the Orange Free State. With this connection, it is not surprising that WP resolutely opposed the British high commissioner, Sir Alfred Milner's attempts to foment war with the two Boer republics. WP engaged in unsuccessful efforts at negotiation with both the Free State and the Transvaal in an effort to forestall conflict, but, when conflict came, Milner and Schreiner clashed bitterly over the use of the Cape Colony's volunteer forces and mounted police for imperial ambitions. The high commissioner set about isolating the Cape prime minister, but it took until 1900 for Milner to manoeuvre WP out of office and out of parliament.

While in office as prime minister, WP visited the Transkei, newly incorporated into the Cape Colony, and met John Tengo Jabavu, editor of the isiXhosa newspaper *Imvo Zabantsundu*. Jabavu was an activist for African rights and he strongly influenced WP, who later called for equal rights to be extended to all 'civilised' men, regardless of colour.[21]

WP returned to the Cape parliament in 1908, at a time when the major issue was the unification of South Africa, a white-dominated South Africa, it must be emphasised. In 1908 and 1909, the negotiations for the establishment of a unified South Africa were beginning and a national convention was held in Durban in 1909. The dominant voices were those of generals Jan Smuts and Louis Botha, of the Transvaal, who argued for a union. WP, whose views inclined towards a federation and towards the extension of the franchise to so-called civilised Africans, was not present.

The governor of Natal, Sir Matthew Nathan, acting on instructions from the Colonial Office in London, headed by Lord Elgin and the young Winston Churchill, and on the urgings of Harriette Colenso in Pietermaritzburg, had persuaded WP to lead the defence team in Dinuzulu kaCetshwayo's trial on spurious treason charges for allegedly encouraging the Bambatha Rebellion of 1906.[22] So, instead of sitting at the centre of the constitutional and political action in the Durban City Hall, WP was defending the son of the last independent Zulu king in the Greytown Town Hall.

After the establishment of the Union of South Africa on 31 May 1910, WP entered the new parliament as a senator, appointed to represent the voteless African majority. Given the interest in women's rights expressed in the family, and particularly by his sister, Olive, it is significant that WP supported and presented a petition to the prime minister in 1914 from black women in the Free State protesting at carrying of passes and other restrictive legislation to which they were subjected.[23]

WP was in London at the outbreak of the First World War and was asked by Louis Botha to stay on as the Union's high commissioner, a role he fulfilled for the duration of the war and until his death, in harness, in 1919. What is noteworthy is that WP did not accept a knighthood to which, as a former colonial prime minster and dominion high commissioner, he would have been fully entitled; he never became 'Sir William Schreiner'. His brother Theo took his seat in the senate after his posting to London. WP was survived by his wife, two daughters and two sons, one of whom was Oliver Deneys (OD), father of the Deneys of this narrative, who has been described by Ellison Kahn as 'the greatest Chief Justice that South Africa never had'.[24]

OD was born in 1890 and as a boy he would have observed his father's clashes with Milner and shared the family anger and distress as war approached. He would have heard his father expressing his opposition to British imperialism and his mother worrying about British oppression and atrocities in the Free State and Transvaal and its effect on her family and friends. By the time he was studying law in Cape Town, he had witnessed his father's adoption of a more liberal policy towards black South Africans and his commitment to principles by representing Dinuzulu at the treason trial in Natal. OD's growing understanding of these events, and the philosophical divides that they exposed, would have been carried with him as he went to England to complete his education at Cambridge. According to Alan Paton, OD could have had the Rhodes Scholarship to Oxford for the asking, but given his father's feud with Rhodes, this would never happen, as 'no Schreiner took such a gift from such a man'.[25]

While OD was still at Cambridge and close to the conclusion of his studies, the First World War broke out. He was trained as an officer and sent on active service to the western front in France, where he was seriously wounded at the Battle of the Somme in 1916. His bravery was recognised by the award of the Military Cross and his academic achievements were recognised by the award of his Cambridge degree, followed by his election to a fellowship at Trinity College, Cambridge.[26] After the war, he qualified for the bar in both England and in South Africa and practised in Johannesburg. In 1923 he was part of a small group of advocates fighting to open membership of the bar to all races.[27] OD also served as a part-time lecturer in law at the University of the Witwatersrand and was remembered as an outstanding teacher.[28]

On 12 December 1923, while OD was a busy young advocate and fighting to open the bar to all races, his youngest son, George Deneys Lyndall, was born. OD's wife, Edna, had already given birth to two other children: a son, William (known as Bill), and a daughter, Jeanie. Jeanie suffered from epilepsy in an era when the condition was not well understood and when treatments were crude and not particularly effective.

In 1937 OD was appointed to the Transvaal bench. However, he hesitated before accepting the appointment, writing to General Smuts, then deputy prime minister, to protest that the position should have gone to Advocate Philip Millin, the husband of writer Sarah Gertrude Millin, biographer of both Rhodes and Smuts: 'I have the clear impression that he would have been appointed had he not been a Jew. If this is so it would be extremely distasteful to me to commence my work as a dispenser of justice by being, in effect, a party to an injustice.'[29]

On receiving the requisite assurances from Smuts, OD took the post and joined the bench to which Millin was also elevated as a judge a few months later. Eight years later, in 1945, OD was further elevated to the Appellate Division in Bloemfontein (now the Supreme Court of Appeals), where he spent the rest of his judicial career and faced the greatest judicial challenge of his life, requiring as much courage as he had shown under fire during the Battle of the Somme. However, what is often overlooked is the fact that he presided over one of the major political trials of the Second World War, the trial of South African Olympic boxer, Afrikaner nationalist and Nazi spy, Robey Leibbrandt, for treason.[30] Leibbrandt was freed by the incoming National Party government in 1948 and perhaps this incident prompted the hostility towards OD, long before he ruled on the issue of coloured people and the common voters' roll.

In 1948, the National Party was elected as the government of the Union of South Africa, with a very small parliamentary majority, although it received fewer votes overall than the United Party. The delimitation of constituencies in the House of Assembly favoured less densely populated, conservative, rural areas over the more densely populated, possibly less conservative urban areas. The National Party set about strengthening and entrenching racial segregation, which became known as the policy of apartheid and, equally importantly, entrenching itself in power. One way of doing both was by effecting the removal of coloured voters from the common voters' roll in the Cape province. However, this was one of the entrenched clauses in the South Africa Act of 1909, which had established the Union of South Africa, and the National Party did not have the required two-thirds parliamentary majority to amend the franchise in the Cape province.

Nevertheless, DF Malan's government rammed a law through parliament, the Separate Representation of Voters Bill, which passed with a simple majority. The matter was quickly referred to the courts and ended up before the Appellate Division, where OD and his colleagues struck down the act in April 1952 (just as white South Africa celebrated the 300th anniversary of Jan Van Riebeeck's arrival at the Cape).

In retaliation, the government passed a new law through parliament, the High Court of Parliament Act, which made parliament itself the highest judicial authority in the country. This new high court then overruled the previous judgement of the Appellate Division. The Appellate Division responded by ruling that this High Court of Parliament Act was as unconstitutional as the Separate Representation of Voters Act had been. But the Malan government was not to be beaten; it resorted to packing the senate with extra nominated members, so that it could secure a two-thirds majority in parliament. Also, as additional insurance, it increased the number of judges on the bench of the Appellate Division from five to ten, thus enabling it to load the court with its own supporters.[31]

OD told Edna that the appellate judges first heard about the appointment of the five new colleagues from the court registrar, who had heard it announced over the radio: 'There it is – and the only course is to take things philosophically, reminding oneself of the relative unimportantness of the affair in the general scheme of things.'[32] With the playing field thus tilted, the battle was finally over. In 1956, the bill became law, with the acquiescence of the Appellate Division, and from then until 1994, coloured people could only vote on a separate voters' roll for a handful of white MPs to represent them and later (from 1984) for their own toothless House of Representatives under the tricameral system of PW Botha. The last challenges to the legislation failed in the enlarged Appellate Division by nine votes to one. Justice Oliver Deneys Schreiner was the only dissenter.

This gallant stand has led to the Law School at the University of the Witwatersrand bearing his name and a bust of him was unveiled in the Supreme Court of Appeal building in Bloemfontein. It is also why Justice Schreiner never became chief justice of the Union of South Africa.

Delivering the annual Oliver Schreiner Memorial Lecture in 2008, Deputy Chief Justice Dikgang Moseneke, of the Constitutional Court, said he was fascinated by 'the steadfast stance Oliver Schreiner took in the Trilogy Cases that gave rise to the constitutional crisis of the mid 1950s'. Moseneke emphasised OD's illustrious family background, his place in the ruling white elite and his privileged education:

> He did not need a social conscience or public spiritedness. He could have lived his life without the political fallout that led to the stunting of his bright judicial career by political executive disapproval. If he had stayed within his elitist confines he would have risen to become the Chief Justice, which he never was. He is said to have had 'boundless powers of work (and) was blessed with great intelligence'.[33]

This account of OD's judicial and moral stand in the 1950s takes us well into the adulthood and professional rise of his son, Deneys, and it is time to turn to his story. Although OD was a member of the Appellate Division, based in Bloemfontein, he kept his main residence in Johannesburg, which is the city where Deneys and his young family were for most of the 1950s. As a mark of solidarity with his father and in protest against the removal of coloured voters from the common roll, Deneys grew his formidable and iconic beard, vowing not to shave again until these voters, indeed all South

Africans, were placed on a common democratic voters' roll. His beard remained a defining feature for the rest of his life, except for a few important days in 1994.

Notes
1. Else Schreiner, Reminiscences, 2016.
2. Tom Sharpe, *Riotous Assembly* (London: Secker & Warburg, 1971).
3. Fatima Meer (ed.), *The South African Gandhi: An Abstract of the Speeches and Writings of MK Gandhi, 1893–1914* (Durban: Madiba Publishers, 1995), p.32.
4. Sheila Meintjes, 'Edendale 1850–1906: A Case Study of Rural Transformation and Class Formation in an African Mission in Natal', PhD thesis, University of London, 1988.
5. Sheila Meintjes, 'Farmers to Townspeople: Market to Labour Reserve' in *Pietermaritzburg 1838–1988: A New Portrait of an African City*, edited by John Laband and Rob Haswell, pp.66–9 (Pietermaritzburg: University of Natal Press, 1988).
6. Karel Schoeman (ed.), *The Missionary Letters of Gottlob Schreiner 1837–1846* (Cape Town: Human & Rousseau, 1991).
7. Karel Schoeman, *Olive Schreiner: 'n Lewe in Suid-Afrika 1885–1881* (Cape Town: Human & Rousseau, 1989), p.15.
8. Lyndall Gregg, *Memories of Olive Schreiner* (London: W & R Chambers, 1957), p.7.
9. Schoeman, *Olive Schreiner*, p.15.
10. Schoeman, *Missionary Letters*, p.13.
11. Schoeman, *Olive Schreiner*, p.17.
12. Gregg, *Memories of Olive Schreiner*, p.7.
13. Schoeman, *Missionary Letters*, p.22.
14. Frank Emery, *The Red Soldier: Letters from the Zulu War, 1879* (London: Hodder & Stoughton, 1977). The quote is from the title page.
15. Gregg, *Memories of Olive Schreiner*, p.35.
16. Schoeman, *Missionary Letters*, p.42. The girl referred to in this passage was one of Olive's older sisters.
17. Schoeman, *Missionary Letters*, p.147.
18. Schoeman, *Olive Schreiner*, pp.410–11.
19. Gregg, *Memories of Olive Schreiner*, p.34.
20. This section is largely based on Eric Walker, *WP Schreiner: A South African* (London: Oxford University Press, 1969).
21. Walker, *WP Schreiner*, p.131.

22. Anthony Haydon, *Sir Matthew Nathan: British Colonial Governor and Civil Servant* (St Lucia: University of Queensland Press, 1976), pp.146–8.
23. National Archives of South Africa, Governor General's Papers, GG 1542 (ref 50/384), 'Natives: Pass Laws: Petition for Repeal of Laws Affecting Native Women in Orange Free State', 1914.
24. Ellison Kahn, *Fiat Iustitia: Essays in Memory of Oliver Deneys Schreiner* (Cape Town: Juta, 1983).
25. Alan Paton, *Hofmeyr* (Cape Town: Oxford University Press, 1964), p.16.
26. Ellison Kahn, 'Oliver Deneys Schreiner: The Man and His Judicial World', *South African Law Journal* 97 (1980), pp.566–615.
27. RL Selvan, 'Early Days at the Johannesburg Bar', *Consultus* (October 1994), pp.115–27.
28. Ellison Kahn, 'The Wits Faculty of Law, 1922–1989: A Story with a Personal Touch', *Consultus* (October 1989), pp.103–12.
29. OD Schreiner Letters: File 1939–43, OD Schreiner to General Jan Smuts, 10 February 1937. Copy of letter – misfiled. See also Kahn, *Fiat Justitia*, pp.25–6.
30. Kahn, 'Oliver Deneys Schreiner', p.574.
31. René de Villiers, 'Afrikaner Nationalism', in *The Oxford History of South Africa, Vol. II: South Africa 1870–1966*, edited by Monica Wilson and Leonard Thompson, pp.405–6 (Oxford: Clarendon Press, 1975).
32. OD Schreiner Letters: File 1955, OD Schreiner to Edna, 26 March 1955.
33. From Justice Dikgang Moseneke's lecture, 'Separation of Powers, Democratic Ethos and Judicial Function', delivered at the University of the Witwatersrand on 23 October 2008. https://www.sahistory.org.za/archive/separation-powers-democratic-ethos-and-judicial-function-oliver-schreiner-memorial-lecture.

2

From Boyhood to Battle via Wits (1923–42)

George Deneys Lyndall Schreiner, the second son and youngest child of OD Schreiner and his wife Edna (née Fincham), was born in Johannesburg on 12 December 1923. His elder siblings were William (Bill) and Jeanie. Deneys was a healthy baby and when he was about four months old, Edna wrote to her husband, while he was absent from home, grinding away at the law:

> And you can think of your family here as thoroughly well & happy, though missing you. We got Ben to adjust the scal[e] most carefully & make out that Deneys is now 11¾ lbs a gain of 12 ounces in a little over two weeks, which is quite satisfactory, considering he has had the change & journey thrown in. He looks splendid – pink & fresh & well & is as happy and contented as possible out in the trees among the Cape canaries.[1]

Although little Deneys's father was heavily involved with building up a legal practice, he remained engaged with the children and was not a distant parent. His mother was interesting and well informed, with an active and enquiring mind. Her interests ranged through art, music, philosophy, politics – almost everything that made the world tick – and she read widely, perhaps a twentieth-century version of Rebecca Lyndall. Else Schreiner, Deneys's wife gave a cautious assessment of her mother-in-law: 'I recognised in her the warmth of her nature, her patient enjoyment of her kids, her patent love for all three – Jean, Bill and Deneys – and the love between her and her husband.'[2]

This helped to create a happy and stimulating home life for the young Deneys. Edna kept a beautiful garden and she liked to tend it herself. She also devoted herself to philanthropic work in the community. However, the letters that passed between Edna and OD also show that while she was a very loyal wife and devoted mother, she was somewhat prone to anxiety. In 1936, when OD was musing about entering politics, she wrote to him:

> But what is good & right for you is good & right for me & for your children & we can be relied on to feel it so. You do realise that? The dread I let myself express of your going into politics wasn't entirely or even mainly selfish. I've always hated the thought of the dislocation of your professional life.[3]

Edna was a strong influence on her youngest son and perhaps Deneys's diffidence can be partly attributed to his mother. Given WP Schreiner's untimely death in London in 1919, there was no Schreiner grandparent to influence his upbringing.

The Schreiner family lived in Rhodes Avenue, close to Jan Smuts Avenue in Parktown, and it was from there, in January 1929, that the five year-old Deneys began his education at St Katharine's Preparatory in Escombe Avenue, less than a kilometre from their home. The founding principal, Mrs Ethel Fielding, encouraged freedom of thought and action, rather than regimentation. Children were to be given freedom of expression and taught respect for others. This would have fitted well with Deneys's home upbringing, which taught similar values and where freedom had to be exercised in a context of moral responsibility and fairness to others.[4]

Even during his childhood, Deneys demonstrated an understanding of the concept of fairness. Once, when his parents were elsewhere or otherwise engaged, the boy was obliged to sign the permission papers, the 'pass', which allowed the family's domestic servants to leave the premises and go out on to the Johannesburg streets. Young Deneys recognised and recalled for the rest of his life, the distorted morality of a ten-year-old white boy being able to control the movements of adults who happened to be black.[5] Helen Suzman, the redoubtable Progressive Party MP, also recalled that as a twelve-year-old girl, she had to sign a pass, known as a 'special', for her family's domestic worker to remain out after the 9 pm curfew.[6]

Some years later, the Schreiners moved to a house, which they named 'Lyndall', at 24 Sixth Avenue in Lower Houghton. Their home was in a leafy suburban street occupied by the well-to-do inhabitants of the 1886 mining town that had turned into a brash twentieth-century city, with many of the social pretensions related to the pursuit of wealth. In January 1931, Deneys entered St John's Diocesan College, an Anglican private school, in the lower preparatory classes, as a day boy. He had just turned seven and he was to remain at the same school until he matriculated at the end of 1939.

St John's had been established under the auspices of the Anglican Church in 1898.[7] From modest beginnings, the school had grown to a complement of more than 400 boys and around 20 teachers by the time the young Deneys put on the characteristic claret and blue colours of the school uniform. Private church schools offered an elite education; they were attended by the sons of the wealthy and influential in business and the professions. The ethos was that of an English public school, such as Eton or Harrow. The architecture was imposing and the buildings had been designed by Sir Herbert Baker, architect of empire and, more specifically, of the imposing Union Buildings in Pretoria.

The shadows of the First World War were cast over the school and permeated its routine. The headmaster, the Reverend Charles Runge, was a decorated war veteran and the chapel was dedicated to the memory of staff and pupils who had fallen in battle, with those who fell at the Battle of Delville Wood on the Somme, taking pride of place. Needless to say, the school cadet corps played an integral part in school activities, which strengthened the strict discipline of the school. Deneys played a full part as a cadet, being appointed as a corporal in his final year at school. He was also a prefect of Alston House and won colours for boxing.

Deneys sailed through his lessons, sang in the choir and played cricket and later rugby. A report card from 1935 lists his academic standing as being 'very good' for spelling and arithmetic, good for most other subjects, but only 'fair' for History, Geography and Writing. The headmaster's comment was: 'Does promising work, but must be more particular about neatness'.[8] An undated childhood letter to his father confirms both the promise and the need for neatness. Deneys describes his brother, Billy, as having a tick on him and an article in the newspaper claiming, 'West Rand beat Pretoria eight three, aren't you glad that your rotten team won?' Deneys was also impressed by Cedile, a little friend of his sister's, 'who had a cheatah [sic] as a pet'.[9]

Deneys's heart was probably leaning more towards the sports field than the classroom at the age of eleven. In later life he wrote that he had always derived, 'very high levels of enjoyment from a large number of different sports played at least at a reasonable level of competence'. He made the First Eleven at cricket and played as a flyhalf in the Under 15A rugby team. He began playing golf during the school holidays.[10]

Family reminiscences describe Deneys as being a boisterous boy, a character trait he kept into at least his middle years, which was coupled with his love of jokes and practical pranks.[11] He played cricket for St John's against King Edward School and faced Russell Endean, later a formidable South African test cricketer. Deneys damaged his thumb playing cricket at school and later boasted that his famous opponent had done the damage. His enthusiasm for the game shines through in a letter he sent to his parents in 1935, after four years at the school:

> I have heard from the Hartshorns that you will arrive back on the 17th of April. Is that right? I hope so. We are

going to stay with the Hartshorns during the holidays. I have played three matches and my average batting is 21 per innings. I made 19 against Marists, 6 against Pridwin and as I have already told you 39 against KEPS. We played PTPS yesterday, but I did not bat. It was a draw. I came fourth in the fortnightly marks. I am sorry to see by your last letter that you are having bad weather and I suppose you are looking forward for good old South African weather again. With lots of love from Deneys.[12]

This also appears to have been the year that the Schreiner children accompanied their parents on a visit to Britain. On his later arrival there, in 1945, Deneys recognised landmarks in London from his memories of a trip to the city a decade or so previously. That trip also gave him the status of having already 'crossed the line', the equator, before he sailed north to Egypt in 1943. Thus he was able to avoid the ceremonial mayhem on the troopship taking him to war, thanks to his adolescent baptism by King Neptune.

Soon after he had turned twelve, young Deneys, a very junior boy at St John's College, started smoking. He kept up the habit virtually his entire life, only giving up cigarettes when he was in his seventies. Else recalls that he had smoked Van Rijn filter cigarettes and, when they were withdrawn from the market, he decided to give up smoking altogether, rather than accustom himself to another brand.[13]

Although St John's was (and still is) a school for the privileged, it was a school with a social conscience. The school was involved with the Community of the Resurrection Mission in vibrant, polyglot Sophiatown, later made famous by Father Trevor Huddleston who, in the 1950s, fought the forced removal of his parishioners to Meadowlands in Soweto and the bulldozing of the suburb to make way for housing for whites in the area, which was renamed Triomf.[14]

The school focused on teaching and learning and on preparing their boys to understand the wider world. Boys were taken on so-called industrial tours of Johannesburg to learn about the City of Gold in all its variety and diversity, from mines and factories to townships and reformatories. Sophiatown was visited in 1939, as was Diepkloof Reformatory (where Alan Paton was headmaster).[15] There were debates in and around the school on the benefits of improving education for black people and the pernicious influence of racial prejudice. Given the fact that OD Schreiner had protested to Jan Smuts, a mere year or two earlier, about possible discrimination against Jews, and the fact that the ten-year-old Deneys had felt acute discomfort at having to give permission for the movements of adult domestic workers, the teenager would have developed an early sensitivity about discrimination in all forms. With his lively and retentive mind, he would have observed and absorbed all the contradictions laid bare during the 'industrial tours'.

One way in which St John's focused on broadening the pupils' understanding of the world was by emphasising reading. By 1935, 'form libraries' had been introduced, with the idea of suiting the books to the ages of the boys. 'All boys are thereby enabled and encouraged to read good literature without any risk of being out of their depth,' explained Reverend SH Clarke, the headmaster who succeeded Charles Runge in 1935 and led the school until 1954. Shortly after his arrival at St John's, Clarke had commented on the absence of ideas in the essays that had been put before him: 'This absence of ideas stemmed from the boys' failure to read reputable literature.' He believed that the test of an educated man was very largely the kind of books he read. 'Education is something more than passing Matric. I do want you, then, to get some decent reading done.'[16]

Deneys was an avid reader and a staunch supporter of libraries throughout his life and it began at St John's. However, Deneys was still a boy, not an adult, nor was he a political or social commentator. He enjoyed his sport and he was a talented student, excelling in Mathematics and Science, although Latin was a burden. He took extra lessons with a Miss Williams and wrote to his mother in mid-1939, his Matric year, describing the lesson time as 'torture'. He added, 'At present I am just sweating my soul out trying to learn things. This week however, barring Latin is comparatively easy.' After this nod to academic subjects, he went on more enthusiastically about his rugby matches, but concluded: 'The rats in William's room had a rugby match yesterday and really something must be done about them. The running around is not so bad but squeaking is a bit beyond a joke.'[17]

The following day he wrote to his father, worrying about the impending Matric exams: 'I get less confident and less confident every day.' The major events of his life were his brother's Afrikaans oral exam and St John's rugby match against Parktown Boys High School. To his delight, the team he played in, the second team, won 3–0.[18] Despite Deneys's concentration on the rugby field and his worries, particularly about Latin, he passed Matric with flying colours just a few days before his sixteenth birthday. The last entry in the school register against his name was, 'First class matric in December 1939.'

He was ready to make his mark on the world, but it was to be in a world newly at war and South Africa was deeply divided as to its role in the war. Adolf Hitler and Josef Stalin, the Nazi dictator of Germany and the Communist dictator of Soviet Russia respectively, had signed a pact that enabled the Germans and the Soviets to invade Poland. Britain and France went to war with Germany in support of Poland and the colonies and dominions of the British Empire and Commonwealth lined up with the mother country. Black South Africans gave cautious support to the war effort, but white South Africa was divided. Prime Minister JBM Hertzog advocated neutrality, but Smuts supported South African involvement on the side of Great Britain. Parliament voted in favour of war and Hertzog resigned, asking the governor general, Sir Patrick Duncan, to call a general election. Duncan declined to accept Hertzog's advice and, instead, asked Smuts to form a government, which he was able to do with the support of a majority in the House of Assembly.[19]

That fateful September, 1939, Deneys was wrapped up in his approaching matriculation examinations. As he was not yet sixteen, he was too young to join up after he finished school and, instead, he decided to go on to university. At the beginning of 1940, he registered at the University of the Witwatersrand (Wits) for a BSc degree. This kept him in Johannesburg, the city where he had lived since birth and where he had received all his education.

He selected first-year subjects that could have led to an engineering degree (and Wits, of course, began as the South African School of Mines and Technology until elevated to full university status in 1920). However, in his second year, Deneys switched his focus to chemistry. Many decades later his daughter, Barbara, asked him why he had studied chemistry and he answered: 'Because it wasn't law!'[20] However, he told his younger son, also Deneys, who studied civil engineering at the University of Natal, Durban, that chemistry was 'fundamental to everything else'.[21] He amplified the remark he had made to Barbara in a retirement interview with the *Sunday Tribune*, in December 1987: 'I have trouble with the law in relation to the logic of it. How do people administer laws that they consider unjust?'[22]

Student life on a university campus during wartime was necessarily more constrained and less boisterous than on a peacetime campus. Phillip Tobias, the renowned palaeoanthropologist, and, later, a friend of Deneys and Else Schreiner, entered Wits as an undergraduate a year or two after Deneys. Tobias describes a studious lifestyle, rather than a political, social or sporting lifestyle. Deneys, however, would have taken full advantage of the constricted social and sporting opportunities available during wartime. He would not have been aware of the secrecy surrounding some of the research work being undertaken at the university.[23] The Bernard Price Institute on the campus, where he would become a research scientist in the 1950s, devoted its energies to the development of radar, which had major military applications.[24]

Wits academic staff and young male students joined up and the exodus of young men allowed women to play a more active role in student politics and campus affairs.[25] The student body was also divided on the issue of the war. The minority of Afrikaner students gravitated towards the Afrikaner Nasionale Studentebond, which trenchantly opposed the Union's involvement in the conflict (and some members secretly hoped for a Nazi victory). The main English student organisation was NUSAS (the more liberal National Union of South African Students), while even more left-wing student organisations also flourished. Ruth First was a stalwart member of the Young Communist League and characterised national issues as being the student affairs that mattered. She found the ferment on the wartime campus an empowering experience.[26] More medical students tended to be radical and students with Eastern European antecedents (many of whom were Jewish) were righteously militant. By contrast, engineering students were more conservative. Perhaps this partly explains why Deneys lost interest in engineering and turned to chemistry.

In 1941, Deneys's second year at Wits, before he had even turned eighteen, he began part-time military training on the campus, being assigned to the Transvaal Scottish Regiment. In 1941 he spent 30 days undergoing military training, supplemented by scattered short periods in 1942.[27] This training would have consisted of parading, marching, handling firearms and learning a semblance of military discipline. Deneys also kept up his sporting activities, particularly rugby, and he played for Wits in the Under 19A side and was also selected for the Central Reef Under 19 side.[28] While he was at Wits, his path crossed that of a young female student, Else Kops, but neither of them showed much interest in the other at that stage of their lives.

Deneys completed his degree at the end of 1942 and immediately joined the army as a full-time recruit. He was then nineteen years old and a university graduate, but, for the next few years, square-bashing and the drudgery and dangers of army routine and campaigning would consume his life.

Notes

1. OD Schreiner Letters: File 1923–4, Edna to OD Schreiner, Hopewell, 16 April 1924.
2. Else Schreiner: comments to David Robbins, 2014.
3. OD Schreiner Letters: File 1936–7, Edna to OD Schreiner, 17 December 1936.
4. Jenny Schreiner: comments on familial values to Graham Dominy, 2017.
5. Else Schreiner: comments to David Robbins, 2014.
6. Helen Suzman, *In No Uncertain Terms: Memoirs* (Johannesburg: Jonathan Ball, 1993), p.8. Gavronsky was Helen Suzman's maiden name.
7. The following paragraphs are drawn from notes made by David Robbins using KC Lawson, *Venture of Faith: The Story of St John's College, Johannesburg, 1898–1968* (Johannesburg: Council of St John's College, 1968).
8. OD Schreiner Letters: File 1935(2), St John's College Report Card, 24 April 1935.
9. OD Schreiner Letters: File 1930-3, undated letter.
10. University of KwaZulu-Natal (UKZN) Archives: SP 25/1/1/1, Schreiner, GDL (Prof & Vice Principal UNP), 1976–87, Newspaper cuttings: Deneys Schreiner, 'Sporting Autobiography', *NU Sport*, June 1984, p.6.
11. Else Schreiner, Reminiscences, 2016.
12. OD Schreiner Letters: File 1935, Deneys to his parents, undated.
13. Else Schreiner, Reminiscences, 2016.
14. Trevor Huddleston, *Naught for Your Comfort* (New York: Doubleday, 1956).
15. Peter F Alexander, *Alan Paton: A Biography* (Oxford: Oxford University Press, 1994), chapters 8 and 9.
16. Lawson, *Venture of Faith*.
17. OD Schreiner Letters: File 1939–43, Deneys to Edna, 20 June 1939.
18. OD Schreiner Letters: File 1939–43, Deneys to OD, 21 June 1939.
19. Monica Wilson and Leonard Thompson, eds, *The Oxford History of South Africa, Vol. II: South Africa 1870–1966* (Oxford: Clarendon Press, 1975), p.382.
20. Comments of Barbara Schreiner, 2015.
21. Comments of Deneys (Neys) Schreiner, 2015.
22. UKZN Archives: SP25/1/1/1, Schreiner, GDL (Prof & Vice Principal UNP), 1976–87, Newspaper cuttings: *Sunday Tribune*, 12 December 1987, Interview with Georgina Hamilton.
23. Phillip Tobias, *Into the Past: A Memoir* (Johannesburg: Wits University Press, 2005).

24. BA Austin, 'On the Development of Radar in South Africa and Its Use in the Second World War', *URSI Radio Science Bulletin* 358 (September 2016), pp.69-81.
25. This paragraph is largely drawn from Bruce Murray, 'World War II and Wits Student Politics', seminar paper, African Studies Institute, University of the Witwatersrand, 1993.
26. Donald Pinnock, *Writing Left: The Radical Journalism of Ruth First* (Pretoria: UNISA Press, 2007), pp.13-14.
27. South African National Defence Force (SANDF) Documentation Centre: 'Record Card: Coast, Garrison and Citizen Forces', Schreiner, GDL (No. 116992).
28. UKZN Archives: SP 25/1/1/1, Schreiner, GDL (Prof & Vice Principal UNP), 1976-87, Newspaper cuttings: Deneys Schreiner, 'Sporting Autobiography', *NU Sport*, June 1984, p.6.

3

'Up North'
The Army and the Shaping of His Character (1943–5)

Like many ex-servicemen, Deneys did not talk much about his wartime service, except to his adopted grandson, Monde Schreiner, who had an interest in military history and to whom Deneys, in later life, gave his medals. Given the exigencies of wartime censorship, his letters home are lively, but references to his activities and locations are largely oblique. According to family recollections, he refused a commission, preferring to serve in the ranks. This would have annoyed the military hierarchy, as he was a university graduate, the son of a distinguished father, who had served as an officer in the First World War, and he clearly had leadership potential. He also enthusiastically participated in the team sports that the army, since Victorian times, believed imparted officer-like qualities.[1]

Deneys enlisted on 4 January 1943, shortly after his nineteenth birthday. According to his military service record card, George Deneys Lyndall Schreiner had blue eyes and fair hair and was pronounced medically fit for active service. He was not a large young man, measuring only 5 feet, 9½ inches in height and weighing 164 pounds, with a chest measurement (deflated) of 34 inches.[2] The military also recorded his religious denomination as Church of England.[3] The army in those days was suspicious of atheists and order in church parades was as important as order in any other parade. The thought of non-believers being able to do nothing while believers marched off to endure tedious sermons from pastors, priests or rabbis, stuck in every sergeant-major's craw. The Church of England, or Anglican Church, was virtually the default religion for English-speaking soldiers in those days and for a decade or two thereafter. Having been to a church school, Deneys was marked as Anglican.

The new recruit was first posted to Potchefstroom for three months of basic training at the artillery school. He would have done elementary square-bashing during his Citizen Force training days while he was still a student. With his quizzical, wide-ranging and enquiring mind, Deneys had a detached and cynical attitude towards army bombast, an attitude later shared by his son Deneys. While a university student, this Deneys was obliged to undergo several days of army training a year in the militia formation known as the commandos. Once at shooting practice he was ordered to aim for the bullseye, but instead he placed his shots precisely in the four corners of the target. This, according to the shooting instructor, was appalling shooting and Deneys was ordered off the range, thus escaping further days of duties.[4] His father would have been delighted by the incident.

Back in Potchefstroom in January 1943, Deneys was tired out by almost continuous guard duty, which was a very unpleasant experience in the rain. The new recruits were also shifted around almost nightly between different tents and bungalows. One minor compensation was that Potchefstroom was not very far from Johannesburg, but very little leave was given. An occasional night out at the local cinema, the 'flicks' was virtually their only relaxation. However, Deneys made a point that being in the army made him appreciate commonplace amenities such as the 'wireless', or radio, which were taken for granted in 'civvy street'.[5]

Deneys managed to get a five-day pass in February, which he spent at home with his parents and this marked the last time they could be together as a family until the end of the war. Bill had joined the army signal corps in 1942, so both boys were in military service and both went north and were able to keep in touch with each other, as did their close friend Geoff Nichols, who also served 'up north'. It seems that some strings were pulled to achieve this and Deneys thanked his mother for her support: 'I know how you hate approaching people for favours and that sort of thing.'[6]

Deneys was attached to the 4/22nd Field Artillery Regiment under the command of Lieutenant Colonel FJ Harpur.[7] From Potchefstroom, his unit moved to Pietermaritzburg, where troops destined for the battlefront were housed in transit camps in Hay Paddock (now the suburb of Hayfields) and Oribi camp, near the city's small airfield. This was his first prolonged exposure to the city where he would spend most of his life. The camp was within walking distance of the tram line between the city centre and the university along King Edward Avenue, but Deneys did not leave a record of his impressions of the city at this time. However, in 1951, in a letter to his parents sent from the United States of America, he remarked: 'I only knew Pietermaritzburg as a contrast to the foul, muddy transit camp there in which we spent a short eternity and it seemed to be a really pretty little town with a somewhat soggy climate and mental outlook.'[8]

The transit camp was not a particularly pleasant experience. Hay Paddock was known to the troops as 'Clay Paddock' or 'Flea Paddock' and it was hot, dusty and overcrowded. At the time Gunner Deneys Schreiner was billeted there, it accommodated 25 000 men in facilities intended for 20 000.[9] This discomfort was a precursor of what he would face in Egypt and Italy, but he took it philosophically, writing to his mother: 'Well I must polish my boots before going on parade, and so I am afraid I must abandon you to your duties at Alexandra Township. Lots of love to all, Deneys.'[10]

The Union of South Africa was preparing to send the 6th Armoured Division 'up north' to the Mediterranean theatre of the war. Soldiers who had agreed to serve outside the borders of the Union wore a red tab and Deneys wore it with pride, but, outside the major cities and English-speaking areas, they were controversial, and ardent Afrikaner nationalists referred to the soldiers who wore them as *'rooi luisies'* (red lice).[11] In 1943 the Smuts government was acutely aware of the shortage of available white manpower for war service, especially overseas. The majority of the Afrikaner population was against the war effort; industrial and agricultural production had to be maintained at home and sufficient police and military reserves had to be maintained in the Union in case of a black uprising, despite the fact that the black population was generally more supportive and loyal than many of the nationalists in the Afrikaner population.

Young white school-leavers and university graduates who were prepared to serve overseas were a godsend to General Smuts. The 'Oubaas' was one of the leading statesmen of the Commonwealth and a member of the Imperial War Cabinet. For Smuts, it was a matter of grave importance that South Africa should strain every nerve to support the Allied war effort. South Africa had already experienced the humiliation of having a division surrender to the German General Erwin Rommel, known as the 'Desert Fox', at Tobruk in 1942, and the 1943 recruitment drive was based on the slogan 'Avenge Tobruk'.[12] Deneys and his brother Bill were setting out to war with Smuts's avengers.

The South African 6th Armoured Division embarked from Durban in April 1943. Thousands of men were packed into the troopships for the voyage up the east coast of Africa and through the Red Sea to disembark in Egypt at the eastern end of the Suez Canal. It is most likely that Deneys sailed on the famous French transatlantic liner, *Ille de France*, which had been pressed into Allied trooping service and lifted a large proportion of the men of the 6th Division.[13] The soldiers were serenaded out of Durban harbour by the famous operatic soprano Perla Siedle Gibson, known to the men as 'The Lady in White'. She always stood on the North Pier at the end of The Point, dressed in white with a red hat, singing popular and patriotic songs to the departing ships through a brass megaphone presented to her by grateful Royal Navy sailors.[14]

Deneys described a tedious voyage to his father: there was the usual 'crossing the line' ceremony, 'a pretty barbarian affair', which Deneys avoided since he had crossed the line before as a boy. There were ferocious boxing matches, with the participants being 'more concerned with slaughter than with boxing', and there were latrine fatigue duties. There was little else to do during the day, except to watch porpoises and flying fish and read, but one of Deneys's precious stock of books had been stolen. At night the ship was blacked out and intensely hot. He included the date that the ship crossed the equator in the letter, but this was cut out by the military censor.[15]

The convoy of troopships arrived at Port Twefik, at the Red Sea end of the Suez Canal, on 30 April 1943.[16] The South Africans were then sent to Khataba in the Egyptian desert for intensive training before their deployment into the line of battle.[17] A post-war reminiscence describes Khataba as 'an area of desert in the most basic sense: flat, sand, sand everywhere and nothing else but the perennial, pestilential fly. Geographically Khataba was between Alexandria and Cairo; physically it was in the middle of nowhere.'[18]

Strict orders were issued to men writing home not to divulge their location. Deneys circumvented this elliptically, as this letter addressed, as they all were, from the huge Army Post Office in Durban, to his friend 'Hardy' (actually the family's pet dog), illustrates:

> A lot of news has turned up which would have been of great interest to you folk but an order came out today limiting very greatly what we can put in letters. Nothing can be said of where we are, no description of places which might be recognised so that there is very little that can be said.

Deneys describes diseased children and 'nasty dirty flies' and the camp as being 'set in a very sandy part'. He visited the signallers and found that Bill was comfortably set out in a tent with fly screens! In a final clue as to his whereabouts, he eulogised the Jaffa oranges he had just eaten: 'They are the juiciest and sweetest oranges that I have ever eaten and they make a thoroughly good meal in themselves. I only hope that the supply of them maintains its present level and, even better, tends to increase.'[19]

Some days later, permission was given for the news to be released that the troops were in Egypt and Deneys was a lot more forthcoming in a letter to his father. He described the country as 'interesting', but 'extremely depressing' and it is clear that he was also homesick. He notes the 'great change in the space of a few yards from fertility to desert in which literally not a blade of grass or the vestige of a bush grows' – which he found amazing.

Deneys watched a water buffalo plodding round and round a water wheel with fascination and examined the mechanics of this age-old method of irrigation dating back to the era of the pharaohs. Then while the men rested, watching the canal slip by, 'there was a sudden brown flash [and] in the path nearby settled a breath of South Africa. He flew off very soon but it was good to see this jolly little hoepoe.'

Deneys was also distressed by the apathetic Egyptian peasants emerging from their 'sordid' houses, which destroyed the pleasure he felt at the novelty of his experiences. He concluded the letter with his opinions on South African politics, a general election campaign was being waged and all men on active service were eligible to vote. The Allies had just taken Tunis and driven the Germans and Italians out of North Africa while the Russians were advancing after the epic Battle of Stalingrad. Deneys was upbeat about the progress of the war, but less so about the state of South African politics:

> With Tunis and Bizerta just taken and the Russians pushing in the Kuban it certainly looks as if the Hun is having a very thin time. I expect that we will be overseas on the continent very soon and that the S. Africans will get there in time to score some big victories over a defeated enemy for the sake of some very good propaganda in South Africa for the strengthen[ing] of the present government.[20]

This letter also contains Deneys's comments on South African parliamentary politics in the run-up to the 1943 general election, especially on a deal between the ruling United Party and the smaller Labour Party:

> I don't like the U.P. particularly but the present policy of the Labour Party seems to be to make the most out of the war and criticise the government for allowing profiteers to do the same. I wouldn't mind if I had any confidence in the Labour Party or its leaders but neither seem to warrant any support. The Springbok Legion is functioning in this div[ision] and I hope that from it there may come an intelligent influence in S.A. politics after the war. It does seem to be a dangerous organisation which might turn Fascist. But I think that its system of democratic election precludes this. The people in it seem to think clearly even if they are idealists and in their post war efforts to see that soldiers get a decent deal they may have quite a big effect. Any how I am going to continue to support them until I see something funny turning up in their midst.

The Springbok Legion was an organisation formed by soldiers to push their interests, both in the army and after demobilisation at the end of the war. Unlike many other such organisations, it was non-racial from the outset and attracted coloured and African members. Several of the leaders, such as Jack Hodgson and Jock Isaacowitz, were communists and Joe Slovo (later the leader of the South African Communist Party) has described it as a 'brave attempt to keep alive the spirit of the anti-fascist struggle among white ex-servicemen, and to wean them away from the extremes of racism'.[21] Slovo also served in the 6th Armoured Division, but as a signaller. There is no evidence that he and Deneys crossed paths, but it is likely that Slovo and Bill Schreiner, also a signaller, may have known each other, or had regular radio contact with each other. Joe Slovo claims not to have seen action at close quarters, but to have heard the impressive Allied artillery bombardments, in which Deneys played a small part, from afar.

Deneys's letters to his mother, Edna, reflected similar themes to those to his father. He wrote of soldiers whose rampant South African racism was tempered by encounters with the Egyptians: South African black people were seen as more honest than the Egyptians, who were offensively called 'Gippos'. He also described his experiences of a sandstorm, playing rugby, barefoot, in the desert sands, his doings and outings with his brother Bill and his friend Geoff. He and Geoff borrowed a set of hair clippers and set about cutting each other's hair: 'We are getting quite expert and are now capable of giving hair cuts which don't look as if a dog had chewed them up.'[22]

Deneys was more reticent about his health, but he suffered from various serious ailments in the army: measles during basic training in Potchefstroom and jaundice in Egypt. These diseases were probably encouraged by the close quarters in which young men from all parts of the country and social conditions were crammed. Many accounts of the history of the 6th Armoured Division mention how widespread diseases such as jaundice, or hepatitis, were.[23]

In June Deneys wrote to his mother describing a short leave period in Cairo.[24] This visit was much anticipated, as his first effort to get there had been thwarted when 'religion reared its ugly head and ably backed up by a bloomin' general succeeded in whittling away the best part of a Sunday. We had a slap up parade with a blooming march past and the complete issue was nothing but a blooming nuisance.'

When they eventually arrived in Cairo, one of the highlights was a visit to a facility for soldiers called Music for All because it played live music all day while offering its patrons baths, shaves and shampoos, as well as food and comfortable chairs. Deneys, Scotty and their mates hired a car and driver in Cairo and visited the great pyramids and monuments near Memphis.

The stepped pyramid of 'Djoser' struck Deneys as rather unimpressive and the pharaoh who built it must have been poor or 'stingy'. However, he was more impressed by the nearby tomb to the sacred bulls with its enormous coffins, but with one missing from the sequence. This was never made because, as Deneys told his parents, a change in rulers resulted in a change of worship from bulls to cats.[25]

The 6th Division remained training in Egypt for most of the rest of 1943. Deneys spent a month on sick leave for jaundice, but recovered fully. There was a brief sideways move to Palestine, but before the division settled down near Gaza, it was diverted to Italy where the final assault on the German stronghold in the ancient Benedictine monastery of Monte Cassino was being prepared.[26]

The South Africans were joining one of the most cosmopolitan of all the Allied armies. There were the Americans under General Mark Clark; British Commonwealth troops came from Africa (East, West and South); Britain itself; Australia; Canada; New Zealand and India. There were also Free French and Free Polish troops and, later, even a Brazilian contingent. In total, troops of some eighteen nations fought their way up the Italian peninsula.[27] The South Africans landed in Taranto, on the heel of Italy, at the end of April 1944 and were transported to the front line facing the German defences in the Gustav Line, the key stronghold of which was the monastery of Monte Cassino. The Allies believed that the Germans had fortified the monastery and consequently bombed it heavily, whereas the Germans only moved in once it had been reduced to ruins and then fortified the rubble.

Accommodation for the troops near the front line was rudimentary and squalid.[28] Family legend has it that Deneys objected to being billeted in a stable and when a sergeant-major roared at him that Jesus Christ had been born in a stable, Deneys replied that he had no such exalted aspirations.[29] Regrettably, Deneys's 1944 letters home do not appear to have survived. However, there is sufficient information to provide an adequate picture of his activities when family lore is correlated with the recorded historical information about the activities of the 6th Division and the 4/22 Field Regiment.

The South African artillery supported the final assault on Monte Cassino, which was made by Polish troops. This enabled the Allies to break through the German defences and dash for Rome. The heavy bombardment of the monastery resulted in much destruction of architectural and religious heritage and may have influenced the subsequent orders not to bombard Florence.

The 4/22 Field Regiment was initially equipped with 'Priest' self-propelled guns, but later re-equipped with 'workmanlike' Sexton self-propelled guns.[30] These were vehicle platforms designed to move artillery under their own power, rather than having the guns dragged behind a truck and then having to unlimber before going into action. The relevance of this technical detail is that Deneys had his left foot injured when it was trapped under the track of his Sexton self-propelled gun and he was out of action for much of June and July 1944.

The accident seems to have happened on 7 June, a day after the great Allied landings in Normandy, in northern France. This was also a day or two after the American commander, General Mark Clark, marched into the undefended city of Rome. This propaganda victory had serious consequences for the rest of the campaign, as Clark had failed to cut off retreating German forces and thus enabled the enemy to regroup behind the strong defences of the Gothic Line further north. On 7 June, the 6th Armoured Division was in hot pursuit of the retreating Germans and the sense of urgency, confusion and crisis may have contributed to Deneys's accident. The German army successfully escaped to their prepared positions in the Gothic Line where, helped by the onset of a severe winter, they prolonged the campaign into 1945.[31] On their way north to the Gothic Line, the Allies had to liberate the city of Florence.

Schreiner family lore has it that Gunner Deneys Schreiner disobeyed a direct order from a superior officer during the advance on Florence. According to the legend, as the self-propelled guns hove into view of the ancient city, the commanding officer provided the 11/66 battery of the 4/22 Field Regiment with a set of co-ordinates on which to open fire. The gunners realised that they would be firing on the dome of the Cathedral of St Mary of the Flower (Il Duomo di Firenze). The dome of this Renaissance masterpiece was completed in 1436 by Filippo Brunelleschi and the building is now a United Nations Educational, Scientific and Cultural Organization (UNESCO) World Heritage site. The family story has it that Peter Braun, the commander of Deneys's gun, refused to obey the order and the officer who had given the order then demanded that Deneys open fire and he refused. For a soldier to disobey a direct order from a superior officer on a battlefield would normally have the direst consequences, including a court martial and possible firing squad. However, there is no mention of the incident in Deneys's military records and the officer concerned does not seem to have been the 4/22 Field Regiment's commanding officer, Lieutenant Colonel Harpur, who was regarded as an outstanding officer and picked for advanced staff courses in Britain.[32] This would not have happened if he had blotted his copybook outside Florence.

The accuracy of this story is questionable. The Allied Supreme Commander in the Mediterranean theatre, Field Marshal Sir Harold Alexander, with the important moral support of the German consul in Florence (a non-Nazi) and the weight of the Geneva Convention behind the decision, had given orders that Florence was to be regarded as an open city, which meant it was not to be defended by the retreating Germans, nor was it to be bombed or shelled by the advancing Allied forces. South Africa's Major General Everard Poole had passed the emphatic order on to all the troops under his command.[33] Therefore, any artillery officer ordering the shelling of one of Florence's architectural and religious masterpieces would have been committing a war crime. At the time the 4/22 Field Regiment was heavily engaged on the flank of the forces advancing on Florence in support of a New Zealand contingent, the members of which were bitterly disappointed that the South Africans were the first of the Allied troops to enter the city, which they did on 4 August 1944.[34] If the incident ever happened, it was quickly hushed up and is possibly an early demonstration of Deneys's lifelong moral courage.

One of the 4/22 Field Regiment's observation officers climbed the steeple of the church of Santo Spirito to reconnoitre the bridges over the Arno and came under fire from the Germans who were busy destroying all but one of the bridges, the famous Ponte Vecchio, which was too narrow to allow tanks to cross it. Some version of this incident may have formed the basis for the family legend. The citizens of Florence welcomed the South Africans with 'wine, flowers and kisses', but the Allied advance halted further north of the city in the foothills of the Apennines where the Germans had built the Gothic Line.[35] As summer turned into autumn and then into a wet and freezing winter, the fighting became seriously bogged down. Deneys wrote to his father in early January 1945: 'Of course at the moment you are lolling around in the sunshine on the beach or battling against the south-easter at the royal Cape. Sounds pretty good to me, but what could really be better than sitting in the Appennines watching the snow fall.'[36]

During these cold months of static warfare, Deneys began preparing himself mentally for the post-war world. He read the letters of TE Lawrence (Lawrence of Arabia) and told his mother how little there was to do and how the troops were handing over their basic domestic chores to Italian families, eager to earn some cash.[37] Already his thoughts were turning to studies at Cambridge and he was refreshing his knowledge of chemistry. Deneys asked his father to find out from the relevant authorities what his chances were of going straight from Italy to Cambridge, rather than returning to South Africa first.[38] He also commented with insight on military tactics and strategy in the closing days of the war and his remarks on world affairs, particularly the meeting between the Big Three (Churchill, Stalin and Roosevelt) at Yalta showed a similar insight into high politics. However, perhaps his new temporary promotion to lance bombardier went to his head somewhat and he had the temerity to give his father a lecture on how to improve his golf.[39]

He also shared his thoughts on his future with his mother and told her of his wish to follow the natural science tripos for his first year at Cambridge until he could get a sense of direction. The most important news in the letter, was the death of President Franklin Roosevelt: 'It seems horribly unfair that Roosevelt, having led the Americans for so long should not live to see his greatest efforts come to fruition.'[40]

A few days later Deneys wrote again to his father, once more under conditions of strict censorship, but he was able to hint at the dramatic developments of the final Allied offensive:

> Obviously I can't tell you where we are but I think I am allowed to say that we are no longer up in the mountains. The country round here is really very lovely with the flat plain rising steeply into the mountains. This censorship business makes things very difficult because I have much that I would like to write about but nothing that I can say without being insecure. We are billeted in houses with the local population and we have been very fortunate in both our house and our family. The locals are only too willing to cooperate even to the extent of being embarrassing and there is very little that we can do for them in return.[41]

In the last days of the war in Europe, the German army in Italy was desperately retreating and many units were trapped against the banks of the Po River where they were pounded by South African and other Allied artillery.[42] However, after this grim task, the mood changed and the South Africans were sent into north-west Italy as the fighting ended. A victory parade was held on the motor racing circuit at Monza.[43] Thereafter, the division was sent to the region along the Swiss and French frontiers, in the foothills of the Alps near Lake Como. It was, as one of the military padres said, 'a lovely finish to the war'.[44]

Deneys wrote to his father: 'We are in one of the most beautiful places in Italy with a lake and boats and everything one could possibly want.'⁴⁵ He met a young Italian woman while rowing on the lake and spent several days rowing up and down near the pier where he had seen her. According to the family legends, she was the heiress to a chocolate fortune, but as Deneys was also seriously investigating the possibilities of going on to Cambridge, he left Italy before the lakeside courtship developed very far.⁴⁶

Deneys had learnt some Italian and he loved Italy, the people, the wine and the food. He had visited Rome, he had frozen in the winter of 1944-5, but he had endured and reached the therapeutic, almost idyllic conclusion at Lake Como. It was a life-moulding experience for a homesick, 21-year-old, who began his war in the fly-bitten desert and ended it two years later on the shores of one of the most beautiful lakes in Europe.

His wartime letters show his sense of humour, his acute powers of observation and his sense of commitment to his family (both to his parents and to his brother Bill), to his comrades and to the task at hand. These strengths enabled him to endure, but the war inevitably left some wounds, as shown by his reluctance to speak about his war service later in life and, perhaps, by his refusal to participate in the reminiscences and group activities of ex-servicemen such as the MOTHS (the Memorable Order of Tin Hats).

Notes

1. Edward M Spiers, *The Late Victorian Army, 1868–1902* (Manchester: Manchester University Press, 1992), pp.98–9.
2. Height: 177 centimetres; weight: 76 kilogrammes; chest: 86 centimetres.
3. South African National Defence Force (SANDF) Documentation Centre: Second World War Service Record, GDL Schreiner (Force Number 330219V).
4. Heather Schreiner, Reminiscences, 7 April 2017.
5. OD Schreiner Letters: File 1939–43, Deneys to Edna, 10 January 1943.
6. OD Schreiner Letters: File 1939–43, Deneys to Edna, 14 April 1943.
7. Neil Orpen, *Victory in Italy: South African Forces in World War II*, Vol. V (Cape Town: Purnell, 1975), p.15.

8. OD Schreiner Letters: File 1950-2, Deneys to his parents, 16 September 1951.
9. James F Bourhill, '"Red Tabs": Life and Death in the 6th South African Armoured Division, 1943-1945' (PhD thesis, University of Pretoria, 2014), p.57.
10. OD Schreiner Letters: File 1939-43, Deneys to Edna, 8 April 1943.
11. Bourhill, 'Red Tabs', p.2.
12. Andrew Stewart, '"The Klopper Affair": Anglo-South African Relations and the Surrender of the Tobruk Garrison', *Twentieth Century British History* 17, 4 (2006), pp.516-44.
13. Young George Bizos, later Nelson Mandela's lawyer, sailed to South Africa in 1941 as a child refugee from Nazi-occupied Greece, aboard the *Ille de France*. See George Bizos, *Odyssey to Freedom* (Cape Town: Random House Struik, 2007), p.47.
14. John Barkham, 'Dockside Diva', *Life*, 13 March 1944.
15. OD Schreiner Letters: File 1939-43, Deneys to OD Schreiner, 24 April 1943.
16. Orpen, *Victory in Italy*, p.7.
17. Orpen, *Victory in Italy*, p.8.
18. Jack Kros, *War in Italy: With the South Africans from Taranto to the Alps* (Johannesburg: Ashanti Publishing, 1992), p.6. Reminiscences of Private Albert Watson.
19. OD Schreiner Letters: File 1939-43, Deneys to 'Hardy', 2 May 1943.
20. OD Schreiner Letters: File 1939-43, Deneys to OD, 9 May 1943. The continent in this context refers to Europe.
21. Joe Slovo, *Slovo: The Unfinished Autobiography* (Johannesburg: Ravan Press, 1995), p.29.
22. See, for example, OD Schreiner Letters: File 1939-43, Deneys to Edna, 8 April 1943 and 2 June 1943.
23. Kros, *War in Italy*, see, for example, pp.82, 90.
24. OD Schreiner Letters: File 1939-43, Deneys to Edna, 2 June 1943.
25. OD Schreiner Letters: File 1939-1943: Deneys to Edna, 7 June 1943.
26. Orpen, *Victory in Italy*, pp.24-5.
27. Bourhill, 'Red Tabs', p.50.
28. Orpen, *Victory in Italy*, p.30; Kros, *War in Italy*, pp.51-2.
29. Else Schreiner, comments to author, 2016. See also Else Schreiner, Condolence Folders, 2008: Deneys Schreiner (Neys), 'Eulogy', 1 June 2008.
30. Orpen, *Victory in Italy*, p.17.
31. Kros, *War in Italy*, p.85. Else Schreiner: comments to David Robbins, 2014 for information on the foot injury.

32. Orpen, *Victory in Italy*, p.159.
33. Orpen, *Victory in Italy*, p.166.
34. Orpen, *Victory in Italy*, p.162.
35. Orpen, *Victory in Italy*, p.164.
36. OD Schreiner Letters: File 1945, Deneys to OD, 5 January 1945.
37. OD Schreiner Letters: File 1945, Deneys to Edna, 9 January 1945.
38. OD Schreiner Letters: File 1945, Deneys to OD, 15 February 1945.
39. OD Schreiner Letters: File 1945, Deneys to OD, 8 February 1945.
40. OD Schreiner Letters: File 1945, Deneys to Edna, 13 April 1945.
41. OD Schreiner Letters: File 1945, Deneys to OD, 21 April 1945 (?) (date unclear owing to water damage).
42. Kros, *War in Italy*, p.284.
43. Orpen, *Victory in Italy*, p.309.
44. Kros, *War in Italy*, p.293.
45. OD Schreiner Letters: File 1945, Deneys to OD, 18 May 1945.
46. Heather Schreiner, Reminiscences, 7 April 2017.

4

Science and Romance
The Cambridge Years (1945–51)

In order to register at the beginning of the 1945 academic year at Cambridge, Deneys's departure from Italy was so hasty that he was not properly demobilised. He had to rectify matters and complete all the paperwork retrospectively when he tried to cadge a military flight back to Johannesburg from Britain the following year.

Cambridge, in the post-war years, was attempting to re-establish its academic glory, but in the context of a beleaguered and impoverished Britain. It was also having to cope with integrating eighteen-year-old school-leavers into classes and colleges together with men in their mid-twenties who had served in the war and endured gruelling or traumatic experiences. Deneys, the war veteran, travelled to Cambridge by train with a boy straight out of school, who was also planning to do the Natural Sciences Tripos.

Deneys was fortunate enough to have had many of his courses from the University of Witwatersrand (Wits) recognised, so the time he needed to spend on undergraduate studies could be curtailed and he began to think about postgraduate studies at an early stage in his Cambridge career.[1] Some may regard it as heretical to extrapolate from an Oxford experience to a Cambridge experience, but the opinions of Ludovic Kennedy, a well-known writer and broadcaster, who had spent a year at Oxford before war broke out and who returned afterwards, are instructive:

The indolence and hedonism that had characterized the pre-war period, at least for some, had given way to application and austerity. Rationing was still in force and those of us – in 1946 the great majority – who had come back from the war and felt that time was not exactly on our side, wanted to make full use of the opportunity offered.[2]

The university authorities had to find accommodation for many more students than usual. School-leavers, British and Commonwealth ex-servicemen and foreign students poured in. Deneys was fortunate, as both grandson and son of Cambridge graduates, in being accepted for a place at Trinity College. The research work done by Cambridge scientists during the Second World War brought a flood of eager young researchers into the university to use the facilities in the expanding laboratories, the most famous being the Cavendish laboratory. Cambridge was becoming a modern research university at the centre of post-war Anglo-American academic dominance.[3] Cambridge science also played a complex role in underpinning the network of relationships between Britain, the Commonwealth and the dependent colonies. South Africa, certainly in the post-war period, was involved and Deneys's Cambridge studies can be placed in a broader dimension than that of simply individual choice and familial tradition; he was studying as part of an expanding international scientific network. But there was also another side to Cambridge: although the university shone in the academic cosmos, it could also be profoundly inward-looking. A historian of the university says: 'A scholar can step in a moment from international discussion in his seminar or lab to the parochial atmosphere of his college's Senior Combination Room – or vice versa, from lofty discourse in the SCR to instant coffee in the lab.'[4]

Deneys and his brother Bill arrived in Britain on 18 September 1945 and made their way to London. Deneys had vague memories of the battered city from the visit he had made with his parents in 1935. After reporting to the offices of the Union Defence Force,

Deneys found South Africa House a 'very frightening place', but nevertheless he and Bill felt like civilians again. They struggled to master the rationing coupon system so that they could buy clothes and look respectable when they applied in person for study grants. They worked out that they had sufficient funds to launch their academic studies; in fact, they may have had more money than they were able to spend in the tightly rationed country.[5]

Bill, who was at Cambridge to study law, wrote to their father describing their arrival and the allocation of rooms in Portugal Street, at The Lion, a hotel, he said, that was probably unchanged from his father's day. What had changed, of course, was that the two young Schreiners had to report to the town hall to obtain identity cards, ration books and clothing coupons. They also applied to be put on a waiting list for transport back to South Africa in 1946, a list that already had 7 000 names on it.[6] In a letter home Deneys mentioned a conversation with Mr Maskell, the Trinity Lodge porter, who not only remembered OD Schreiner, but also remembered a visit by WP.[7]

Deneys described his daily routine to his mother. His competent and efficient landlady, a 'sensible soul', woke Bill and Deneys at 7 am and they used the communal bathroom to shave and wash. They cycled up Portugal Street, carrying jugs to collect their daily milk ration (enough for six to eight cups of tea), then a walk or cycle up to college for breakfast at 8 am. Deneys had a full programme of lectures and laboratory work until 1 pm when he returned to Trinity for lunch. The afternoon activities were either rugby, laboratory work or free time. In the evenings were dinners in the Hall of the College, with age-old ceremony and tradition, but the meal was based on what could be produced under rationing conditions. Deneys, with his lifelong interest in food, grumbled frequently and loudly about the grimness of Cambridge meals under post-war conditions.[8]

His Cambridge letters demonstrate an expanding consciousness of both world affairs and social problems. Deneys wrote to his parents about British politics, the beginnings of the Cold War and racial prejudice. He clearly saw fear as the basis for racial prejudice and remarked that even liberals did not recognise 'the native as a fellow man'.[9] Yet, for all his philosophising, he lived student life to the full, playing rugby and squash, soaking up the atmosphere of Cambridge, but also concentrating on his studies; juggling physics and cutting back on mineralogy to focus on core subjects. He worried about being behind in his studies, no doubt because of his wartime service, and struggled to keep up with the pace. He played cricket for his college and rugby for Cambridge with great enthusiasm and was elected captain of the Trinity College Field Club, which controlled most sport at the college, except rowing. However, because he never played against Oxford, Deneys was never awarded a 'Full Blue'.[10] Much of his time was also devoted to planning a return trip to South Africa during the mid-year break, summer in England, winter in South Africa.

This trip was particularly significant because Deneys had not been home since leaving for Italy in 1943. It was on this trip too that he began his lifelong relationship with Else Kops, his future wife. Else was born in the eastern Free State, near Ficksburg. Her family moved to Johannesburg when she was twelve and she went to school at Parktown Girls High School and later at Potchefstroom Girls High School as a boarder. This move was apparently made to instil some discipline in her.[11]

Else had studied for a BSc at Wits, which was regarded as a useful degree that offered good career prospects for a young woman. However, in later life, she bemoaned the fact that she had not studied for a BA degree since her real interests were people, the past and the arts. As already mentioned, her path crossed with Deneys's during their undergraduate days, but no sparks flew at that stage. In 1946 when Deneys flew back to Johannesburg, he was not only reunited with his parents and family, but he met Else again and, this time, there was a spark after they met at a party.

However, it was not a party for young adults, but a birthday party for a twelve-year-old girl and Deneys and Else were invited separately to help control the children and make it a success. The hosting mother had invented a novel method of pairing children. She gave each girl the end of a coloured thread and a boy got the other end. They were in separate rooms and were to pull towards each other until they met up with their playmate. Deneys, the ever-enterprising, grabbed all the threads out of the hostess's hands and told the girls that they were all his! Else enjoyed his enthusiasm and they hit it off and began dating, or courting, in the terminology of the time.[12]

Deneys returned to Cambridge for the Michaelmas term, beginning in October 1946, and once again worried about his studies. Else, in the meantime, began making plans to join him in England. Deneys took himself off to Cornwall at the end of the year and saw the New Year in with much revelry. Remorse, perhaps even a case of drunken melancholy, set in and he began to worry about his chances of academic success and future prospects. He mused to his father:

> I don't suppose it's much good thinking out plans for after June, in the event of my being slung out, in anything more than tentative terms. My qualifications will most certainly not be of the highest then but it wouldn't appear that I am going to make an [missing word] success on the academic side. This doesn't, I hope, mean that I will of necessity spend the rest of my life as a stooge chemist – an automaton rather than a maker but the question arises as to whether it is best to settle down in a job in some particular field rather than to continue equipping myself.[13]

Whatever his faults, Deneys was certainly neither an automaton nor a stooge scientist.

OD Schreiner was on the edge of the limelight in early 1947. The British royal family visited their South African dominion between February and May to thank the Union for its contribution to the war effort. King George VI, Queen Elizabeth and the princesses Elizabeth (the present queen) and Margaret, included

Bloemfontein in their itinerary. The judges of the Appellate Division of the Supreme Court were involved in all the pomp and circumstance attendant upon such an occasion. The Appeal Court buildings were specially decorated and Chief Justice Watermeyer, accompanied by Appeal Judges Schreiner, Greenberg and Tindall, were part of the high-level delegation that met the White Train and the royal party on the platform of Bloemfontein Station. Then followed gun salutes, receptions, parades and garden parties in which the judges had to play their full part.[14]

The year 1948 was a significant one for Deneys. He wrote the final examinations for the Natural Sciences Tripos and began planning both his serious academic research and a major cycling trip to Italy with Else and Bill. However, Italy was in the throes of an acrimonious election campaign, which the Communists seemed likely to win. Fortunately, the results swung in favour of the Christian Democrats, largely as a result of the intervention of the Pope. Deneys made a wry comment to his father:

> It seems almost to be a proof that the Catholic Church is God's own church and the Pope is very highly commended for having given the right instructions to to his superstitious flock at the appropriate moment. The apparently widely used threat of excommunication for incorrect voting was regarded as a master stroke on behalf of the forces of truth and decency.[15]

In the next paragraph, Deneys commented on South African politics, with a general election imminent on 26 May, a month later, reporting that the British newspapers were predicting a victory for the United Party led by Jan Smuts. The narrow victory of the Afrikaans nationalists (Herenigde Nasionale Party), winning more seats in Parliament, despite winning fewer votes than the United Party (shades of the American elections in 2016), set South Africa on the apartheid path for decades to come.

OD Schreiner wrote to Edna, as Afrikaans nationalist supporters, dressed in Voortrekker costumes, celebrated in the streets of Bloemfontein, telling her that he had written to Bill and Deneys to calm them down. As for Deneys's plans to return and do scientific research in South Africa, OD had advised him to consult with Basil Schonland, the founder of the Council for Scientific and Industrial Research (CSIR), who would presumably be considering his own position in the wake of the election. However, OD, continued, all things being equal, there was no reason for Deneys not to return as his son's, 'line of country [*sic*] has nothing to do with repressing blacks or fighting the British'.[16]

However, Deneys was busy with his final examinations and they were preying more on his mind than the state of South African politics. Bill wrote to OD:

> Neys finished his exams yesterday rather gloomy about what occurred in the practicals and cursing himself for an oaf. Solid bloke though he is, exams get him really worked up and having done rather well in the written exam when he came a cropper in the first practical he wasn't feeling too good ... Failure seems out of the question but getting a II (1) is now according to him, very doubtful indeed.[17]

However, Cambridge had a system of taking into account laboratory work from the whole year and all hoped that this would help Deneys. OD told Edna that it was too soon to worry:

> We can't tell yet. I have always at the back of my mind that Neysie's strongest quality is his ability to deal with other people and I have the idea that if he goes out into a job of the right kind, in which he is not only looking at apparatus, he is more likely, *perhaps*, to find the best opportunities for his special faculties.[18]

Deneys did not get a stellar degree at Cambridge in 1948, but he consoled himself with the long-planned trip to Italy with Else and Bill. They left Cambridge before the final results were announced and appear to have missed the installation of Jan Smuts as chancellor of Cambridge University. OD described the reports of Smuts's speech as being of a 'highish grade' and he hoped that the boys did not leave for France before hearing it. The speech was indeed particularly far-sighted. Smuts often recognised, when out of South Africa, shifting world realities that he rarely acknowledged so explicitly when harassed by the nationalists back home. In his speech at Cambridge he said: 'We do not realise that we are in fact passing through one of the great secular revolutions of history, and that deeper forces are at work which – war or no war – may completely reshape our world, and are already in fact transforming our human scene.'[19]

Deneys was a member of the generation that would live through these revolutions, the deeper forces Smuts referred to. Deneys's great-grandfather Gottlob had been an extremely devout man, but his many progeny followed differing religious and secular persuasions: WP's descendants were firmly secular within two generations. The science Deneys studied was the instrument for a new understanding of the world and he dedicated himself within his sphere, to use Smuts's words, to the transformation of the 'human scene'.

Else and Deneys's holiday travels began with a very rough trip across the English Channel from Newhaven to Dieppe. Bill took seasickness pills and survived the storm sitting in a lounge in a stupor. Deneys refused the pills and suffered the consequences, although he did enjoy standing on deck in the gale, with the spray from the enormous waves whipping around them. They were then able to take a more tranquil train trip from Dieppe to Paris and enjoy a meal there because they had booked their bicycles through to Milan. However, when they arrived in Milan, there were no bicycles; they only arrived the following day.[20] This gave them time to visit the cathedral in Milan, which Deneys thought was the most beautiful in the world, and to attend an outdoor opera performance, albeit in poor weather.

In a letter to his mother, written in Milan, Deneys reported that he had sought out the top physical chemist at Cambridge and asked him what he should do and whether he would get a postgraduate position. Dr Dainton did not exclude Deneys from consideration, but warned that there was a great deal of competition for very limited places. He categorically warned Deneys off going to London. The letter concluded with rejoicing at the final arrival of the bikes, but they could only be retrieved after a battle with the Italian bureaucrats who had run out of the relevant forms and had to get new ones made before anything could happen.

Then it was up through the mountains to Lake Como and the villages Deneys had come to know so well in 1945. Else remembered their rapturous welcome and Deneys's easy rapport with the Italians.[21] Family members often queried this, arguing that the South Africans were an occupying army, but, by 1945, northern Italy had suffered a two-year occupation by the Germans, so easygoing South Africans were seen as liberators and were far more welcome, particularly as their arrival signified the end of conflict.

Returning to Cambridge, Deneys set about putting his life in order. He had several options: one was to work in an organic chemistry research laboratory with a senior scientist, but while this was potentially interesting, it did not seem to hold out good long-term prospects. The second option was to join a queue with several other research students with Dr Dainton and the third was to take up an offer from Dr Kemball to do research on adhesive and surface chemistry. Deneys had to reassure himself that it would not be a waste studying under a young and relatively unknown supervisor. He was relieved to discover, however, that Dr Kemball was highly regarded in both Britain and the United States of America and that Deneys would get a British government grant for his research work under his tutelage.[22]

Else had come over to England in 1948 to take up a research position at the Department of Scientific and Industrial Research (DSIR) and her relationship with Deneys continued to grow and deepen. He proposed the day before a rugby match involving his London Club, Richmond. His new fiancée went down to watch the match. As Deneys ran out on to the field, some of the young women sitting nearby remarked on his legs in highly flattering terms. Else turned to them and said, 'Hands off, girls, he's mine, we got engaged yesterday!'[23]

On 7 August 1948, a telegram was sent to Johannesburg, which read: 'Hooked and Happy Much Love from Both Else and Deneys'.[24] Deneys also wrote to his parents, exclaiming that he was lucky to have

> you folks for parents and your other two children as sister and brother; lucky too in parents-in-law-to-be although I know them very little at the moment; and lucky to be going to marry Else... You people have set a pretty high standard to live up to in the line of building a happy family and a fine home but if we didn't think that we could come more or less close to it we wouldn't be going to get married.[25]

Deneys's next letter was on an entirely different theme, as he tried to explain to his father, in non-technical terms, the meaning and importance of his doctoral research in inorganic chemistry. The occasion for the cogitation was a bout of rheumatoid influenza, 'of game reserve fame', through which Else nursed him. His PhD dissertation was titled 'The Absorption of Vapours on Metal Oxides' and was submitted in June 1951. He explained the complexities in language he hoped that his parents would understand. To simplify even further, the activities between molecules on a surface and molecules in the gas surrounding it are affected by temperature and a variety of other complex factors. His analysis and observations were based on careful calculations, but 'the set up for doing it is liable to all sorts of errors and the difference between good and bad work lies in (a) the elimination of the errors (b) a realisation of the errors and adjustment for them in analysing the results'. Deneys also took the long view that, over time, research would have so advanced that there would be a very different picture, 'with very little side tracks and dead ends'.[26]

Else settled into the post-war British way of life well and her life centred around Deneys's research, his sporting activities (including his golfing trials and tribulations), and her drawn-out laboratory research on bees. She was asked by the BBC to give two radio talks in Afrikaans. The couple were still meeting over weekends, as Else's work kept her in London, but they went to sporting events and to the opera at Covent Garden, one of their favourites was *La Traviata*. They aimed to get her laboratory work on bees transferred from London to Cambridge in 1949.[27]

The wedding was scheduled for January 1949 and the couple made excited preparations. Among the most important logistical arrangements was acquiring enough ration coupons to allow for a decent wedding cake to be baked. This proved a major exercise and Else and Deneys's friends chipped in with their ration coupons to help with catering for the reception. The two mothers back in South Africa sent food parcels and Else and her friends prepared a trifle, a great luxury at the time. It was so large that Deneys and Else were eating it for weeks after the wedding.[28]

Else confessed to her future mother-in-law that she felt moments of 'exultant joy' that she was going to marry Deneys and that her life was a whirl of shopping in London with her friend Janet Mollison, who was to be her maid of honour, and weekend trips to Cambridge to see Deneys. A literary event that made an impact on Else, despite the wedding excitement, was the arrival, hot off the press, of a copy of Alan Paton's *Cry, the Beloved Country*, which was rapidly becoming an international sensation. Else thought it was too heart-rending to read through all at once, partly because Paton had captured black South African speech patterns so accurately.[29]

Else and Deneys were married in the registry office in Cambridge on 22 January 1949. Neither the Kops nor the Schreiners were able to make it to the wedding and it was a small affair. Bill described the event for his parents, describing the couple as 'very controlled outwardly but clearly bubbling over inside'. The ceremony was quietly and tastefully performed and the reception was held in Deneys's friend Bob Smith's rooms at

Trinity. According to Bill, it was 'small and very friendly because only friendly folk had been asked'. Deneys made a serious but good speech and toasted their absent parents before he and Else headed to London. Bill said that the only flaw in the arrangements was the 'distinct shortage of parents'.[30]

On returning from their very abbreviated honeymoon (punctuated by Deneys's appearances on the rugby field), they moved to 33 Victoria Park, with Deneys's fellow students helping to move their goods in the Trinity College hand cart. Among their earliest visitors was a South African veterinary researcher from Onderstepoort, who had met Else in her laboratory, and on discovering that her maiden name was Kops, declared himself to have been her mother's first boyfriend.[31]

Else and Deneys embarked on their life as a young married couple, juggling his research schedule with her work commitments, building a circle of friends, acquiring new kittens and entertaining in their tiny Cambridge flat. Deneys's irreverent sense of humour and desire to poke fun at pomposity had ample scope in Cambridge. One example was his written suggestion to the university authorities that his rugby club, the Hampstead Raiders, should receive an honorary degree. As a result of his audacity, Else and Deneys were invited to tea with the master of Trinity College, the eminent historian of Italian unification and also of eighteenth-century England, GM Trevelyan, and Mrs Trevelyan, whom Else regarded as the more formidable figure. Else happily recounted to Edna that Deneys had fired off his letter in the evening and woken up the following morning in a cold sweat saying, 'Good God woman! I must be mad! Why did you let me post it?'[32]

Although Deneys had missed Smuts's great address to Cambridge when he was inaugurated as chancellor in 1948, he met the ex-prime minister on his next visit to Cambridge in 1949. This time, the South African students were more critical of the 'Oubaas' than they had been in 1948. Deneys described him as unimpressive and out of touch, particularly in his remarks on the 'colour problem'. Smuts seemed uninterested in the affairs of the Union and was enjoying spending his time, 'banqueting about England'. The South African students, according to Deneys, were utterly disillusioned as they left the meeting.[33]

As his research neared completion, Deneys began thinking of further career moves and one option was a year in the United States, before heading back to South Africa.[34] He also applied to various British and Commonwealth agencies for direct funding, or for a fellowship that would enable him to continue at Cambridge. However, nothing came of this and so he accepted a visiting professorship at Pennsylvania State College, beginning in August 1951.[35]

Else and Deneys spent their last New Year in London, joining in the revelry in Trafalgar Square to see in 1951. They took up a position under the tall Norwegian pine tree (donated by the people of Norway each year, to this day, to thank the British for their efforts at liberating Norway during the Second World War) and watched the 'hilarious and not very sober crowds' enjoying themselves.[36]

In March 1951, Else gave birth to their first son, Oliver Conrad, described by his Kops grandmother, Bertha, as a 'lovely baby'. The Kops parents had gone to England for the big event. Deneys was bursting with pride. Bertha described how he wanted to walk up one street and down the next, so that he could tell more friends about his new son.[37] Three months later, the gestation period for Deneys's PhD ended and he submitted his dissertation in June. In August the little family left for the United States.

Between 1945 and 1951, Deneys completed his Cambridge Natural Sciences Tripos and mastered the art of postgraduate research, receiving his PhD within three years. Despite the wobbles in his undergraduate studies, he had succeeded at Cambridge, one of the leading research institutions in the English-speaking world. He followed this by taking his first steps in his academic career at a fast-growing American university where research was well funded. He had been exposed to the intellectual environment in post-war Britain where a socialist government (of which he did not entirely approve) was building a welfare state. It was a country where social and political experiments were taking place; Else described how, on their New Year's Eve visit to Trafalgar Square, they were shaken by the amount of indiscriminate kissing that went on all around them. She wrote: 'A girl wandering along would fight much harder to prevent some strange young man pricking her balloon than she would struggle to prevent some strange and probably not very sober young man kissing her.'[38]

The Second World War had wrought immense changes in British social mores and Deneys and Else, brought up in the more conservative environment of South Africa, had to adjust fast, but they adapted well and accepted the changes with the tolerance for which they would later become known.

Notes

1. OD Schreiner Letters: File 1945(2), Deneys to Edna, 24 September 1945.
2. Ludovic Kennedy, *On my Way to the Club* (Glasgow: Fontana, 1990), p.174.
3. Heike Jöns, 'The University of Cambridge, Academic Expertise and the British Empire, 1885–1962', *Environment and Planning A*, 48 (2016), pp.94–114.
4. Christopher NL Brooke, *A History of the University of Cambridge 1870–1990*, Vol. IV (Cambridge: Cambridge University Press, 1993), p.xv.
5. OD Schreiner Letters: File 1945(2), Deneys to OD, 20 September 1945.
6. OD Schreiner Letters: File 1945(2), Bill to OD, 24 September 1945.
7. OD Schreiner Letters: File 1945(2), Deneys to OD, 24 September 1945.
8. OD Schreiner Letters: File 1945(2), Deneys to Edna, 12 October 1945. Confirmed by Else Schreiner, Reminiscences, 2017, and Jennifer Schreiner, Reminiscences, 2017.
9. OD Schreiner Letters: File 1946, Deneys to OD, 6 January 1946.
10. Else Schreiner, Reminiscences, 2016. See also University of KwaZulu-Natal (UKZN) Archives, SP25/1/1/1, Schreiner, GDL (Prof & Vice Principal UNP) 1976–1987, Newspaper cuttings, Deneys Schreiner, 'Sporting Autobiography', *NU Sport*, June 1984, p.6.
11. Schreiner, 'Sporting Autobiography'.
12. Else Schreiner, Reminiscences, 2016.
13. OD Schreiner Letters: File 1947, Deneys to OD, 5 January 1947.

14. J. Haasbroek, 'Die Britse Koningsbesoek aan Bloemfontein, Maart 1947', *Navorsinge van die Nasionale Museum Bloemfontein* 16(8) (2000), pp.213–59.
15. OD Schreiner Letters: File 1948, Deneys to OD, 25 April 1948.
16. OD Schreiner Letters: File 1948, OD to Edna, 28 May 1948.
17. OD Schreiner Letters: File 1948, Bill to OD, 6 June 1948.
18. OD Schreiner Letters: File 1948, OD to Edna, 13 June 1948. Emphasis in the original.
19. Richard Steyn, *Jan Smuts: Unafraid of Greatness* (Johannesburg: Jonathan Ball, 2015), p.160.
20. OD Schreiner Letters: File 1948 (2), Deneys to Edna, 18 June 1948.
21. Else Schreiner, Reminiscences, 2016.
22. OD Schreiner Letters: File 1948 (2), Deneys to Edna, 9 July 1948.
23. Else Schreiner, Reminiscences, 2016.
24. OD Schreiner Letters: File 1948, Telegram, 7 August 1948.
25. OD Schreiner Letters: File 1948, Deneys to parents, 2 August 1948.
26. OD Schreiner Letters: File 1948, Deneys to OD, 30 August 1948.
27. OD Schreiner Letters: File 1948, Deneys to Edna, 8 September 1948; Deneys to OD, 8 October 1948.
28. Else Schreiner, Reminiscences, 2016.
29. OD Schreiner Letters: File 1948, Else to Edna, 22 November 1948.
30. OD Schreiner Letters: File 1949, Bill to Edna, 24 January 1949.
31. OD Schreiner Letters: File 1949, Deneys to OD, 17 February 1949.
32. OD Schreiner Letters: File 1949, Else to Edna, 30 May 1949.
33. OD Schreiner Letters: File 1949, Deneys to OD, 21 June 1949.
34. OD Schreiner Letters: File 1949, Deneys to Edna, 25 July 1949.
35. OD Schreiner Letters: File 1950–2, Deneys to parents, 14 February 1951.
36. OD Schreiner Letters: File 1950–2: Else to parents, 10 January 1951.
37. OD Schreiner Letters: File 1950–2: Bertha Kops to Edna, 28 March 1951.
38. OD Schreiner Letters: File 1950–2: Else to parents, 10 January 1951.

5

Research on a Cold War Campus
Pennsylvania State College (1951–2)

Once he had completed his PhD, Deneys took the opportunity to spend a year or so in the United States of America and he, with Else and baby Oliver, crossed the Atlantic in August 1951. He had received several tentative offers from Ivy League campuses, but the firmest one came from Pennsylvania State College, home to the cutting-edge Low Temperature Laboratory. He was offered a post that paid US$4 800 per annum, a greater sum than the more prestigious universities were offering.[1] This was a significant consideration for a scientist with a young family. Deneys always saw his time in the United States as a temporary move to enrich his career, before his planned return to South Africa. However, the move also fixed Deneys's personal career into a post-war web of expanding international scientific and academic networks.

The United States was important for Deneys's direct research experience as a part of the international family of organic and inorganic chemists, or physical scientists, but his interests were always broader: he was a reflective and thoughtful person who absorbed ideas and the atmosphere of his context. The American sojourn also influenced his broader intellectual and even political development. His wartime, Cambridge and American experiences all played their part in moulding him into a defender of academic freedom later in South Africa. He thought deeply about society in general and about the role of the university in society in particular.

While his ideas developed over his lifetime, the experiences he had in the United States were critical to the development of his intellectual approach, for it was there that he first had personal experience of state interference in academic freedom, of the compromises related to applied research and of discrimination against African Americans.

The Cold War may be said to have begun, or have been proclaimed, in 1946 when the British wartime prime minister, Winston Churchill, visited the United States. Accepting an honorary degree from Westminster College in Missouri, he warned of Soviet influence and encroachment:

> From Stettin in the Baltic to Trieste in the Adriatic, an iron curtain has descended across the Continent. Behind that line lie all the capitals of the ancient states of Central and Eastern Europe . . . all these famous cities and the populations around them lie in what I must call the Soviet sphere.[2]

The Western world, the so-called free world, turned to caution and conservatism in the late 1940s and early 1950s, as the world changed dramatically. India became independent in 1947 and Pakistan broke away as an independent Muslim country. In the Far East, communists had banished the corrupt regime of Chiang Kai-Shek from mainland China to Taiwan (Formosa). The French were losing control of their colonies in Indochina, the Dutch had lost Indonesia and the British were facing a communist insurgency in Malaya. The United States and its allies, authorised by the United Nations, were waging war against North Korea and 'Red' China on the Korean peninsula. Above all, the minor wars were being fought under the threat of nuclear war between the United States (and the West) and the Soviet Union and the Warsaw Pact countries.

France was in a period of prolonged political turmoil that was only ended in 1958 when General Charles de Gaulle returned to power to establish the Fifth Republic. Across the Rhine, West Germany began rebuilding democracy under its conservative chancellor Konrad Adenauer and the Soviets lifted the blockade of the divided city of Berlin after the Western allies (including South Africa) staged a successful airlift of supplies for the civilian population. The European swing to conservatism was strengthened when Churchill was returned to 10 Downing Street in the 1951 British general election.

In the United States in 1950, shortly before the Schreiners arrived, Senator Joseph McCarthy began his campaign against communists, homosexuals and liberals generally, a campaign that turned into a witch-hunt that coined the term 'McCarthyism'. Academics, actors, diplomats, trade unionists and journalists fell victim to his demagoguery. The wartime military leader and war hero General Dwight D Eisenhower won the presidency in 1952, but cautiously avoided confronting McCarthy, until the senator overplayed his hand and attacked the military. Only then did Eisenhower strike back. By that time the atmosphere of anti-communist paranoia had deeply permeated American universities, as well as Hollywood, the State Department and the trade unions.[3]

In South Africa, the new nationalist government had taken power in 1948 and began consolidating its hold on power and implementing ever stricter racial segregation. '*Swart gevaar*' and '*rooi gevaar*' (black and red threats) became the main menaces of the day, much used in nationalist rhetoric and propaganda. In 1950, Prime Minister DF Malan pushed the Suppression of Communism Act through Parliament and the Communist Party of South Africa became illegal and had to dissolve and go underground.[4] It was in this international atmosphere of tension, even paranoia, that Deneys and his family arrived in rural Pennsylvania.

American universities in the 1950s were beginning a period of enormous expansion that would peak in the 1960s and early 1970s. Jacques Barzun, French-American historian and philosopher of education, described the American university of the period thus: 'Its structure, management, sources of support, relation to Church and State, and responsibility to the public are unique and set it apart from all other types – English, Continental or South American.'[5] Universities, Barzun continued, were expected 'to turn out scientists and engineers, foster international understanding, provide a home for the arts, satisfy divergent tastes in architecture and sexual morals, cure cancer, recast the penal code, and train equally for the professions and for a life of cultured contentment in the coming Era of Leisure'.[6]

Pennsylvania State College (now Pennsylvania State University) did not have such grand ambitions in the early 1950s. It was a publicly funded educational institution known as a 'land-grant college'. These were developed to promote teaching and research in practical disciplines such as agriculture, engineering and science, rather than the classical studies of the Ivy League or Oxbridge-style universities.[7] In crossing the Atlantic, Deneys was moving from a musty traditional institution to one with a utilitarian approach; from the spires, quads and traditions of Cambridge to the modern functional buildings, fears and enthusiasms of the United States.

The director of the Low Temperature Laboratory at Penn State, under whom Deneys was to work, was Professor John Aston, a renowned organic chemist whose work led to the production of liquid hydrogen and helium, with applications for the cooling of nuclear reactors, but this latter development was after Deneys's time.[8]

In 1950 Penn State acquired a new president, Milton Stover Eisenhower, younger brother of the soon-to-be president. Professor Eisenhower focused on raising Penn State to full university status. One of the most important ways he did this was by promoting scientific research. Deneys arrived to take up his position as a visiting associate professor of Chemistry at the beginning of this campaign.[9] The arrival of a research scientist with a PhD from one of the oldest and most distinguished universities in the English-speaking world, who also had a distinguished war record, must have delighted the brother of the more famous General Eisenhower.

The core campus of Penn State was situated in College Park, a town that grew out of the farmlands to service the college. It is situated almost at the geographical centre of the state of Pennsylvania, surrounded by rolling hills, streams and fields and

Deneys and Else had to adapt to life in these bucolic surroundings, somewhat different to the fens of Cambridgeshire, with their close proximity to London.

They settled at first in an apartment on the main street of College Park, but later rented a house in Bellefonte, some 15 kilometres to the north-east of the campus. Bellefonte nestled among heavily wooded hills and was a hilly town, filled with trees shedding their many-hued leaves as autumn advanced and with steeply pitched roofs ready to cope with the fairly regular snowfalls that characterised the winter months.

The Schreiners found the Americans almost overeager to be helpful, but, as Deneys informed his parents, they had strange ideas about England, 'where everything pleasurable comes in ½ pints and hardships come by the gallon or more'. Deneys also found that one of the key American words was 'homogenised', which applied to everything from their milk and bread (which he and Else disliked) to the university where the process of 'homogenisation' helped to manage the ballooning student numbers.[10]

Deneys plunged into his research, but, surprisingly, given the stereotypes about go-getting Yankees, he found that the American laboratories were not as well organised as those at Cambridge had been. Penn State was involved in research for the United States Navy that required confidentiality and this had priority in the allocation of resources. Deneys therefore had to compete for access to laboratory equipment and resources with colleagues who were working on secret projects. He was even roped in to help operate equipment for a colleague whose naval research findings were long overdue.[11]

One of the side effects of the Cold War anti-communist fears was that university faculty members, including visiting foreign scholars, such as Deneys, were required to sign oaths of loyalty to the United States. The anti-communist furore in the late 1940s and early 1950s has been described as the 'nadir in the history of American academic freedom'.[12] The Truman administration had imposed loyalty-testing on federal employees and state universities fell within the widely cast net. Penn State College rigorously enforced the federal edict for many years, but, by the beginning of the twenty-first century, it was seldom enforced, although it remained university policy for another decade or so.[13]

The foreign researchers at Penn State in the early 1950s were required to sign the oaths as a condition for continuing their research. This caused consternation and various scientists experienced fits of patriotism and loyalty to their own countries that they may never have felt before. A British scientist refused to compromise his loyalty to the ailing King George VI, a Hungarian experienced feelings of deep Danubian devotion, while several more were worried that they would compromise their standing back home by signing the American documents. It was Deneys Schreiner who thought up a solution, but first he took the document home, discussed it with Else, then slept on it.

The next morning he returned to college and presented a letter to the Chemistry Department stating that he would undertake not to attempt to overthrow the United States government by force, unless, of course, a state of war existed between the Union of South Africa and the United States of America. The anxious university administrators were quite happy with the formulation, national honour was satisfied and, above all, funding was not compromised. The Schreiners had a good laugh and some of the other foreign students took up the idea and decided to submit similar letters.[14]

Penn State College may not have been the most vibrant cosmopolitan academic hub in the United States, but it was demanding of the time and expertise of its faculty members. Deneys was absorbed in his research work and spent long hours in the laboratory, often working deep into the night. He would supervise what he called 'hydrogen runs', which depended on the continuous running of a compressor. He also had to use his allotted quantity of hydrogen in one fell swoop, so he would spend days and nights, sometimes up to a week, working and sleeping in the laboratory. Else was once awoken from a welcome sleep (given the lung capacity of a vocal baby Oliver) by the sounds of what she thought was a burglar downstairs. She rushed to the top of the staircase to defend her home and infant. The burglar, none other than Deneys, switched the light on as he crept up the stairs, only to find his wife at the top, with a chair held on high, ready to smash it over his head.[15]

Else found the adjustment from Cambridge life difficult and her American experience was naturally dominated by toddling little Oliver and her second pregnancy. Although American academic wives were kind, they had little experience of the wider world and the rounds of coffee mornings and baby chatter were cloying for the more cosmopolitan young South African. She found it claustrophobic, very materialistic and snobbish. She recalled a cocktail party held at their home. They had invited their next-door neighbour, a man who happened to be a plumber. The university people were distinctly put out at this disregard for their class and status. Else was also obliged to belong to the university Women's Circle – the 'stitch and bitch club', she called it. She found the women conservative and excessively prudish. Once Else had to entertain them at their home. To torment them, Else hung a painting of a naked woman reclining on a settee, by Jean Dufy, in a prominent position. No one dared raise their eyes from their knitting and needlework to look at it.[16]

Nevertheless, the Schreiners were able to enjoy the rural environment around College Park and rambled in the Catskill Hills around the college. Deneys even started a cricket team with a motley collection of Indians, West Indians, an Englishman, a South African, a New Zealander and three curious Americans, but they had to travel long distances to find any opposing teams to play against. Golf was also not widely played and Deneys found that he used his golf clubs so infrequently that mice chewed off his grips.[17] However, he and Else played tennis in Bellefonte and on the university campus and several times during their stay, they holidayed in the Catskill Mountains. However, they scandalised the 'stitch and bitch club' by encouraging young Oliver to splash around naked in mountain streams and ponds.[18]

The Schreiners had enough space in their allocated home, before little Deneys was born, to take in a lodger to help cover expenses. They were surprised when the first prospective lodger to come knocking on their door was an African American student who was finding that his race stood in the way of his acquiring lodgings. Deneys and Else asked if he knew they were from South Africa and were astonished at his response: 'Yes, but I knew that you would not be here if you were racists.'[19]

Research demands, a toddler and the birth of their second child meant that Deneys and Else were not able to make any sort of grand tour of the United States. The most Deneys thought likely was that they would be able to spend a few days in New York before they left for South Africa.[20] However, he participated enthusiastically in college activities, helping with fund-raising and even running an English-style pub and a cigar bar at events.[21]

Perhaps the most important event in the lives of the Schreiners during their time in the United States was the birth of their second son, Hilson Deneys, on 24 May 1952. This anticipated event prompted grandfather OD Schreiner to apply to the chief justice for long leave, so that he and Edna could visit the United States to be present when the baby was born. OD also wanted to visit Boston, so that he could have a surgical procedure on his pharynx.[22]

The visit of OD, Edna and Deneys's sister Jeannie came as a constitutional crisis, caused by the efforts of the nationalist government to remove the coloured voters in the Cape province from the common voters' roll, gripped South Africa. The Separate Representation of Voters Act of 1951 had been passed by the House of Assembly and the Senate, without the two-thirds majority required by the South Africa Act, the Constitution of the Union since 1910. It was legally challenged and heard by the Appellate Division in early 1952. Chief Justice Albert Centlivres, with a full bench of judges, including OD Schreiner, concurring, struck down the Act.[23]

To circumvent the constitutional protections of the entrenched clauses, the Malan government retaliated by passing the High Court of Parliament Act in April 1952. This piece of legislation turned Parliament into the highest judicial authority over its own laws. OD Schreiner was on his visit to the United States when this legal abomination was passed. His friend and judicial colleague Oscar Hoexter kept him abreast of developments, highlighting the legal absurdity of the situation in words that must have been relished by the Schreiners:

> If I were an M.P., I would propose an amendment that no member of the Court [meaning Parliament] having a law degree should be allowed to vote, provided that any Cabinet Minister having a law degree would be allowed if he filed an affidavit that, in spite of his degree, he had no knowledge of the law.[24]

OD returned to South Africa after visiting his son and his new family and having had a successful operation in Boston. He resumed his seat on the bench in time to join his colleagues in striking down the High Court of Parliament Act in November 1952.[25]

While Else found her time in the United States an alienating experience, Deneys enjoyed himself. His research was rewarding, the university had a collegial atmosphere and he felt he was laying a worthwhile platform from which to launch an academic career. He liked the Americans of his acquaintance and judged McCarthyism to be an aberration. Perhaps, at that stage, he also saw apartheid as a temporary South African aberration.

Deneys, Else, Oliver and the latest young Deneys (Neysie) returned to South Africa towards the end of 1952. They travelled again by sea, a lengthy voyage, but not as intensely traumatic an experience as carting a toddler and a new baby on a long and noisy intercontinental flight with multiple stopovers.

In January 1953 Deneys took up an appointment as a senior research officer at the Bernard Price Institute for Geophysical Research at the University of the Witwatersrand. He was set to begin his academic career at his alma mater in his home city. He had been a participant in and a direct beneficiary of the Anglo-American academic dominance of the post-war era. He imbibed the tradition and deeper values of the system, surviving Cold War paranoia in the United States. However, as became clearer during the late 1950s and following decades, universities in South Africa, and particularly the English-language universities, were to be squeezed between internal political turmoil and external political and academic isolation. It would be Deneys's role, as a senior university administrator more than two decades later, to try to keep channels of communication open to the outside world and to begin to break down the apartheid barriers within the university and within the country.

Notes

1. OD Schreiner Letters: File 1950–2, Deneys to family, 17 December 1950.
2. Martin Gilbert, *Never Despair: Winston S Churchill 1945–1965* (London: Heinemann, 1988), p.200.
3. Shrecker, Ellen, 'Political Tests for Professors: Academic Freedom during the McCarthy Years', The University Loyalty Oath: 50th Anniversary Retrospective Symposium, 7–8 October 1999, University of California, Berkeley. http://www.lib.berkeley.edu/uchistory/archives_exhibits/loyaltyoath/symposium/schrecker.html.
4. Stephen Clingman, *Bram Fischer: Afrikaner Revolutionary* (Cape Town: David Philip, 1998), pp.185–6.
5. Jacques Barzun, *The American University: How it Runs, Where it is Going* (London: Oxford University Press, 1969), p.1.
6. Barzun, *The American University*, p.2.
7. Barzun, *The American University*, p.3.
8. 'John Aston, 87, Dies, Pioneer in Cryogenics', *New York Times*, 9 August 1990. See also University of KwaZulu-Natal (UKZN) Archives, SP25/1/1/1, Schreiner, GDL (Prof & Vice Principal UNP), 1976–1987, Press Release (PR 92/65), 2 November 1965, New Dean of Science.
9. Email from Meredith Weber, Research Services Specialist, University Libraries, Pennsylvania State University, 11 December 2016.
10. OD Schreiner Letters: File 1950–2, Deneys to parents, 16 September 1951.
11. OD Schreiner Letters: File 1950–2, Deneys to parents, 13 January 1952.
12. Schrecker, 'Political Tests for Professors'.
13. Larry C Backer, 'Loyalty Oaths and the University: Should Penn State

Continue to Reserve to Itself the Power to Terminate "Subversives"?' *Monitoring University Governance*, 27 January 2013. http://lcbpsusenate.blogspot.co.za/2013/01/loyalty-oaths-and-university-is-it-tiem.html.
14. Else Schreiner, Reminiscences, 2016.
15. Else Schreiner, Reminiscences, 2016.
16. Else Schreiner, Reminiscences, 2016. The painting is still hanging in Highwood.
17. UKZN Archives, SP25/1/1/1, Schreiner, G.D.L. (Prof & Vice Principal UNP), 1976–1987, Newspaper cuttings, Deneys Schreiner, 'Sporting Autobiography', *NU Sport*, June 1984, p.6.
18. Else Schreiner, Reminiscences, 2016.
19. Else Schreiner, Reminiscences, 2016.
20. OD Schreiner Letters: File 1950–2, Deneys to OD, 13 January 1952.
21. Else Schreiner, Reminiscences, 2016.
22. OD Schreiner Letters: File 1950–2, OD to Chief Justice, 5 December 1951.
23. Ellison Kahn, 'Oliver Deneys Schreiner: The Man and His Judicial World', *South African Law Journal* 97 (1980), pp.566–615.
24. OD Schreiner Letters: File 1950–2, OH Hoexter to OD Schreiner, 30 April 1952.
25. Kahn, 'Oliver Deneys Schreiner'.

6

Launch into Liberalism and Academia
Johannesburg (1953–9)

The Schreiners moved into a house in Richmond Avenue in the expanding Johannesburg suburb of Auckland Park, a comfortable commute for Deneys, travelling to the University of the Witwatersrand (Wits) campus in Braamfontein. There was a bucolic quality to the white-ruled world of the suburb in the 1950s. John Laband (later a professor of history at the University of Natal in Pietermaritzburg), who lived in the same street as the Schreiners, recalls horse-drawn vegetable carts clopping along the streets and housewives stopping them for their supplies. Milk was delivered to the doorstep, or front gate, in glass bottles sealed with cardboard discs. Children could roam the streets unattended, play in parks and whirl around on their bicycles. Young Oliver and little Deneys (Neysie) played with John and learned to swim in the Laband swimming pool.[1] This idyllic lifestyle was shielded from South African reality by the apparatus of the apartheid state, including the pass laws and influx control and the night-time curfew for black South Africans.

Deneys had been appointed as a senior research fellow at the Nuffield Geochronological Unit of the Bernard Price Institute (BPI) in February 1953. The Institute had been founded by Sir Basil Schonland, a friend of OD Schreiner's. When Deneys arrived Schonland was still an influential figure, but he had largely moved upwards to establish the Council for Scientific and Industrial

Research and was later appointed to the high honorary position of chancellor of Rhodes University. As a rising young scholar, Deneys was fortunate to co-publish a scientific paper with Schonland.[2]

There were also other distinguished scientists associated with the BPI in the 1950s, particularly in the broad field of palaeontology. They included the world-renowned, Australian-born palaeo-anthropologist Raymond Dart, who had identified the first fossil of *Australopithecus africanus*, also known as the 'Taung child'.[3] Other stalwarts were James Kitching and Edna Plumstead and one of the up-and-coming young scientists, Phillip Tobias, later became a close friend of the Schreiners.[4]

The exciting discoveries of pre-human fossils in the Makapansgat area of what is now Limpopo Province, then the northern Transvaal, provided strong evidence for theories of evolution. However, these were not popular with the government of the day, which was not only developing pseudoscientific theories to support apartheid, but also located these within the framework of dominant fundamentalist, Calvinist, religious theories. The BPI had to perform some deft manoeuvres on occasion to acquire and keep state funding.[5] Deneys's contribution related to the chemical dating of rock strata, an essential part of the process of dating the fossils, but not in itself likely to raise the suspicions of the guardians of Afrikaner nationalist orthodoxy.

Outside the university, the political climate was heating up. Deneys had returned to South Africa in January 1953, shortly before the National Party was returned to power in the white Parliament for the second time, despite its continued failure to win an overall majority of votes. Efforts to extend racial segregation and entrench National Party power increased and Dr Hendrik Verwoerd, Minister of Native Affairs, was forging segregationist prejudice into the ideology of apartheid. Verwoerd, Dutch-born, but a more extreme ideological Afrikaner nationalist than most native-born Afrikaners, loathed the English. He quickly became a dominant figure in the National Party during the 1950s, being elected party leader and prime minister in 1958, following the death of JG Strijdom. His segregationist philosophy was not simply the old colonial stratagem of divide and rule, but was formed by a total intellectual conviction. As an anthropologist, his concept of society was that it was an organic whole and each society had a culture, traditions and history so peculiarly its own that it was set apart from all other nations.[6]

Two of the anti-apartheid battles of the 1950s that impinged most on Deneys were the battle to protect the coloured franchise, in which his father played a leading part, and the campaign against the early moves to segregate the universities, culminating in 1959 in the promulgation of the Extension of Universities Act. OD had kept his home in Johannesburg, living at the Bloemfontein Club when the Appellate Division was in session. Therefore, he had the support of his whole family near at hand during the great judicial crisis. What they said to each other has not been recorded for the obvious reason that, living near each other and sharing Sunday lunches, they did not need to put their thoughts on paper. The Schreiner letters of this period are largely between OD and Edna and are of a personal rather than a public or political nature. Correspondence between Deneys and his parents petered out after his sojourn in the United States of America ended.

The struggle to protect the position of coloured people on the common voters' roll was part of a broader struggle against a relentless attack by the National Party on democratic values in South Africa. It prompted a strong reaction and led to the establishment of activist groups such as the Black Sash, originally known as the Women's Defence of the Constitution League (WDCL), and as the Black Sash from 1956 onwards.[7] Else was active in its establishment and took part in its earliest march on 25 May 1955. Some 2 000 women, largely white, marched through the streets of Johannesburg from Joubert Park to the City Hall to protest at the packing of the Senate by the Nationalists, which was their chosen method for manufacturing the two-thirds majority that would enable them to amend the Constitution and remove coloured people from the common voters' roll.[8]

On 28 June Else took part in a smaller march to the Union Buildings in Pretoria to present a petition, signed by one hundred thousand white women, protesting against the government's attacks on the Constitution. As was to happen the following year, during the much better-known Women's March against the Pass Laws, Prime Minister JG Strijdom was not in his office and the petition was presented to the Minister of Transport, Ben Schoeman. Else indignantly remembered that when the petitions were deposited in the minister's office, Schoeman did not even take his pipe out of his mouth.[9] She also participated in an all-night vigil at the Union Buildings, sleeping on the lawns in a sleeping bag.

A national Day of Prayer was planned in August and members of the WDCL called their husbands and other male relatives to action. This resulted in the formation of the Citizens' Committee, which called for a national convention, 'to work towards common ideals in a spirit of harmony and co-operation'.[10] Deneys was an active member of the Citizens' Committee and this was the first time that he participated in a campaign to draft an alternative constitutional structure to that of the apartheid state. This first constitutional attempt was not successful. Deneys and other ex-servicemen performed a more useful role, based on their military experience of sentry duty, by advising the women of the WDCL, who stood for hours 'haunting' Cabinet ministers, how to stand still without cramping muscles, how to rock from heel to toe and how keep the blood circulating.[11]

Deneys's most visible protest against the removal of coloured people from the common voters' roll in 1956 was to grow his beard and he vowed not to shave again until coloureds people, and by extension, all South Africans, could vote on a common roll. John Laband, who encountered the beard as a boy when it was first grown, wrote: 'And then, the beard! Never had I seen such a thing and it impressed me utterly. I was told why he had grown it and that made it something especially notable.'[12]

Colin Gardner, in his obituary for Deneys, written in 2008, described the beard as giving him an appearance that was a 'cross between some of the old-fashioned depictions of God the Father and a well known portrait of Charles Darwin' and, as a result, 'he was able to satisfy, or disturb, unbelievers and believers alike'.[13]

Laband also recalls how the beard served an active political purpose, rather than simply being a hirsute sign of silent protest. A meeting was called in Auckland Park to discuss the conversion of a park and children's playground into a new Dutch Reformed Church:

> When Deneys rose to speak, the Afrikaner worthies noted his Voortrekker beard with delighted satisfaction and leaned back in their chairs fully expecting him to advocate building the church. Not so! Deneys was (I believe) an atheist and no friend of churches squatting over children's playgrounds. He was also a fluent, witty and undaunted orator who pulled no punches and delighted in getting a rise out of his audience. The meeting was soon in uproar as the indignant Afrikaners realized they had a *volksverraaier* [traitor of the people] in their midst. (In the end the church was built over only part of the playground – but it was ruined anyway.)[14]

The second major political issue encroaching on the life of a newly minted academic was the determination of the nationalist government to divide the universities on racial grounds. Wits was one of the so-called open universities, which admitted students of colour: African, Indian, so-called coloured and those from the tiny Chinese community. Not only was complete racial segregation the goal, but also black South Africans were to be de-urbanised where possible and linked to their remote tribal, rural homes by every means that the ingenuity of segregationists such as Verwoerd could devise. Bantu Education was designed to be inferior and to keep black South Africans in an inferior position. For English-language universities to teach black students would turn them into 'black Englishmen', an utter abomination to Verwoerd.[15]

Even before the Orwellian-sounding Extension of University Education Act was passed in 1959, Wits, Cape Town and the somewhat less integrated universities, Natal and Rhodes, were placed under increasing, sometimes petty, government pressure. Every possible obstacle was placed in the way of black and white students socialising together; applications for liquor licences for university functions at which blacks and whites would mix were granted reluctantly and painfully slowly. Many obstacles were also placed in the path of the universities in finding legal residential accommodation for black students and life for those students was often made as difficult as could be.[16]

On 22 May 1957, when Deneys was at the BPI, one of the earliest academic protest marches against apartheid and government interference with the universities took place in Johannesburg. Led by the university's chancellor, members of the senate, professors, members of convocation and students, some 2 000 people in all, marched from the Wits campus to the steps of the Johannesburg City Hall carrying a single banner: 'Against the Separate Universities Bill'. Deneys and his friend Phillip Tobias, who had served as president of the National Union of South African Students (NUSAS), being elected in the fateful year of 1948, also marched.[17] During his career, Deneys was to become a veteran of such marches and protests.

After the segregation of the universities was promulgated into law, ministerial permission (very rarely given) was required for a black South African to attend one of the white English-language universities. Separate universities, the so-called bush colleges, were established in remote rural areas: the University of Zululand at KwaDlangezwa (in the sugar cane fields outside Empangeni) and, in the far northern Transvaal, the University of the North at Turfloop, several kilometres to the east of Pietersburg (now Polokwane). Fort Hare, once the leading light of tertiary education for black students from all over southern Africa, was targeted by a second act tracking the Extension of University Education Act, the University of Fort Hare Transfer Act. This separated the pride of African universities from the ministry responsible for mainstream universities and placed it under the minister of Bantu Education.

Fort Hare was then relegated to the position of being an ethnic college for Xhosa-speaking students.[18]

The Extension of University Education Act also empowered the government to establish separate universities for coloured and Indian students. These colleges eventually grew into the University of the Western Cape and the University of Durban-Westville. This lay in the future, but the hostility relentlessly demonstrated by the nationalists towards integration in general, and in the universities in particular, was prompting stronger opposition in both the black and white communities.

A few months after Deneys's return to South Africa, disparate groupings of liberal thinkers formed themselves into the new Liberal Party of South Africa. The Nationalists had scored their second electoral victory on 16 April 1953 and on 9 May, the Liberal Party, freed from the fear of embarrassing the enfeebled United Party at the polls, was established.[19] One of the first people to join up in Johannesburg was Deneys Schreiner, as did his sister Jean, who rolled up her sleeves and went to help in the Liberal Party offices.[20] Deneys, as one of the new guard of young liberals, attended the inaugural meeting at the Darragh Hall. The meeting was presided over by Margaret Ballinger MP (a friend of the Kops family), Alan Paton, the author of *Cry, the Beloved Country*, and senior lawyers, Harold Hansen QC, and Jack Unterhalter. The party immediately began wrangling over the thorny question of the franchise.[21]

The franchise had been an issue when WP Schreiner was prime minister of the Cape Colony. It was one of the fudged compromises at the National Convention in 1909, when the decision was taken to form the Union of South Africa; it was the constitutional hot potato in the 1950s and it remained a burning issue until the first democratic elections in 1994. The liberals, after some hesitation and much debate, committed themselves to full enfranchisement of all adult South Africans.[22] This was unlike the Progressive Party, which broke away from the United Party in a few years later in 1959, which stuck to a qualified franchise until the late 1970s. Deneys followed the discussions and learned from them, but his major contributions to the political discourse lay in the future. However, these debates directed his thoughts firmly in the direction of a universal franchise. Some twenty or so years later, Deneys wrote in the Liberal Party journal, *Liberal Opinion*, in support of a universal franchise, disputing with party stalwart Ken Hill that such a stand would have a negative effect on the party in the eyes of white voters.[23]

The Liberal Party adopted an ambiguous attitude towards the Congress of the People that met at Kliptown in 1955 to adopt the Freedom Charter. Although they received an invitation to attend, it had been issued half-heartedly because many of the members of the Congress of the People saw the liberals as too tame and insufficiently enthusiastic about radical transformation. The Liberals eventually refused to take part (after heated internal debate) because of the communist influence on the Congress of the People and on the organisation of the event. However, the liberals rapidly realised the significance of the Freedom Charter and the courage of the organisers and participants in the event in Kliptown.[24]

The following year, 1956, the famous Women's March on the Union Buildings in Pretoria took place. A petition protesting against the imposition of the pass laws on African women was delivered to the prime minister's office, but again, Strijdom made sure he was not in the building. The Black Sash took part in the march, but not Else, as she was heavily pregnant with her daughter Jennifer at the time. Back in 1914, Senator WP Schreiner had submitted a petition to Prime Minister Louis Botha from African women in the Orange Free State, protesting at having to carry passes.[25] It was more than 40 years since the first protest, but another generation of the family was still protesting about the same issue and protests would continue until the late 1980s when apartheid began to collapse.

One of the outcomes of the signing of the Freedom Charter in Kliptown and the Women's March the following year was that the government decided to round up as many of the African National

Congress (ANC) and related opposition leadership as possible and charge them with treason. Thus began the long-enduring Treason Trial that was held in the Old Synagogue building in Pretoria. More than a hundred men (including Nelson Mandela, Walter Sisulu, Govan Mbeki and many other struggle stalwarts) and a few women (including Helen Joseph) were charged. Advocate George Bizos did not appear for the accused, but he was asked to assist with arranging support for the families of the accused and with research for the defence. Deneys and Else were among those who came forward to provide food and necessities for the accused.[26] One of the treason trialists who received the food the Schreiners delivered was a Pietermaritzburg medical practioner, Dr Chota Motala, a member of the Natal Indian Congress, who was also associated with the Liberal Party. Motala and his wife Rabia later became close friends with Deneys and Else in Pietermaritzburg.[27]

The size of Deneys's family doubled in the 1950s, with the birth of two daughters: Jennifer Ann on 30 October 1956 and Barbara Gay on 22 November 1958. It seemed as though Deneys's Johannesburg childhood experiences would be repeated in the new generation, particularly as Oliver and Deneys were sent to their father's alma mater, St John's. Part of the family routine while they were living in Johannesburg was for Deneys, Else and the children to visit OD and Edna at Lyndall for Sunday lunch. This happened even when OD was staying in Bloemfontein during the court sessions.

Edna described to her husband in Bloemfontein a typical Sunday visit from the younger Schreiners that was more abbreviated than usual, as Deneys had to leave immediately after lunch to do battle with an infestation of rats in the roof of their house in Auckland Park. On the advice of the municipality he had set a series of traps, but failed to catch a single rat: 'They all seemed – the humans, not the rats – very cheerful & very well, although Neys hadn't had as much sleep as he would like as he had attended the Varsity Boat Race dinner the previous night.'[28]

Despite his carousing at university celebrations, Deneys's time at the BPI was highly productive. He co-published four major scientific papers and attended three international conferences in South Africa and what was then Southern Rhodesia (Zimbabwe), at which he presented papers. He had also joined the South African Association for the Advancement of Science on his return to the country in 1953.[29] One of his most important conferences was the International Geophysical Conference at Wits in 1955. The International Geophysical Year was one of the earliest major postwar efforts at international scientific collaboration and it continued into the following year with projects lasting until 1958.

The conference was part of South Africa's contribution to the international and Commonwealth effort. One of the most dramatic projects was the Commonwealth expedition that made the first crossing of the continent of Antarctica. It was headed by Sir Vivian Fuchs and the first man to climb Mount Everest, the New Zealander, Sir Edmund Hillary.[30] Deneys, the rising academic, was playing an important role in the international scientific networks he had begun developing in Cambridge and furthered in Pennsylvania.

However, back at the BPI, Deneys found himself in conflict with colleagues in related disciplines over what he felt was a lack of proper acknowledgement and citation of his research by others. Deneys did not have a confrontational personality, but he nevertheless felt some unhappiness in his working environment.[31] When, in 1959, the opportunity to apply for a professorial post at the University of Natal, Pietermaritzburg, arose, Deneys submitted an application and was offered the post. It was a more senior position than his current one at the BPI and he would have more contact with students. As his father had said to Edna in 1948, when Deneys was worrying about his results at Cambridge, his strongest quality was his ability to deal with other people.[32] His new job in Pietermaritzburg would play to that strength. He was appointed professor of Inorganic and Analytical Chemistry in August 1959.[33]

Notes

1. John Laband, 'Some Reminiscences of Deneys Schreiner', email of 14 October 2016.
2. See RT Jamieson, GDL Schreiner and B Schonland, 'Age Measurements on a Pegmatite Mica from the Rhodesian Shield', *Nature* 175 (1955), p.464.
3. Raymond Dart (with Dennis Craig), *Adventures with the Missing Link* (London: Hamish Hamilton, 1959).
4. Else Schreiner, Reminiscences, 2016.
5. Phillip Tobias, *Into the Past: A Memoir* (Johannesburg: Wits University Press, 2005).
6. Henry Kenny, *Architect of Apartheid: HF Verwoerd; An Appraisal* (Johannesburg: Jonathan Ball, 1980), p.89.
7. Mary Kleinenberg and Christopher Merrett, *Standing on Street Corners: A History of the Natal Midlands Region of the Black Sash* (Pietermaritzburg: Natal Society Foundation, 2015), p.1.
8. Kleinenberg and Merrett, *Standing on Street Corners*, p.2.
9. Kleinenberg and Merrett, *Standing on Street Corners*, p.4.
10. Kleinenberg and Merrett, *Standing on Street Corners*, p.5.
11. Kleinenberg and Merrett, *Standing on Street Corners*, p.6.
12. Laband, 'Some Reminiscences of Deneys Schreiner'.
13. Colin Gardner, 'George Deneys Lyndall Schreiner (1923–2008)', *Natalia* 38 (2008), pp.83–5. This obituary contains an incorrect reference to OD becoming chief justice.
14. Laband, 'Some Reminiscences of Deneys Schreiner'.
15. Kenny, *Architect of Apartheid*, pp.136–7.
16. George Bizos, *Odyssey to Freedom* (Cape Town: Random House Struik, 2007), pp.90–1.
17. Tobias, *Into the Past*, p.185.
18. WM Kgware, 'The Role of Black Universities in South Africa', in *The Future of the University in Southern Africa*, edited by HW van der Merwe and David Walsh (Cape Town: David Philip, 1977), pp.225–36.
19. Randolph Vigne, *Liberals against Apartheid: A History of the Liberal Party of South Africa, 1953–68* (London: Macmillan, 1997), p.19.
20. OD Schreiner Letters: File 1956, Letter from Edna to OD, 24 May 1956.
21. Vigne, *Liberals against Apartheid*, p.29. Deneys's status as a founder member is mentioned on p.147.
22. Michael Cardo, *Opening Men's Eyes: Peter Brown & the Liberal Struggle for South Africa* (Johannesburg: Jonathan Ball, 2010), pp.86–9.
23. Vigne, *Liberals against Apartheid*, p.217.
24. Vigne, *Liberals against Apartheid*, pp.48–9.
25. See Chapter 1.

26. Bizos, *Odyssey to Freedom*, pp.174–5. On the Schreiner's involvement, see Else Schreiner, Reminiscences, 2016.
27. Goolam Vahed, *Chota Motala: A Biography of Political Activism in the KwaZulu-Natal Midlands* (Pietermaritzburg: University of KwaZulu-Natal Press, 2017). Dr Motala became the first person to register as a voter on the new democratic municipal voters' roll in 1995, according to Anne Dominy, then the voters' roll officer and deputy returning officer for the Pietermaritzburg-Msunduzi Local Transitional Council.
28. OD Schreiner Letters: File 1956, Letter from Edna to OD, 25 March 1956.
29. GDL Schreiner, Curriculum Vitae.
30. The International Geophysical Year, http://www.nas.edu/history/igy.
31. Else Schreiner, Reminiscences, 2016; Deneys (Neys) Schreiner, Reminiscences, 2017.
32. OD Schreiner Letters: File 1948, Letter from OD to Edna, 13 June 1948.
33. Bill Guest, *Stella Aurorae: The History of a South African University, Volume 2, the University of Natal (1949–1976)* (Pietermaritzburg: Natal Society Foundation, 2017), p.46.

7

Science Faculty and Family
Pietermaritzburg (1959–75)

'Soggy' was the word Deneys had used to describe Pietermaritzburg's climatic conditions and human outlook in a letter to his father in 1951. Eight years later he settled in the city, perhaps intent on teasing the sogginess out of the place. The university he was joining was unusual in that there were three campuses in two cities, one in Durban, one in Pietermaritzburg and the Medical School, on a separate site in Wentworth, to the south of Durban. The principal and vice chancellor was Dr EG Malherbe, a noted educationalist who had served as General Smuts's director of military intelligence during the war. Ernie Malherbe became head of Natal University College after the war ended and shepherded it through its transformation into a full university in 1949.[1] He stayed in the post until 1965. As university principal he was noteworthy for his 'broadmindedness, his receptivity to new ideas and his gift for friendship'.[2] It appears that the nationalist government handled Malherbe with both caution and suspicion as, given his intelligence background, he knew many secrets about government members from his wartime days.[3]

Malherbe also earned the undying enmity of many Pietermaritzburg academics and citizens by moving the centre of the university's administration to Durban three years before Deneys arrived.[4] One of the long-term consequences of this was the development the position of vice principal on the Pietermaritzburg campus into one of considerable power. This was the post that Deneys was to fill for nearly twelve years.

The University of Natal was not a fully 'open' university, as were the universities of the Witwatersrand and Cape Town. Indian and African students were admitted to the Medical School and limited residential accommodation was provided. Black students in other disciplines were taught in segregated classes in the Durban city centre, with Mabel Palmer and Leo Kuper playing leading roles.[5] Bernard Magubane, a leading social scientist, who was later to go into exile in the United States, was a student there during the 1950s, although his graduation ceremony was on the Pietermaritzburg campus, indicating some degree of ceremonial integration even in the 1950s.[6] Malherbe fought hard for the university to keep control of the Medical School against Pretoria's efforts to place the facility under the authority of the more docile University of South Africa.[7] As it was a segregated facility, the battle was fought on the principle of university autonomy, rather than on the principle of integration.[8] Deneys would later fight battles in defence of both principles.

But first, he had to establish himself as a teacher and as a scientist. There were only four teaching staff members and a laboratory assistant in the Department of Chemistry when he arrived. As was common with lecturers in many other departments, Deneys had to teach on both the Durban and the Pietermaritzburg campuses for many years until the departments were separated and he thus had a very heavy teaching load. However, Pietermaritzburg was a small university and a collegial one. Academic, technical and administrative staff took tea together in the tearoom behind the Council Chamber, behind the Main Science Lecture Theatre (known as the MSLT).[9] The chemistry staff stuck together and, until he became vice principal, Deneys almost always drank tea in a huddle with his chemistry colleagues in the staff common room.[10]

Christopher Forsyth, initially a chemistry student, and then a BSc graduate, who later completed an LLB (and was a contemporary and rival of Oliver, son of Deneys and Else) described Deneys's lectures as 'crystal clear and ruthlessly logical'. He claims that he can still remember a lot of the periodic table, thanks to Deneys's teaching and says that at the end of a lecture, all available blackboard space would be 'covered with chemical formulae and equations written in [Deneys's] clear precise hand'. A Schreiner lecture would end, chalk down, precisely when the bell went and his next lecture would begin precisely where he had left off. Forsyth tells the popular story that Deneys had just written 'Na' (for sodium) when the bell rang and his chalk went down. At the next lecture he picked it up and wrote 'Cl' (for chlorine) on a board that had been used and cleaned several times since his previous lecture. Woe betide any student who was not up to speed with what had happened before.[11]

Enoch Sikonje, the departmental laboratory assistant, was deeply impressed by the Schreiner beard and exclaimed that the chemistry department had its own Jesus![12] The chemistry department also, allegedly, had an additional occupant, the ghost of a former chemist named Burnett, who lurked, or wafted, along the mezzanine floor late at night breaking apparatus. Chris Morewood suspected that the superstitious research students, who heard the crashing and felt the wafting, had consumed too much Tassies, the memorable and drinkable cheap red wine that was a student favourite, more formally known as Tassenberg. Apparently, Burnett no longer manifested after Deneys had the mezzanine floor removed in the late 1960s.[13]

One of the key resources lacking in the Pietermaritzburg chemistry department was a mass spectrometer. This instrument measures the exact mass of very small particles to many decimal places. Deneys's colleague and close friend Alistair Verbeek had discovered the wonders of such a machine during a research stint at the advanced British nuclear laboratories at Harwell. On his return, he extolled its virtues. Deneys reported the requirement to the university authorities and requested funding so that the department could buy one. Several requests were refused. Deneys and his team then put their heads together and decided they would build a mass spectrometer themselves.[14]

This was a major undertaking and equipment and parts had to be acquired by fair means and foul from across the country. Alistair Verbeek, George Costello, a glass-blower, and Chris Morewood, the new technician at the mechanical instrument workshop, sat down with Deneys and did the detailed planning and drew up the shopping list of required equipment and various parts. Deneys did not have the time to tinker with the construction, but he was involved in the planning and what would now be called project management.

The pieces of iron pole were machined by a commercial engineering work in the city; the insulators were made from lavite, or Wonderstone, acquired from a mine in the Free State and then vitrified in the kiln in the fine arts department, until Chris Morewood was able to manufacture a gas-fired kiln that could perform to more precise specifications. Alistair Verbeek was responsible for the electronics made in the physics department's electronics workshop, while the mechanical work was done in the mechanical instrument workshop next to the chemistry department. The assembly of the final product really was a joint campus affair. Siegfried Drewes, who lectured with Deneys in the chemistry department before the latter became vice principal, described the mass spectrometer as a 'Heath Robinson' contraption, the construction of which required much dedication, putty, hacksaws, welding and perseverance in the face of all the sceptical remarks from gawking onlookers.[15]

The mass spectrometer guzzled liquid air and Alistair Verbeek had to feed it at all hours – he was as tied to it as Deneys had been to his liquid nitrogen-consuming laboratory equipment in Pennsylvania. Alistair used to take his children with him when he went in after hours and tried to take the family dog, but it sat cowering and whimpering outside, apparently afraid of the ghostly Burnett. The homemade mass spectrometer was a talking point at international chemistry conferences and Alistair and Deneys were treated with jocular awe by their colleagues.[16]

The spectrometer was still working, after a fashion, some ten years later. Its existence allowed Deneys to link research in Pietermaritzburg to the most cutting-edge work at Princeton University conducted by Professor David Waldbaum, one of the leading scholars in the thermodynamic properties of rock-forming minerals.[17] The spectrometer became a topic in their correspondence when Deneys wrote to Waldbaum and warned him: 'We work with a very simple Mass Spectrometer which is now some ten years old and has for the past year given us very considerable trouble.'[18]

childhood memories

Deneys had a lifelong interest in geology and geomorphology, what the world looked like and how it had been formed. This transcended the laboratory and the classroom; the whole world was very much his laboratory. When the family travelled in the car, he used to chat to the children about the landscape and how it was formed. They regularly went on fossil hunts. Some of these were close to home and not even in holiday time. When the N3 highway between Durban and Johannesburg was under construction, fossil beds were unearthed on the route, particularly on the steep slopes of Town Hill. Deneys would be contacted at the university and would invariably go and inspect them, often taking the children with him. They would come home with various rocks and when they cracked them open, they would find fossilised leaves millions of years old and other evidence of ancient life embedded in the rocks.[19] Several rock samples and cores from his more formal investigations into the rocks of southern Africa remained on the verandah of Highwood until Else's death, when the house was sold.

On long car journeys when frazzled children, corralled on a large mattress in the luggage section of the famous Schreiner Peugeot station wagon, were beyond being educated on the environment, Deneys became a storyteller of sublime imagination and invention. Invariably his stories centred upon a family of rabbits – the 'Bee Rabbits', as he called them, were furry things with long legs and striped wings like bees, and with versatile '*sterts*' (tails), which could become telescopes and a variety of other useful things. They faced many emergencies and had experiences that the children could relate to, but the hero was the Baby Bee Rabbit, who always saved the day.[20]

The children grew out of these stories, but remembered them into their teenage years and adulthood. Oliver and Deneys (Neys) spent their junior school years at Cowan House, but were sent to high school in Johannesburg, at St John's, where their father had been before them. Jennifer and Barbara both received their schooling in Pietermaritzburg and matriculated from Epworth, the private Methodist girls' high school near the university campus. All four of the Schreiner children studied at the University of Natal. Oliver completed a BSc degree, before studying for an LLB and served as president of the Pietermaritzburg Students' Representative Council (SRC). Deneys studied engineering on the Durban campus. Jenny began a BSc degree in Pietermaritzburg, but completed her studies in the social sciences in Cape Town. Barbara completed a BA in Pietermaritzburg, majoring in speech and drama.

The Schreiners' family life had a strong element of routine to it. They took two holidays a year: in winter at the Hluhluwe Game Reserve in Zululand, or to the Kruger National Park, and to Betty's Bay on the Cape coast in the summer. The summer visit to Betty's Bay was the time for fishing; sea fishing from the rocks, rather than the beach, was favoured by the Schreiners over fishing in rivers or dams. The family could cut themselves off from the world, be themselves and destress by fishing and family antics on the beach. Deneys relied doggedly on old fishing gear: bamboo rod when the rest of the family were using fibreglass; old wooden reels in preference to the new ones with gears and brakes. He wanted it to be a fair fight – man against fish.[21]

Betty's Bay also became the favoured holiday destination of none other than Hendrik Verwoerd, the prime minister and architect of apartheid. He owned a holiday cottage there called Blaas 'n Bietjie that was proclaimed a monument by a sycophantic National Monuments Council in 1973.[22] On one occasion Deneys and his sons were up early and already settled on the rocks casting their lines out to sea when Deneys was approached by a small group of security policemen. Would he kindly leave the beach immediately, as the prime minister was about to come down and fish? In perfect Afrikaans, Deneys refused, firmly stating that the rocks were part of the Admiralty Reserve and, therefore, public land and anybody was entitled to fish there. Besides, he added, there is plenty of space for other people. Stymied, the police withdrew and some time later, a rather grumpy-looking Verwoerd appeared, with the police carrying his fishing gear. The two exchanged chilly nods and Verwoerd settled down on another part of the rocks and began fishing.[23]

Another favourite holiday destination was further along the coast to the east at Noetsie, beneath the imposing Potberg mountains, where the Schreiners had part ownership of a cabin right on the sea. It was a wonderfully wild place, with a shack built largely out of driftwood and other material that had washed up on the small beach between two headlands. The shack was completely isolated and could only be accessed after a long walk, carrying booze, food, fishing rods, backpacks and cases. The shower had to be connected on arrival, by putting a piece of hosepipe into another piece of hosepipe that was fixed in a small waterfall. That was it. The toilet facilities were a loo with a view. It was carefully placed so that one could sit with the door open and look out across the beach to the sea. It took the Schreiners no time at all to fall into a wonderful state of isolation from human rules and social behaviours. The family, including Deneys in particular, shifted into a different way of thinking as they absorbed the simplicity of the life they led there.[24] Although their holidays were in isolated places and they roughed it, they never went camping, perhaps because Deneys had spent too much time under canvas during the war.[25]

However, Deneys's love of the outdoors took him to primitive fishing haunts, particularly at Mkhambathi on the Wild Coast. These trips were arranged as chemistry department outings. Julian Riekert remembers an encounter on a dirt road near the Wild Coast. He was returning from his parents' home in Bizana in the Transkei and came across a Peugeot station wagon with a flat tyre on the side of the road. Alistair Verbeek and a senior student, Mike Robinson, were trudging down a hillside to the car with a wattle tree branch. This was used to jack up the Peugeot and the wheel was changed, only for the travellers to find that the spare was also flat. Julian handed over an ancient foot pump. Deneys was delighted and described him as a 'very well-equipped young man'. Julian claims to have retorted something witty based on the double meaning.[26]

The other favourite holiday was the winter trip to the Kruger National Park. On these trips Deneys was in his element, expounding on the natural environment and the importance of conservation. While they admired wild animals, their lunches were venison sandwiches, prepacked and brought from Pietermaritzburg.[27] The Kruger Park was also a favoured venue for Deneys's research field trips. He was often accompanied on these expeditions by his colleague and close friend, Alistair Verbeek, a lecturer (later professor) in inorganic and analytical chemistry.[28] The high cliffs above the Olifants River gave them the ideal opportunity to examine the different clearly exposed rock strata in a magnificent natural environment with the animals and the wilderness all around them. One of their expeditions was in October 1970 and some of the minor mishaps resulted in Deneys submitting a claim for R7.50 (worth considerably more in 1970 than in today's money), for accommodation, beer and the loss of a geological hammer.[29]

When they were out on expeditions in the park, they were accompanied by an unarmed game guard. On one occasion they were walking along a narrow path on a steep slope between the Olifants camp and the Olifants River when they were confronted by an approaching herd of elephants. The matriarch was alarmed by the intruders and confronted them with trumpeting and flapping ears, while the younger mothers and elephant calves secured themselves behind her. While Deneys and Alistair cowered (perhaps this is when the geological hammer was lost), the game guard walked quietly up to the matriarch, gently slapped her on the base of her trunk and murmured to her in his home language of Tsonga, usually referred to as 'Shangaan' in those days. The elephant began making responsive noises and, with a toss of her head, led the herd off into the bush. Deneys turned to Alistair and complained that it was a pity that his children were not as obedient as the elephants.[30]

However, Deneys was very good with small children. If they became fretful in his presence, he would often pick them up and engage with them face to face and calm them if they were distressed. One of his grandsons, also a Deneys, known as Neysie, recalls that when he was at school in Pietermaritzburg, his grandfather would always come and watch him play cricket. Despite the fact that Neysie was completely useless as a batsman, rarely staying in for much longer than two or three balls, his grandfather would always be there.[31]

Deneys was intrinsically high-spirited with boundless energy and sometimes his humour burst out in strangely adolescent form. The serious man, the intellectual, would suddenly behave like a schoolboy. Once, the family was gathered in the concourse of Cape Town airport to bid farewell to Deneys, who was flying off to a conference and the children had been ordered to behave. There was a momentary lull in the noise of the crowd that Deneys filled in a loud, carrying voice, with the words: 'I'm an impala: plonk, plonk!' He looked around innocently as though nothing had happened while Else and the children shuffled in embarrassment.[32]

Family life at Highwood was also boisterous and dominated by Deneys's sense of fun. Once, he and his sons staged a fake but apparently serious argument that turned physical. Else had banned the males from karate contests in the lounge and the two Deneyses plotted their revenge. The younger Deneys slapped his father across the face with a table napkin and a major battle commenced. It ended when the elder Deneys had been pushed into a window seat by his son and accidentally shoved his elbow through the glass in the sash window. Else and the girls were in a state of panic until Deneys and the boys turned round to them and burst out laughing. Only then did the female Schreiners realise that they had been hoodwinked, although the broken window was collateral damage.[33]

Barbara remembered that her parents had a strong and happy relationship. Given their backgrounds, they did not parade any disagreements in front of their children or outsiders. Else consciously decided to be a full-time mother and supportive academic wife. Deneys was naturally shy and he had to force himself to attend the frequent social and public engagements that were the lot of a professor and then the more onerous lot of a university vice principal, so Else's constant support and sharing of the social load was a godsend to him.³⁴

Else, however, was not a stay-at-home wife, she worked vigorously for the Black Sash and the local community feeding scheme, Kupugani, that was founded in 1962 by, among others, Leslie Weinberg, a city lawyer and a close friend of the Schreiners.³⁵ Else worked as Kupugani's office manager for several years. She was also an office-bearer in the National Council of Women, becoming the national chairperson in 1982.³⁶ This was almost the only women's organisation open to all races that survived the banning of non-racial organisations in the early 1960s, even the Black Sash was restricted to white women. It was this unique status that prompted Else to eventually devote her energies to the National Council of Women, rather than the Black Sash.³⁷ However, in the 1970s, the African membership of the National Council of Women decided to establish their own organisation, in order to develop their self-confidence and empower themselves. Else attended the meeting in Edendale and was saddened by the split, although she was elected as an honorary member of the Edendale Branch of the National Council of African Women.³⁸

A picture of Schreiner family life would not be complete without acknowledging the important role of Evelyn Mkhize and her extended family in caring for them. Their life was supported, and to some extent managed, by an extended family of workers with Evelyn as the matriarch. Generations of the family lived and worked at Highwood. The Schreiners supported their children's education and the two families lived surprisingly intertwined lives for apartheid South Africa. Evelyn and her successors also coped with the succession of large and boisterous dogs that inhabited Highwood and chased the hadedas and neighbouring cats across the large, wooded garden.

In 1962 Deneys, presumably inveigled into the duty by Else, was guest speaker at the annual meeting of the National Council of Women at the St John's Ambulance Brigade Hall, in Old Fort Road, Durban. The Sharpville Massacre had occurred in 1960; the ANC, the Pan Africanist Congress (PAC) and other liberation movements had been banned and Umkhonto weSizwe (MK) had launched the armed struggle in 1961. Internationally, the Cold War was at it height, with the Berlin Wall having been built in 1961. Tension between the young American president, John F Kennedy, and the veteran Soviet leader, Nikita Khrushchev, was at its most intense.

Deneys spoke on the important, but apparently uncontroversial topic of 'Science Training for Girls'. He confronted his audience with the crises of the moment, asserting that science training would help girls and young women understand the 'dreadful world which we have arranged as their home', adding that scientists themselves had created a difficulty in communication between those trained in the sciences and those not so trained.[39] A week or so later, a newspaper correspondent, 'Christian Recorder', commented on the speech, complaining that 'science is pure no more'.[40]

Family discussions ranged from sport and science to education and politics and the arts. In common with many liberal white South African families in the 1960s, the prism through which politics was viewed was that of the white political world: the struggle against the 'Nats', the inadequacies of the United Party, the scope for the Progressive Party and the hopes for a resurgence of liberal values that would solve the nation's problems. The discussions did not often dwell on South Africa's harsh economic realities and extreme contrasts of wealth and poverty, let alone on the system that underpinned this.[41] However, perhaps something must have begun rubbing off on Jenny, who later became a committed Marxist. She remembers that her views did not distress her parents and that, as long as she could sustain her views by rational argument, Deneys and Else were prepared to accept them, even if they did not necessarily share them.[42]

Deneys was, however, very argumentative and, despite his shyness, he revelled in provocative debate. Barbara recalled that he used to drive her insane, picking on specific words, playing with semantics, but, if all else failed, he would simply move the goal posts.[43] Deneys, or Neysie, as he was known as a youngster, remembers that his father used to play devil's advocate and argue for the sake of argument.[44] Julian Riekert quoted a Schreiner guest describing Deneys as 'very counter-suggestible'.[45] However, there was always a glint in his eye and he relished the verbal jousting, although some, even in his own family, thought that he went too far. He formalised his enjoyment of debate by becoming one of the first members of the Pietermaritzburg Parliamentary Debating Society, acting as the first 'prime minister'. This was a multiracial organisation and its first meeting was held in the Lotus Hall, in the Indian area of the city, so that luminaries such as AS Chetty and Chota Motala could also attend.[46] However, the Parliamentary Debating Society barely survived the decade and it died off even before the advent of television, which smothered interest in many such organisations in the mid- to late 1970s.

Schreiner family legend recalls a meeting with a pompous anti-government politician at a social gathering when Deneys, gleefully and eloquently, advanced all the possible arguments in support of the National Party and apartheid. The politician grew more and more angry and when Deneys was finally introduced as Professor Schreiner, a well-known liberal, his victim was positively apoplectic with rage.[47] Once, at one of the Sunday evening soirées at Highwood, two self-important academics from the arts faculty were discussing Samuel Beckett's play *Waiting for Godot*. Deneys listened attentively and joined the debate, shredding the arguments put forward by the two supposed experts. Else watched in amusement until the two guests had left and then turned to her husband and reminded him that he had never seen the play. Deneys ruefully confessed that, indeed, he had not seen the play, but the opportunity for mischief was too good to resist.[48]

The regular Sunday evening soirées were a Schreiner institution. Highwood would be open to all: academic colleagues, students, personal friends of parents and children, visitors from out of town and Pietermaritzburg townsfolk. They were among the earliest regularly racially integrated social gatherings in the city. Friends like Chota and Rabia Motala and AS Chetty attended. Motala had strong links to many of the white liberals in Pietermaritzburg, including Peter Brown and other Schreiner friends such as Leslie and Pessa Weinberg.[49]

Terry King, from the Department of Fine Arts, described the evenings as 'wonderful', with 'witty and interesting and entertaining discussions surrounded by sculpture and other works reflecting the vibrancy of art-making in this region'. Former students Peter and Hilde Colenbrander (who emigrated to Canada in the 1980s), described the Sunday suppers as relaxed and lively, 'with much laughter, a great deal of vigorous discussion and a lot of good fellowship'. Dr Blade Nzimande, later a colleague-comrade of Jenny's in the South African Communist Party (SACP) and minister of higher education under Jacob Zuma, until he was suddenly dismissed in October 2017, appreciated the warm welcome he received as a young twenty-year-old from an impoverished township background and he vividly remembered Deneys's incredible sense of humour in the face of adversity.[50]

Julian Riekert recalls that he and two other students, Ecky Eckhart and Richard Sturdee, were engaged in a dispute of 'global significance' and Julian declaimed that he would not change his position, even if his life depended upon it. Deneys, who was probably egging on the verbal combatants, declared, 'Don't misunderstand me, I have nothing against a yearning for crucifixion, but I would be choosy about who was hanging on the cross on each side of me.' Julian concluded ruefully that these were wise words: Ecky Eckhart was exposed as a security police spy on the campus in June 1972 and confessed to spying on the National Union of South African Students (NUSAS), the SRC and, of all absurd student organisations, the League of Empire Loyalists. The vice principal at the time, Ronnie MacMillan, issued an official statement banning Mr JCPP Eckhart from the campus and from participating in any university activities.[51]

Spying on university campuses was widespread during the 1970s and 1980s and young, impressionable and financially vulnerable students were often easy pickings for the recruiters in the Security Police.[52] Deneys's own daughter led a double life, but for the other side and Deneys certainly confronted the issue of campus spies on many occasions during his time as vice principal.

On another occasion Deneys was complaining on a Sunday evening that he had to declare his religion on an official form and decided to put down 'Anglican: Lapsed'. One of the guests, Colleen Irvine, newly arrived in Pietermaritzburg and, despite being a little nervous in the new environment, retorted: 'Is that the religious equivalent of BA Failed?'[53] This delighted Deneys and Else and a lifelong friendship between the Schreiners and the Irvines began.

Many students in the chemistry department and in other disciplines were close to Deneys and sought his advice and counsel. He tried to structure interactions by supporting a forum for discussions between science students and the faculty. One student of whom Deneys was particularly fond was Mike Robinson. He was a chemistry student and went on the departmental fishing expeditions to the Wild Coast. He served as SRC president between 1967 and 1968, but shortly afterwards he was killed in a tragic car accident. His parents asked Deneys to assist with funeral arrangements and Deneys asked Robinson's successor as president, Patrick Stilwell (known as Pat), to speak on behalf of the students. Pat, who had not delivered any eulogies at that stage of his life, anxiously consulted Deneys and was invited to Highwood the Sunday evening before the funeral. A lifelong bond between Pat and the Schreiners developed.[54] A trust fund was established by Mike Robinson's parents to acknowledge student leadership and all-roundedness. On one occasion in the 1970s, an award was made to an individual whom Deneys considered unworthy and he made his strong views known to the award committee's chairperson. He spoke in private, but argued in no uncertain terms, that it would have been better not to have given an award at all that year.

Pat Stilwell adopted Deneys as his mentor and Deneys reciprocated by inviting him on the chemistry department's fishing expeditions to Mkhambathi. Pat frequently consulted Deneys about SRC problems, one of which was the relationship with the vice chancellor, Professor Owen Horwood, successor to the liberal Malherbe. Horwood was an economist and had taught at what was then the University of Rhodesia and Nyasaland in Salisbury (now the University of Zimbabwe in Harare). Horwood was married to the sister of Ian Smith, who became the hard-line prime minister of rebel Rhodesia.[55] Horwood also joined the National Party while vice chancellor and became the target of much student hostility. The Pietermaritzburg campus student newspaper, *Nux*, was vociferous in its criticism of him and, as SRC president, Pat Stilwell received a demand from an angry Horwood that all articles in *Nux* be sent to him for prior approval. Torn between disobeying an instruction from the vice chancellor and violating his own principles by censoring *Nux*, Pat consulted Deneys. The advice he received was that he should inform Horwood that he was consulting his colleagues and then do nothing further. Pat did so and heard no more from the vice chancellor.[56]

As SRC president, Pat faced another dilemma. There was a tradition of an annual photograph of all SRC members with the vice chancellor. Most of the SRC were adamant they they would not pose with Horwood and Pat again consulted Deneys, who advised him that the SRC should stick with tradition and the presence of Horwood did not signify agreement or disagreement with his political views. Pat strong-armed his colleagues into posing for the picture, which was taken in the Students' Union building. As they emerged after the event, Pat was greeted by a crowd of students protesting against him for having invited Horwood to sit for the photograph. Deneys was philosophical: life, he told Pat, is not always just.[57] As a chemistry professor, Deneys did not have direct contact with Horwood, although the Schreiners were decidedly in the anti-Horwood camp, as the cartoons in the understairs toilet in Highwood attested.

A few years later Deneys supported another humorous student endeavour at free speech. The 1973 Rag magazine, *Nucleus*, appeared with a caricature of Queen Victoria in saucy 'cheeky pants' that revealed her buttocks on its cover. The mayor of Pietermaritzburg, Councillor Cecil Wood, a man of such reactionary views that he had returned his OBE to Buckingham Palace, either when Rhodesia made its Unilateral Declaration of Independence (UDI) or when the Beatles received their MBEs, was incandescent with rage. He announced to the media that as mayor he was a member of the university council and he would be demanding strong action against the students who had perpetrated this atrocity.

Councillor Wood was even more apoplectic when the editor of *Nux* reproduced the image on its front page, but with the head of the queen replaced by the head of the mayor. Deneys was gleeful and used his influence in the councils of the university to ensure that no action was taken against the students. He also supported SRC President Tim Dunne's public defence of the student journalists.[58] Even the vice principal, Ronnie MacMillan, was greatly amused. He summonsed the editor to his office and said: 'My boy, I have not laughed so much in years, consider yourself severely reprimanded.'

Deneys progressed up the ladder at the University of Natal. He was highly regarded for his committee work and chaired both the library and the research committees. Colleen Vietzen, the university librarian for several years when Deneys was vice principal, remembered that, even before he became vice principal, he was a staunch supporter of the library and did everything in his power to get it sufficient funding and resources. Deneys also backed the efforts of the Pietermaritzburg campus library to circumvent the government censorship of 'undesirable publications' and politically subversive books.[59] In the sixteen years before he became vice principal, Deneys served on the research committee, where his even-handedness was much admired. He retained the chair of this committee throughout his period as vice principal and had many jocular confrontations with Professor Waldo Meester of the zoology department. In the late 1970s, when the Islamic revolutionaries took over Iran, Meester began referring to Deneys as the Ayatollah because of the similarity in their beards.[60] Deneys also served on the senate and the council, the most important decision-making bodies in the university. He was a member of the Academic Staff Association for several years and chaired it between 1968 and 1969.[61] It was clear that his academic peers had confidence in him as a person and as a leader.

In 1968 the government appointed a committee to investigate the white universities, focusing particularly on subsidies, funding and managerial matters – to use the word 'governance' would be a slight misnomer. This commission was chaired by Judge J van Wyk De Vries and the unloved (by the University of Natal, at least) Professor Owen Horwood was a member.[62] The Van Wyk De Vries Commission was more technocratic in its approach and more even-handed in its investigations than the Schlebusch Commission (which is discussed in the next chapter). In his curriculum vitae, Deneys notes that he played a major role in drafting and editing the two volumes of evidence submitted by the academic staff association. The senate and the council accepted the submission and a special Senex subcommittee finalised a comprehensive document that was submitted to the commission.[63]

Deneys was a member of the delegation that presented the University of Natal's evidence to the commission and his hand is very apparent in the style and wording of the documentation. The submission mentions the impact that the dual campus system has on the 'obvious desiderata in arriving at a staff/student ratio of 10.5' (a very Schreiner-like turn of phrase) and argues passionately for improved library facilities, stressing the importance of maintaining full library facilities in both Durban and Pietermaritzburg. There is also a strong argument for improved specialised equipment for the physical sciences, 'the provision of which is extremely costly'.[64] Perhaps Deneys's experiences with the chemistry department's mass spectrometer were behind this argument.

Judge Van Wyk De Vries produced an interim report in 1969, but his final report was only published in 1974, as he had been recalled to the bench of the Transvaal Supreme Court.[65] By this stage, university emotions had been scraped raw by the furore over the reports of the Schlebusch Commission and, perhaps unfairly, the Van Wyk De Vries report was tarred with the same brush.

Deneys was becoming what is known in British politics as a 'big beast' – he served as deputy dean of science and then as dean. The deanships rotated between the Durban and Pietermaritzburg campuses and Deneys took his turn accordingly, succeeding Desmond Clarence, Professor of Physics in Durban (and later principal and vice chancellor) as dean of science in June 1966.[66] At the beginning of 1976, six months before the Soweto Uprising, Deneys became the biggest beast on the Pietermaritzburg campus when he was appointed vice principal.[67]

Notes

1. Bill Guest, *Stella Aurorae: The History of a South African University, Volume 2, the University of Natal (1949-1976)* (Pietermaritzburg: Natal Society Foundation, 2017), pp.3-4.
2. Edgar Brookes, *A South African Pilgrimage* (Johannesburg: Ravan Press, 1977), p.107.
3. Personal communication to the author by his late father EJ Dominy. EJ served under Malherbe in military intelligence in a civilian capacity during WW2 before he joined up and proceeded north with the SA 6th Armoured Division, probably in the same ship as Deneys Schreiner, the French transatlantic liner turned troopship, *Ille de France*.
4. Guest, *Stella Aurorae, Vol. 2*, pp.18-19.
5. Guest, *Stella Aurorae, Vol. 2*, pp.139-40. See also Shula Marks, ed., *Not Either an Experimental Doll: The Separate Worlds of Three South Africa Women; Correspondence of Lily Moya, Mabel Palmer and Sibusisiwe Makhanya* (Pietermaritzburg: University of Natal Press and Killie Campbell Africana Library, 1987), p.6.
6. Bernard M Magubane with Mbulelo V Mazmane, *My Life & Times* (Pietermaritzburg, University of KwaZulu-Natal Press, 2010), pp.75-7.
7. Guest, *Stella Aurorae, Vol. 2*, pp.39-40.
8. Guest, *Stella Aurorae, Vol. 2*, p.146.

9. The Main Science Lecture Theatre is now the Deneys Schreiner Lecture Theatre (DSLT).
10. Douglas Irvine, Reminiscences, 15 January 2018.
11. Chris Forsyth, Reminiscences, email of 12 September 2017. Forsyth retired as a distinguished law professor at Cambridge in 2016.
12. Jennifer Verbeek, Reminiscences, email of 6 September 2017.
13. Chris Morewood, Reminiscences, email of 1 October 2017.
14. Jennifer Verbeek, Reminiscences, 2017.
15. Chris Morewood, Reminiscences, email of 1 October 2017. See also Siegfried Drewes, Reminiscences, email of 10 June 2017.
16. Jennifer Verbeek, Reminiscences, email of 6 September 2017.
17. Lincoln S Hollister, 'Memorial of David Robert Waldbaum: March 22, 1937–April 11, 1974', *American Mineralogist* 60 (1975), pp.514–17.
18. University of KwaZulu-Natal (UKZN) Archives: SP25/8/22, Schreiner, GDL Documents VP's Office, Chemistry – Correspondence with academic peers re 'Variations in K39/K41 ratio and movement of K in A Granite Shale Contact Region' (by Schreiner and Alistair Verbeek); University of Natal-Princeton co-operation: Deneys Schreiner to Prof DR Waldbaum, Princeton, 8 November 1971.
19. Barbara Schreiner, Conversations with David Robbins.
20. Else Schreiner, Reminiscences, 2016.
21. Deneys (Neys) Schreiner, Reminiscences, 2017.
22. Franco Frescura, 'National or Nationalist? A Critique of the National Monuments Council, 1936–1989'. N.d. http://www.sahistory.org.za/franco/historical-conservation-nationalist.html.
23. Else Schreiner, Reminiscences, 2016.
24. Else Schreiner, Reminiscences, 2016.
25. Barbara Schreiner, Reminiscences, 2016.
26. Julian Riekert, Reminiscences, email of 9 April 2017. Julian is now a prominent labour lawyer in Melbourne, Australia.
27. Deneys (Neys) Schreiner, Reminiscences, 2017.
28. Alistair Verbeek, curriculum vitae, courtesy of Jennifer Verbeek.
29. UKZN Archives: SP25/8/25, Schreiner, GDL Documents VP's Office, Schreiner, GDL (Prof & Vice Principal UNP), 1976–1987, 'Report on Geological Expedition to the Olifants River, October 1970'.
30. Jennifer Verbeek, Reminiscences, 2017. Another version of the story is that the game guard scared the matriarch away by shouting and waving his arms.
31. Deneys (Neys) Schreiner, Reminiscences, 2017.
32. Barbara Schreiner, Reminiscences, 2016; Deneys (Neys) Schreiner, Reminiscences, 2017.

33. Else Schreiner, Reminiscences, 2016; Deneys (Neys) Schreiner, Reminiscences, 2017.
34. Barbara Schreiner, Reminiscences, 2016.
35. 'Leslie Weinberg' (obituary), *Natal Witness*, reproduced in *Natalia* 40 (2010), pp.158–9.
36. Else Schreiner, Reminiscences, 2017.
37. Mary Kleinenberg and Christopher Merrett, *Standing on Street Corners: A History of the Natal Midlands Region of the Black Sash* (Pietermaritzburg: Natal Society Foundation, 2015), p.45.
38. Kleinenberg and Merrett, *Standing on Street Corners*, p.71.
39. UKZN Archives: SP 25/1/1/1, Schreiner, GDL (Prof & Vice Principal UNP), 1976–1987, Newspaper cuttings, *Natal Mercury*, 2 May 1962.
40. UKZN Archives: SP 25/1/1/1, *Natal Mercury*, 11 May 1962.
41. Barbara Schreiner, Reminiscences, 2016.
42. Jennifer Schreiner, Reminiscences, 2016.
43. Barbara Schreiner, Reminiscences, 2016.
44. Deneys (Neys) Schreiner, Reminiscences, 2017.
45. Julian Riekert, Reminiscences, email of 9 April 2017.
46. *Natal Witness*, 19 August 1961.
47. Else Schreiner, Reminiscences, 2016.
48. Else Schreiner, Reminiscences, 2016.
49. Goolam Vahed, *Chota Motala: A Biography of Political Activism in the KwaZulu-Natal Midlands* (Pietermaritzburg: University of KwaZulu-Natal Press, 2017). See also https://1860heritagecentre.com/2018/10/23/chota-motala-a-biography-of-political-activism-in-the-kwazulu-natal-midlands-by-goolam-vahed/.
50. All these comments are taken from Colin Gardner, 'Tribute to Deneys Schreiner, 9th Dec 1923–27th April 2008', delivered at a memorial gathering at Tembaletu, 1 June 2008. This is an unpublished, more comprehensive version of tributes published in the *Natal Witness* and *Natalia*.
51. Julian Riekert, Reminiscences, email of 9 April 2017. See also *Nux*, 23 June 1972.
52. Jonathan Ancer, *Betrayal: The Secret Lives of Apartheid Spies* (Cape Town: Tafelberg, 2019), p.238.
53. Colleen Irvine, Reminiscences, 15 January 2018.
54. Pat Stilwell, Reminiscences, email of 3 October 2017.
55. Guest, *Stella Aurorae, Vol. 2*, pp.370, 372.
56. Pat Stilwell, Reminiscences, email of 3 October 2017.
57. Pat Stilwell, Reminiscences, email of 3 October 2017.

58. *Nux*, 18 April 1973.
59. Colleen Vietzen, Interview, 28 October 2016. See also Bill Guest, *Stella Aurorae: The History of a South African University, Volume 3, The University of Natal (1976–2003)* (Pietermaritzburg: Natal Society Foundation, 2018), p.38.
60. Guest, *Stella Aurorae, Vol. 3*, p.108.
61. GDL Schreiner, Curriculum Vitae.
62. National Archives of South Africa, Pretoria: *Commissions of Enquiry*, Vol. No. K 263/7, Department of Higher Education, 'Kommissie van Ondersoek na die Universiteitswese [Van Wyk De Vries Commission]', 'Memorandum to the Commission of Enquiry into Universities, in Connection with Financial Matters', submitted by the University of Natal, March 1969.
63. Guest, *Stella Aurorae, Vol. 2*, pp.384–5.
64. National Archives of South Africa: K 263/7: University of Natal Memorandum.
65. Guest, *Stella Aurorae, Vol. 2*, p.385.
66. UKZN Archives: SP 25/1/1/1, *Natal University News*, June 1966.
67. GDL Schreiner, Curriculum Vitae.

Defending principles and a prince: the Greytown Prison yard, 1909. Left to right: WP Schreiner, Eugene Renaud, Dinuzulu kaCetshwayo, RC Samuelson and Harriette Colenso. (*KZN Provincial Museum Service*)

Schreiner Family, Johannesburg, *c.*1940. Back row left to right: Bill, Judge OD and Deneys; seated: Edna (left), unknown (right); front: Jeannie and family dog.

* Unless stated otherwise, all images are from the private Schreiner collections.

Gunner Deneys Schreiner, Union Defence Force, c.1943.

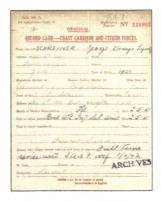

Deneys's Union Defence Force military record while a Wits student, 1941. (*SANDF Documentation Centre*)

Deneys with family dogs, Laurel and Hardy, c.1935.

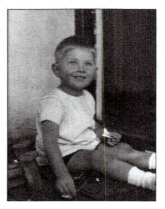

'He looks splendid – pink & fresh & well': Deneys as a toddler.

The Young Deneys in Cambridge.

The Cambridge Rugby Team in chilly weather, post-war period. Deneys is in the back row, 2nd from left.

Deneys and Else on their wedding day, 21 January 1949.

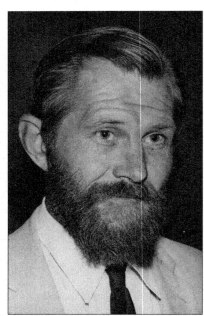

New professor, new protest beard: Deneys in Pietermaritzburg, *c.*1959–60.

'I am about to buy a tree; and, oh yes, there is also a house.'
Deneys and Else in the garden of Highwood, c.1961.

'Highwood' sketch by Harold Bailey.

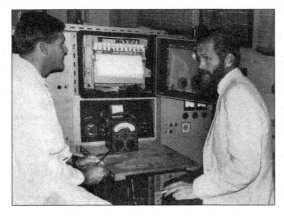

Natal University Chemistry Department: Deneys and technician HH Basson, with the famous mass spectrometer, 1964.

Deneys the fisherman, who faced down Hendrik Verwoerd, Architect of Apartheid, at Betty's Bay.

Family Tree: three generations of male Schreiners, under the Highwood mahogany tree. From left to right: Deneys (Neys), Judge OD, Deneys (standing) and Oliver.

Justice OD Schreiner with Deneys, when OD was awarded an honorary doctorate by Wits University (1961).

University and family luminaries, 1972. From left: EG Malherbe (first VC of Natal University), Bertha and Conrad Kops (parents of Else), Else, Deneys, and Janie Malherbe.

'Mrs S' and 'The Aged P', as the Schreiners were affectionately known to generations of students, at a Gala Ball in the Students Union.

Jock Leyden cartoons on the walls of the downstairs toilet at Highwood.

Owen Horwood – talking tripe.

Owen Horwood standing on toilet, in the genre of the notorious Wits Student cartoon of John Vorster in a toilet bowl.

The New Republic Party 'treed' by the Buthelezi Commission.

March against the Quota Bill, June 1983. From left to right: Piet Booysen (UND Vice Principal), Alan Paton, Des Clarence (Vice Chancellor) and Deneys Schreiner. (Natal Witness, *3 June 1983, courtesy of UKZN Archives*)

The Buthelezi Commission: Prof Deneys Schreiner and KwaZulu Chief Minister Mangosuthu Buthelezi. (*Courtesy of Arthur Konigkramer and* Ilanga *newspaper*)

A *Nucleus* cartoon from the 1970s showing Queen Victoria in cheeky pants.

A *Nux* cartoon depicting Mayor Cecil Wood's head superimposed on Queen Victoria in cheeky pants.

Showing the strain of the trial: Deneys and Barbara in Kirstenbosch Gardens, trying to de-stress.

Cape Town Supreme Court, November 1990: Jenny Schreiner released on bail. Left to right: Nomonde Nkwandla, Jenny, Else and Deneys.

Home at last! Deneys and his daughters, Jenny and Barbara, at Highwood, December 1991, after Jenny's release on bail.

The two Professors Deneys Schreiner, with Else and Jenny in the Margaret Kirkwood Room at an Alan Paton Centre function for the launch of Else's book, *Time Stretching Fear*, in September 2000.

Deney's Retirement Party, 1987. Left to right: Miriam Gqubele and Rev Simon Gqubele (Principal of the Federal Theological Seminary), Else, Dr Chota Motala, Rabia Motala and Deneys.

Prof Colin Webb with Else and Deneys. Webb succeeded Deneys as Vice Principal in Pietermaritzburg.

A photo collage of the Schreiner Clan at the end of the 20th century: Deneys and Else (top) with their children, grandchildren and various spouses and partners, December 1999.

End of the beard: clean-shaven Deneys after the first democratic elections, April 1994.

'Don't let the bastards grind you down.' Deneys's memorial plaque, 2008. Maitland Cemetery, Cape Town: Schreiner family plot.

8

Academy and Activism (1959–75)

For a scientist, Deneys had a profound interest in things political and constitutional. His tidy mind dwelt on systems, both scientific and political. Human systems, particularly the South African political system, were acutely unjust and Deneys was always ready to challenge the injustice.

His wartime letters as a young soldier demonstrate that he was a profound student of current affairs, but had a somewhat cynical view of his fellow humans, particularly those in authority or those striving politically to get into positions of authority. His Cambridge years coincided with Clement Attlee's reforming the Labour government and the establishment of the British welfare state. He was not an ardent Labour supporter, but he observed the reforms closely. His time in the United States coincided with the tail end of the Truman administration and he watched the first tentative steps towards desegregation. He also experienced the anti-Communist fervour and the Cold War paranoia upon which it was based. He was able to gently poke fun at and undermine the absurd demands of the academic Cold War warriors. The lesson of the loyalty oath and the strategy he used to circumvent it served him well when resisting and out-thinking apartheid machinations on South African campuses.

In Johannesburg in the 1950s Deneys joined the Liberal Party and Else joined the Black Sash. He supported his father during the court battles over the common voters' roll. By 1959, when Deneys and his family moved to Pietermaritzburg, Hendrik Verwoerd was prime minister, ever more onerous restrictions were being placed on Africans in particular and freedom of speech was increasingly curbed. Moving to Natal, the Schreiners were in the one province not totally controlled by the National Party, but the Provincial Council had restricted powers and functions and the United Party was almost as racist and paternalistic as the nationalists. However, in its limited and overly cautious way, tiny steps at desegregation and the amelioration of the grossest abuses of apartheid were attempted in the early 1980s.[1] Deneys's work on the Buthelezi Commission provided a road map for transformation at a time when the provincial council system, as set out in 1910, was being abolished.

The big issue for white Natalians in 1960 was the advent of the republic and the threatened break with the Britain and the Commonwealth. The big issue for liberals was that the republic would further divide South Africa's citizens and isolate the country internationally. Verwoerd held a whites-only referendum in 1960, with an outcome in favour of the establishment of a republic. Natal was the only province to vote overwhelmingly against the proposal, but its opposition was based more on residual pro-British nostalgia (and anti-Afrikaner prejudice) than on liberal principles.[2] The republic was proclaimed on 31 May 1961, but given the total lack of consultation with African, coloured and Indian South Africans, the seeds of its own destruction were within it from the beginning, although they took until the 1990s to germinate.

Some resistance was planned in Natal and there was semi-serious talk of seccession. A mysterious organisation, calling itself the Horticulturalists, was formed in 1959 to co-ordinate opposition to the coming republic. Apparently, Deneys was a member.[3] The Horticulturalists alarmed the government and the police raided homes and offices and hideaways and found documents indicating that subversive activities, including sabotage, were being planned. Military action may have been fantasised about: even a mutiny by the Royal Natal Carbineers (about to lose their 'Royal' appellation) was whispered about. However, the Horticulturalists were primarily a pressure group of middle-class white men in Natal, many of them ex-servicemen, with careers, homes and families, not militant Bolsheviks with nothing to lose. Their main objective was to embarrass and infuriate the nationalist government.[4] Deneys fitted the profile and, with his 'counter-suggestible' nature, the tweaking of nationalist noses delighted him.

Closely associated with the Horticulturalists was Freedom Radio (not to be confused with the later broadcasting operation of the African National Congress (ANC) in exile), a clandestine radio transmitter that broadcast anti-nationalist and anti-republican propaganda from various locations around Pietermaritzburg and its environs. Rumour had it that the government detection apparatus was in the Post Office in Longmarket Street and that the reason Freedom Radio could not be located was because it used the next door Victoria Club for its broadcasts and the apparatus could not pick up something that was so close to it. A mobile detection van was sent from Pretoria to roam the Pietermaritzburg streets, but never managed to pin down the source of the broadcasts. One night several activists broke into the Post Office premises and manipulated the antenna on the detection van so that it would not read accurately. It was so inaccurate that a police raid was launched on the Bernard Price Institute's field research station near Piet Retief in the south-eastern Transvaal.[5] The field station used to radio data back to the University of the Witwatersrand (Wits) using a frequency close to that of Freedom Radio. Does one detect Deneys's hand in this?

Of greater significance were the efforts to chart an alternative course for Natal. The Natal Convention was held at the University of Natal, Pietermaritzburg, from 17 to 19 April 1961, less than six weeks before the proclamation of Verwoerd's republic. Some 67 organisations were represented and more than 220 people of all races attended, but there were no representatives of the United Party.[6] The conference was opened by Edgar Brookes, former Native Representative senator (as WP Schreiner had been), clergyman, former diplomat, history professor and liberal icon. Deneys was one of the organisers. The conference was handicapped by the absence of the United Party – as Brookes put it, the United Party opposition often 'failed to oppose and by its abstention ... made the task of other opponents of the government harder than it needed to be'.[7]

This convention, Brookes emphasised in his keynote address, was not 'a Natal Stand of the old type', but its purpose was to make a stand that 'we and our children after us shall share the future as friends and fellow-citizens'.[8] Deneys was a junior member of the organising committee and one of his duties was ensuring the availability of ashtrays.[9] However, he clearly impressed the convention leadership with his ashtray-organising abilities because after the convention, he was elected to the continuation committee whose main purpose was to take matters further and try to arrange a South African convention in Johannesburg before the end of November 1962.[10] Although the Natal convention organisers pushed, there was an atmosphere of timidity and lethargy in the Transvaal.

A meeting to rally the Transvaal liberals was planned in Johannesburg in June 1962 and the Natal liberals sent Edgar Brookes and Deneys to attend and to stiffen morale, which had been dented by the sudden departure into exile of one of the key Transvaal liberal leaders, John Lang.[11] Unfortunately, despite the efforts of Edgar Brookes and Deneys, neither a Transvaal nor a South African convention took place and the momentum faded away.[12] Brookes bemoaned the fact that he had sat waiting for the Johannesburgers to 'recover their morale and in the meantime [I] let the Natal Committee lapse. I feel that this was one of the lost opportunities of the struggle and I regret my share in it.'[13]

On 16 December 1961 the ANC's armed wing, Umkhonto weSizwe (MK), launched its campaign of armed struggle, but by the middle of 1963 the top leadership had been swept up in a police raid on Liliesleaf farm in Rivonia, north of Johannesburg. Nelson Mandela had already been arrested near Howick, outside Pietermaritzburg. The Rivonia Trial lasted from October 1963 until June 1964 and the internal leaders of the ANC were sentenced to long years of imprisonment on Robben Island. For the rest of the

1960s, resistance was crushed; a few illegal strikes began in the early 1970s, but it took the rising of the youth in Soweto in 1976, to pose another major challenge to the nationalist government. Meanwhile, the repression of the great mass of the South African people and the targeting of specific individuals continued. John Aitchison, a young Anglican theology student in Pietermaritzburg and a neighbour of the Schreiners in Wendover Road, was banned, as was the Liberal Party's most effective leader in Natal, Peter Brown.[14] Brookes describes Brown as unafraid, calm, cheerful, sane and, 'unfalteringly loyal to democratic principles'.[15] Deneys exhibited many of the same characteristics, except for the fact that he disliked the limelight of the political stage.

However, Deneys was a father with a dependent family and wide responsibilities. He would be in a difficult position if he took an open stand that resulted in a banning order being served on him. How would he support his family? What would be the response of the university authorities? Certainly Professor Stock was not a supportive principal. Deneys was a gentlemanly liberal and he conducted himself as such. The Aitchisons and Browns had his full and committed support, but Deneys was more of the engineer who prepared the trench and reconnoitred for the enemy, rather than the fiery subaltern who led the charge over the top.

Peter Brown's banning order was signed by John Vorster, then the minister of justice, two days before Liberal Party member John Harris planted a bomb in the main concourse of Johannesburg Park Station that killed two people when it exploded.[16] This coincidence seriously weakened the Liberal Party, not only by silencing Brown's voice, but also exposing the splits between the constitutional wing and the more militant wing of the party.[17] Debates of this nature also occurred within the Schreiner family itself, in the late 1980s, when Jenny was arrested.

In 1966 a brief, inspirational window opened, United States Senator Robert Kennedy, brother of the assassinated President John F Kennedy, visited South Africa at the invitation of the National Union of South African Students (NUSAS) and delivered the Day of Affirmation Address at the University of Cape Town. In a key passage of his address, he claimed that when a man stands up against injustice 'he sends forth a tiny ripple of hope'.[18] These words, spoken in oppressed South Africa to rally opponents of apartheid, are engraved on Kennedy's tomb in Arlington National Cemetery, outside Washington, DC. Kennedy also visited Natal and spoke to a packed hall at the University of Natal in Durban. His audience included Deneys and Else Schreiner.[19] Thereafter, he took a quick helicopter trip up the north coast to visit Chief Albert Luthuli, the president of the ANC, who lived under house arrest at Groutville.[20] Helen Suzman described the effect of the visit in her memoirs: 'Robert Kennedy's visit and his passionate espousal of liberal values were immensely encouraging to those under siege. He boosted the morale of all of us under attack, and for once we felt we were on the side of the angels.'[21]

Verwoerd was assassinated in 1966, soon after the Kennedy visit, and was replaced as prime minister by former justice minister BJ Vorster. In 1968, the Vorster government passed the Prohibition of Political Interference Act, which made multiracial membership of political parties and organisations illegal. This killed off the Liberal Party, many of whose leaders had been steadily picked off and served with banning orders.[22] The parliamentary-based Progressive Party restricted itself to whites-only membership in compliance with the new law. Protest meetings were held, but to little avail. In Pietermaritzburg, in March 1968, a final requiem meeting for the Liberal Party was held and Pat Stilwell, a Progressive Party member and, at that time, the president of the Pietermaritzburg Students' Representative Council (SRC), shared the platform with Colin Gardner (professor of English) and Deneys Schreiner, both Liberal Party members.[23] Other vehicles for opposition needed to be utilised and an obvious one for Deneys was the South African Institute of Race Relations (SAIRR), of which his father had become honorary president after his retirement from the bench. Deneys never again joined another political party.

Deneys was active in the affairs of the Pietermaritzburg Branch of the SAIRR. The SAIRR became an important haven for liberals, as the government steadily moved to close down organisations offering alternative thought to apartheid. Viewing their authoritative annual race relations surveys from the perspective of the twenty-first century – with the meticulously researched and dispassionately presented statistics of deprivation – takes readers back into a world of petty-minded cruelty and systemic oppression. Deneys, with his questioning mind and calm demeanour, helped to support and facilitate the critical research work that exposed the contradictions and hollowness of the apartheid system.

In the mid- to late 1960s the assistant director of the SAIRR was Peter Randall, a former lecturer at the Natal Teachers' Training College in the former British governors' residence in Pietermaritzburg. Randall was very close to most of the leading liberals in Pietermaritzburg, including the Schreiners, Peter Brown, Colin Gardner, Alan Paton and Edgar Brookes. After his stint at the SAIRR, he was selected to head an investigation into the evils of the apartheid system called SPRO-CAS (Study Project on Christianity in Apartheid Society), which was established by Beyers Naudé of the Christian Institute and the South African Council of Churches. Several academics at the University of Natal, including Colin Gardner of the English department, Tony Mathews of the law faculty, Lawrence Schlemmer and Rick Turner of the Durban social sciences were involved. SPRO-CAS produced several incisive and radical research publications that enraged the government. Rick Turner was later assassinated by apartheid operatives and Peter Randall was banned. The Christian Institute found itself a target of the government. Constitutional issues were not the main focus of SPRO-CAS research, but their reports provided ammunition and ideas that Deneys was to use later in his constitutional investigations.[24]

The main attack on the remaining liberal organisations took place in the early 1970s, when Vorster appointed a parliamentary commission of inquiry, headed by Alwyn Schlebusch, MP for Kroonstad, into the 'subversive activities' of liberal or radical organisations such as NUSAS, the Christian Institute, the SAIRR and the University Christian Movement. To give the commission a veneer of objectivity, the nationalist government invited the United Party to nominate members to the commission. Helen Suzman warned the United Party not to touch the commission with a 'bargepole', claiming it was a 'McCarthy committee, a witch hunt, and would lead the United Party to disaster'.[25]

The Schlebusch Commission met in secret. Witnesses could not be cross-examined and were usually unaware of what other witnesses were saying. When its report was released in 1973, Vorster announced the banning of sixteen student leaders: eight from NUSAS and eight from the black consciousness student movement SASO (the South African Students Organisation, of which Steve Biko was a leading figure). Some of those banned were associated with the University of Natal, in particular, Durban political science lecturer Rick Turner and former SRC president and NUSAS president, Paul Pretorius and his partner, Paula Ensor.[26] The English-language campuses were thrown into turmoil.

In Pietermaritzburg, students were particularly outraged because Bill Sutton, the United Party MP for nearby Mooi River, had been a member of the Schlebusch Commission and had endorsed the report. Sutton accepted an invitation to address students on the report, but made sure that his wife accompanied him, in a forlorn effort to curb the emotions of the students by appealing to their better nature, or to an already out of date code of gentlemanly conduct. The effort failed and Sutton was castigated in very forthright and increasingly emotional terms. The presence of Mrs Sutton had no effect on the gathering.[27] Deneys, who had coolly and clinically eviscerated Sutton's feeble arguments, had to calm the audience down and physically escort the Suttons out of the hall and safely off the campus.

Bill Sutton's protector characterised himself in a retirement interview as a conservative liberal – a liberal but a slow-moving chap: 'I always find myself on the cautious side of things.' Deneys always encouraged students to find out how other communities think: 'They should even go to Pofadder. I've been to Pofadder and while it may not be the most *vooruitgaande plek* [advanced place], it helped me understand why people there think the way they do.'²⁸ Deneys undoubtedly understood what made Bill Sutton tick, even though he totally disagreed with him.

Three senior professors were most prominent in standing with students during protests in the 1970s: Colin Gardner (English), Colin Webb (History) and Deneys Schreiner (Chemistry). They stood in the student picket lines along the boundaries of the university, since it was illegal to protest off the campus. They marched with the students and addressed mass protest meetings in the Students' Union Hall, or in what was then the Main Science Lecture Theatre, or MSLT (now the Deneys Schreiner Lecture Theatre). The trio were affectionately parodied in a 1973 Rag variety concert Gilbert and Sullivan skit composed by Michael Lambert. It was based on *The Mikado* and Webb, Gardner and Schreiner were described as 'a giggling tall historian, an English pwof who lisps and a bearded scientist – they never will be missed, they never will be missed, I've got 'em on the list.'²⁹

Deneys's beard and imposing demeanour gave students a sense of comfort and security when facing the police across Durban Road. Sage advice was also dispensed at the Sunday evening gatherings at Highwood. When students wanted to defy the law, Deneys counselled caution, but subtly suggested creative and legal ways of expressing dissent within the confines of the law, perhaps harking back to his creative defiance in relation to the issue of the loyalty oath in the United States. One of the fiercest protests occurred in June 1972 when the police baton-charged students at the University of Cape Town, who were protesting against the government's Bantu Education policy on the steps of St George's Cathedral, and chased them into the cathedral, still wielding their batons and beating the students.³⁰ This provoked a wave of opposition on English-language campuses and there was a large demonstration on the Pietermaritzburg campus. Mass meetings were held in the Students Union Hall to denounce the police action. Deneys joined the students on the picket lines at the university entrance gates and his imposing presence and calm demeanour gave young students courage. He was also able to give the older students, such as the SRC president, Tim Dunne, strategic advice.[31]

Not all Pietermaritzburg students supported the anti-apartheid struggle, the students in the agriculture faculty and the male residents of William O'Brien Hall of Residence being the most conservative. Many of these were white Rhodesians; the Pietermaritzburg and Rhodes campuses being favourite destinations for Rhodesians in search of higher education at the time. They have been criticised for their apathy and conservatism, even forming a 'kind of sub-culture', but this is an oversimplification.[32] Some Rhodesian high schools had limited numbers of African students, living and studying along with whites. In the late 1960s and early 1970s when white South Africans came on to campus without any exposure to Africans, other than through the lens of the master-servant relationship, young Rhodesians often treated African workers in the residences with greater respect than South Africans did.

This changed dramatically in the mid- to late 1970s, as the Rhodesian Bush War, or Second Chimurenga, intensified and male Rhodesian veterans arrived on campus suffering from post-traumatic stress syndrome and uttering bigoted, racist and hostile sentiments. It took all Deneys's tact and people skills to calm several very tense situations. His own boisterous and sporty nature helped him not only to understand, but also to empathise with the mentality of the students he was guiding, even though he was politically poles apart from them.

Deneys had an open-door policy for students of all persuasions, including members of the Sports Union, which was presided over by his friend and fellow chemistry department colleague, Winton (known as 'Wog') Hawksworth.[33] In the mid-1970s, Deneys and Else were invited to the Sportsman of the Year banquet, which was to be held at William O'Brien. In those days, although awards for sportswomen were also presented, the event was known as the Sportsman of the Year Award. This was a time when the international anti-apartheid sports boycott was beginning to bite. To annoy the lefties, the Sports Union decided to invite the minister of sport, Piet Koornhof, an 'engaging' and vaguely enlightened member of the National Party, known as 'Piet Promises' because his well-meaning rhetoric was hardly ever converted into action.[34]

The event was planned as a military operation. Junior 'rugger-buggers', not on the invitation list, were detailed to patrol the car park in front of William O'Brien, armed with their girlfriends' hockey sticks, to ensure that no dangerous lefty attack squad interfered with the glorious event. The lefties were too squeamish to plan a direct confrontation, but they too made their preparations and exploited a major error the Sports Union had made in their battle plans. The master of ceremonies was a large, bearded divinity student, studying for the Anglican priesthood. He was an imposing figure on campus, with a great sense of fun. When approached to be master of ceremonies, he agreed to preside, but warned that he would not be held accountable for what he said.

The lefties ensured that 'The Rev' was sufficiently well oiled before the event not to care about the wrath of this world. When he came to introduce the guest speaker, he lurched to his feet to announce that the minister of sport had asked him to make an announcement: South Africa had a new national game, masturbation: 'Nobody will play with us, so we have to play with ourselves!' There was a deathly hush, until Piet Koornhof giggled and Deneys roared and the entire hall erupted with mirth. The *pièce de résistance*, according to one version of the story, was when Deneys's sleeve was tugged by Mrs Koornhof who asked him to explain the joke. Regrettably, history does not record his reply.[35]

In the early 1970s, liberal students heading for the picket lines, feared gun-toting rugger-buggers from William O'Brien. Deneys was the academic they turned to for support and to mediate with the authorities in the residences and to have the Rhodesians disarmed. After much backroom manoeuvring within the university administration, students were forbidden to keep firearms in their rooms and had to surrender them for secure storage in university-controlled safes. They could only retrieve them for formal target practice and sporting activities.

Else stood as a candidate for the Progressive Party in the 1974 general election, an experience that inoculated her against seeking elected public office for the rest of her life. In the 1970s, when white South Africans went to the polls, they elected both an MP and a member of the Provincial Council. Else stood for the Pietermaritzburg North constituency as the Progressive Party's candidate for the Natal Provincial Council. Her main opponent was Frank Martin, the senior Member of the Executive Committee on the Provincial Executive Committee and the leader of the United Party in the Provincial Council. He was an ex-serviceman and a veteran local politician who knew every string to pull and back to scratch. At each election he ran on his record, rather than on the vague and inconsequential policy platform of the United Party.[36] Martin was not only the political overseer of the Comrades Marathon, but he also kept political control of the horse racing industry in the province to himself. Else entered the provincial election contest severely handicapped.

The election was a disaster, Else's senior running mate, the candidate for the parliamentary seat, withdrew at the last minute. Instead of putting Else forward as the leading candidate, the Progressive Party hierarchy decided to support Theo Gerdener, an ex-National Party member, but a popular former administrator of Natal. Else's campaign was virtually abandoned by her party. In the confusion, and running against the seasoned political pro, Frank Martin, Else lost her deposit. Helen Suzman commiserated with her, not only regarding the loss of the election, but also the patronising way the male party leadership treated her as a female candidate.[37] Deneys, who no longer had a political home, gave moral support and helped Else on election day.

Although Else's campaign failed, the Progressive Party at national level won half a dozen new seats and, for the first time since 1961, Helen Suzman had company in Parliament. The United Party's losses were attributable, in significant measure, to its equivocation in relation to the Schlebusch Commission report.[38] Meanwhile, the first shifts in the tectonic plates of South African politics were beginning, the Soweto Uprising was but two years in the future and the small-scale manoeuvres in the grandiose Provincial Council chamber, behind the statue of Queen Victoria in Longmarket Street, were becoming increasingly irrelevant. The rapid collapse of the United Party was a sign of the changing times.

Nationally, 1975 was the pause before the Soweto Uprising, which was sparked by the government's attempting to force education in Afrikaans on African school pupils. Within the Schreiner family it also marked transitions: Oliver was completing his law degree and preparing to move on to Cambridge. His brother Neysie was nearing the end of his engineering degree in Durban and Jenny and Barbara were both students on the Pietermaritzburg campus. Finally, Deneys was appointed vice principal on the Pietermaritzburg campus, a post he took up at the beginning of 1976.

Issues of academic freedom, student rebels and keeping a liberal flame alive at a time of increasing national and university paranoia would play a major part in Deneys's years as head of the Pietermaritzburg campus. His time as vice principal began a few months before the Soweto Uprising shocked the apartheid regime to its foundations and it ended eleven years later during a time when South Africa was subject to a full-scale state of emergency. It was not in any way a peaceful time. On a personal level, Deneys and Else's eldest son, Oliver, was killed in a freak accident in Cambridge in 1977 and, ten years later, their eldest daughter, Jennifer, was detained for armed MK activities, shortly before Deneys formally retired.

Notes
1. Achilles Bozas, 'The Natal Provincial Council, 1910–1986', *Natalia* 16 (1986), pp.45–50. Bozas, a former United Party and New Republic Party member of the Provincial Council, is kind to the Provincial Council.

2. Paul Thompson, *Natalians First: Separatism in South Africa, 1909–1961* (Johannesburg: Southern Book Publishers, 1990), pp.166–7.
3. Else Schreiner, Reminiscences, 2016.
4. Mark Coghlan, 'The Horticulturalists, Freedom Radio and the Erase Erasmus Society: Pietermaritzburg-Based Protest against the Nationalist Government in the 1950s and Early 1960s', *Natalia* 25 (1995), pp.54–64.
5. Coghlan, 'The Horticulturalists', p.60.
6. Edgar Brookes, *A South African Pilgrimage* (Johannesburg: Ravan Press, 1977), p.127.
7. Brookes, *South African Pilgrimage*, p.127.
8. Randolph Vigne, *Liberals against Apartheid: A History of the Liberal Party of South Africa, 1953–68* (London: Macmillan, 1997), pp.145–6.
9. Alan Paton Centre: PC 101, Ainslie Papers, PC 2/9/5/1, Natal Convention Organising Committee, 1961.
10. Alan Paton Centre: PC 101, Ainslie Papers, PC2/9/5/3, Natal Convention Continuation Committee.
11. Vigne, *Liberals against Apartheid*, p.147.
12. Vigne, *Liberals against Apartheid*, pp.146–7.
13. Brookes, *South African Pilgrimage*, p.130.
14. Vigne, *Liberals against Apartheid*, p.198.
15. Brookes, *South African Pilgrimage*, p.122.
16. Vigne, *Liberals against Apartheid*, pp.203–5.
17. Michael Cardo, *Opening Men's Eyes: Peter Brown & the Liberal Struggle for South Africa* (Johannesburg: Jonathan Ball, 2010), pp.184–5.
18. Helen Suzman, *In No Uncertain Terms: Memoirs* (Johannesburg: Jonathan Ball, 1993), p.120.
19. Else Schreiner, Reminiscences, 2016.
20. Graham Dominy, '"On the Side of the Angels": Helen Suzman and the 1966 Robert Kennedy Tour', Helen Suzman Foundation Brief, 2016, https://www.politicsweb.co.za/comment/on-the-side-of-the-angels.
21. Suzman, *No Uncertain Terms*, p.120.
22. Brookes, *South African Pilgrimage*, p.141.
23. Vigne, *Liberals against Apartheid*, p.223; Pat Stilwell, Reminiscences, email, 3 October 2017.
24. See, for example, Peter Randall, ed., *Anatomy of Apartheid*, SPRO-CAS Occasional Publication No. 1 (Johannesburg: Christian Institute, 1970) and *Education Beyond Apartheid*, report of the Education Commission of the Study Project on Christianity in Apartheid Society (Johannesburg: Christian Institute, 1971), https://disa.ukzn.ac.za/sites/default/files/pdf_files/rep19710000.037.052.005.pdf.
25. Suzman, *No Uncertain Terms*, pp.131–2.

26. Christopher Merrett, *A Culture of Censorship: Secrecy and Intellectual Repression in South Africa* (Pietermaritzburg: University of Natal Press, 1995).
27. Bill Guest, *Stella Aurorae: The History of a South African University, Volume 2, the University of Natal (1949–1976)* (Pietermaritzburg: Natal Society Foundation, 2017), p.354.
28. University of KwaZulu-Natal (UKZN) Archives: S236/1/1, BIO, Retirement interview with Georgina Hamilton, *Sunday Tribune*, 12 December 1987.
29. Guest, *Stella Aurorae*, Vol. 2, p.334.
30. Michael Lambert, *The Classics and South African Identities* (London: Bloomsbury Academic, 2011), pp.73–4.
31. Personal knowledge. This was one of the first demonstrations I participated in.
32. Brookes, *South African Pilgrimage*, p.113. See also Guest, *Stella Aurorae*, Vol. 2, p.306.
33. Guest, *Stella Aurorae*, Vol. 2, p.214.
34. Suzman, *No Uncertain Terms*, pp.202–3.
35. This event was deemed a little too risqué to be included in Guest's *Stella Aurorae*. However, it lives on in university legend and popular reminiscences.
36. University of South Africa (UNISA) Archives: United Party Collection, Natal Provincial Office, 48.1.1, Provincial Election, Pamphlets, 'Martin for North' – Provincial Election 1970. The party propaganda for the 1974 election would have been virtually indistinguishable.
37. Else Schreiner, Reminiscences, 2016.
38. Suzman, *No Uncertain Terms*, p.132.

9

Pietermaritzburg Vice Principal
Challenges and Tragedy (1976–87)

In an interview shortly after his appointment was announced, Deneys explained that the role of vice principal was easy to define, but less easy to fulfil.[1] Within the university the vice principal had to be aware of the academic ambitions of faculties, departments and individual members of staff and attempt to order the internal operation of the university to keep a balance between conflicting ambitions and provide a maximum opportunity for the realisation of academic hopes. Outside the university, the vice principal had to promote understanding of and support for the university throughout the community it served. Experience taught Deneys that the vice principal also had to devote a lot of attention to the critical but mundane problems of infrastructure maintenance. Shortly before he retired, but after Professor Colin Webb had been announced as his successor, Deneys was asked how he thought Webb would cope as vice principal. He replied, with a mischievous twinkle in his eye, 'Colin does not know how much time he is going to have to spend on the drains!'[2]

Deneys was appointed vice principal on the Pietermaritzburg campus of the University of Natal on the retirement of Professor Ronald MacMillan and took office at the beginning of 1976. A scientist was following an educationalist; a rugby player and golfer was following a marathon runner into the campus hot seat.[3] It may also be said that a laconic figure was following a long-winded one. MacMillan enjoyed regaling students and visitors to his office, at great length, with tales of his athletic triumphs at national and international sporting events.⁴ Meetings with Deneys were, by comparison, mercifully brief, although he enjoyed cross-questioning his visitors, probably more than they enjoyed the experience.

MacMillan had nursed a proprietary interest in the Pietermaritzburg campus, to the extent that the principal and vice chancellor, Francis Stock, felt excluded. Else Schreiner recalled that on her first meeting with Mrs Gwen Stock after Deneys became vice principal, Mrs Stock thanked her for the welcome. When Else said, 'This is your campus', Mrs Stock became quite emotional and said how grateful she was to hear this, after years of not being made to feel welcome.⁵

Professor Stock, a British medical academic, with colonial experience in Africa and academic experience in Hong Kong, was not a popular figure with students. After the depressing and divisive experience with Owen Horwood at the helm, the university selectors were looking for a neutral, outside figure. However, Stock proved too technocratic, too aloof and insufficiently prepared to stand up to government attacks on students and staff to be popular with many staff and students. Although Stock was accused of being a second Horwood, he did use the Committee of University Principals as a platform to oppose government censorship regulations that impacted on university libraries.⁶ His ultra-cautious stance was in contrast with the much stronger stance against government interference with the universities taken by the vice chancellors of the universities of the Witwatersrand and of Cape Town. The latter was Sir Richard Luyt, who had even stronger colonial credentials than Stock. Luyt had been governor of British Guiana, the only British colony in South America, before taking up his university post in South Africa, the land of his birth.⁷

The internal tensions over Stock's attitudes may well have influenced the university council's decision to select a resolute liberal for the Pietermaritzburg local leadership, as a counterweight to the conservatism coming from the principal's office in Durban.

Also, the placing of a well-known liberal as a vice principal would prove less of a blatant challenge to the national government than would have been the case if the university elected a liberal as principal or vice chancellor.

After Stock's retirement, Deneys was a candidate for the position of vice chancellor and principal, but the vacancy occurred very early in his term as vice principal, before he had accumulated much experience in the post. According to Professor John Benyon, Deneys and Desmond Clarence had competed for principal and vice chancellor and the race between them was very keen, but swung by the fact that more people on the larger Durban campus knew Clarence (who was the vice principal there).[8] Nevertheless, the two men had a good working relationship and Clarence backed Deneys's initiatives. Their academic careers followed similar paths: Deneys was a chemist and Clarence was a physicist and both had worked with the famous Sir Basil Schonland. Although Clarence's duties as principal did not allow him to participate directly in the Buthelezi Commission, he encouraged university staff to contribute to it and support it.[9]

Before taking up his position as vice principal, Deneys went on a tour of British universities, sponsored by the British Council. He took the opportunity to renew many of the acquaintances and contacts he had made during his Cambridge years. However, the visit provided more challenges than it did nostalgic reunions, although Else and the family joined him for a short holiday that coincided with Oliver going to Cambridge.

The anti-apartheid academic boycott had not been effectively developed by the beginning of 1976, but even so it could be uncomfortable for white South Africans, no matter how liberal, to pay official visits overseas, especially to universities. Deneys's visit was no exception. He was greeted by student demonstrations on several of the campuses. Deneys, who was described by the *Natal Witness* as one of Pietermaritzburg's, 'better known campaigners for racial freedom and equality', was abused as a 'representative of the fascist Vorster regime' by some militant British students.[10] While this treatment was a shock, Deneys's sense of humour (and his long-standing knowledge of British academic and scientific circles) saved him from a display of self-defeating righteous anger.

Although English-language South African universities still regarded British universities as their exemplars and mentors, the situation in the United Kingdom had changed radically since Deneys's time at Cambridge. There had been a massive expansion of British universities during the 1960s, but by the mid-1970s academic ambitions, fuelled by secular and scientific visions, in contrast to the outmoded collegiality of Oxbridge, were outrunning available funding.[11] The late 1960s had been years of student unrest and social conflicts continued in the early and mid-1970s. These culminated in the widespread coal-miners' strikes, which spawned even wider strikes between 1972 and 1974. These strikes disrupted community life, transport, power supplies and, eventually, brought down Prime Minister Edward Heath's Conservative government.[12]

Deneys made an extensive study of the British higher education sector, looking at academic and physical planning; libraries; student subject choices; professional associations; labour management and trade unions; student residences and catering; and the interface between academics and administrators. He took careful note of the rivalries between Oxbridge and redbrick universities, and between universities and polytechnics (the equivalent South African institutions were then known as technikons).[13] In his report to the university council on his return, Deneys gave a perceptive summary of the situation: 'My visit took place then to a beleaguered and, perhaps, bewildered group of Universities rapidly adjusting to a new set of circumstances and forced from a comparatively orderly planning to ad hoc adjustment to meet immediate situations.'[14]

As vice principal, Deneys became used to making ad hoc adjustments, but he had masterminded the construction of the mass spectrometer in the chemistry department many years earlier, so he had demonstrated not only his flexibility, but also his willingness to surmount or circumvent obstacles in his path. He exuded calm and, with his easy manner, he connected with a wide range of students. At the beginning of the 1976 academic year, he welcomed the new first-year students with the words: 'We have something in common. You are first year University students. I am a first year Vice-Principal. I am therefore almost as bewitched, bothered and bewildered as you are.'[15]

This was largely rhetorical. Deneys was experienced and competent and he adapted easily to his new role. He made every effort to keep up with developments in university management and higher education policy. In 1977 he was one of the University of Natal representatives at a conference on the role of universities in southern Africa, held in Cape Town. This brought together representatives of English and Afrikaans universities, the 'black' universities (African, coloured and Indian) and included representatives from universities in other southern African countries. It was opened by the minister of national education, Dr Piet Koornhof, and although no formal resolutions were adopted, the conference expressed a consensus view that, among other issues, a university should be able to teach what and how it thinks best, to whom and by whom it thinks fit.[16] This accorded closely with Deneys's philosophy and, as one of the discussants, he helped to formulate the findings. That such an influential gathering expressed views in close alignment with his own would have given him a degree of quiet satisfaction.

He also wholeheartedly supported the views expressed by Professor George Bozzoli, the principal of the University of the Witwatersrand, who, in his address to the conference, strongly opposed the racial and ethnic segregation of universities and described it as 'a nonsense'. Bozzoli staunchly opposed government censorship of ideas and literature in the 'sociological and political fields'.[17] Censorship, particularly of academic material, was also anathema to Deneys, who had used his position as chairperson of the Library Committee to do as much as possible to circumvent government censorship in as circumspect a manner possible.[18] Librarians on the English campuses were loath to draw the attention of the censors and the police to the so-called subversive material in their collections and cover from senior academics, such as Deneys, who was also a 'real' scientist, rather than an overtly left-wing social scientist, was highly prized.

The matters that reached the desk of a vice principal included the mundane, such as the perennial, but essentially insoluble, problem of parking, and the critical, such as protecting academic freedom. Deneys's personal, egalitarian approach to the parking problem was to refuse to have a reserved parking space near his office. He also disapproved of reserved parking in general and sent out a testy memorandum in response to staff complaints: 'If common sense does not prevail, we will be forced to introduce a system of individually reserved parking places and a corresponding system of law enforcement. Both of these will involve expense which is wasteful, and I hope unnecessary.'[19]

This provoked much discontent from other staff who felt that it compromised their rights to precious parking spaces and also because when Deneys returned from a meeting off-campus or in Durban, during the middle of the day, he often had to park some way down Ridge Road and come running, rather late, into the next meeting. The chaos in Ridge and Golf roads was also unpopular with local residents and the university files are full of acrimonious internal memoranda and irate letters from Scottsville residents. In his responses, Deneys expressed his regrets, shared his sympathy, but opined that there was very little that could be done.[20]

Adjudicating issues of accommodation played an important role in the vice principal's work. A minor instance of this occurred in 1980 when Francis Antonie, a newly arrived lecturer in political science (who was also a fine musician with a sensitive ear) was installed in an office in the Old Arts Block, close to the chemistry department.[21] He complained bitterly that the very loud extractor fan in the chemistry department, which faced directly on to his office, was thumping away an octave off A flat and it was driving him crazy. Deneys had to lead an inspection of the problematic site and solemn deliberations were held with technicians. Finally, Deneys decreed that the extractor plant had to be 'retuned' and Francis Antonie was satisfied.[22]

There was also an exchange of correspondence with Malcolm Macintyre-Reed of the fine arts department, which was housed in utilitarian buildings near the administration building on the Ridge Road side of the campus. Shortly after Deneys's appointment, Macintyre-Reed began agitating for improved accommodation and even sweetened his correspondence by sending a cake over to the vice principal's office.

Deneys was informed that the fine arts department celebrated 30 years in temporary accommodation and Hilda Ditchburn, a lecturer with 30 years of service, cut the first slice. The students and staff decided to send it to Deneys, in the hopes that fine arts might be favourably considered for extra accommodation when most of the arts departments moved to the new Arts Block on the Golf Road campus.[23] Deneys replied:

> Dear Mr Macintyre-Reed,
> I enjoyed my tea this morning more than usual because of the delightful cake that I was able to eat with it. The student who supplied it may possibly be in the wrong department: his/her talents in home economics seem well developed.
>
> I wonder whether there is not something appropriate about a sub-department which is making such a significant contribution to the future of Archaeology being housed in temporary accommodation. It derives some respectability from historical precedent.
>
> It was well understood in late Roman days that bribery and corruption should be conducted on what could be called an improperly proper scale, and that rewards were directly proportioned to the scale of the benefits received. I consider that for the University of Natal to uphold the great Roman tradition would be entirely acceptable.[24]

Nobody would dare to make such a joke in these days of national corruption and state capture.

One of the earliest externally inflicted crises was the petrol crisis of the mid-1970s. The security of the national fuel supply had been unsettled by the conflict in the Middle East, beginning in 1973 with the Arab-Israeli War, but accentuated in 1976, after the Soweto Uprising, when many of the oil-producing states resolved to punish South Africa through sanctions and boycotts. As a result, Deneys had to devote considerable attention to the logistical details of student field trips, which would never normally come to the vice principal's attention. He even had to attempt to co-ordinate staff trips to Durban because a classics lecturer on the coastal campus was on sabbatical leave and a Pietermaritzburg lecturer had to cover the course, without anybody having considered the implications for the university's restricted fuel supply.[25] The fuel crisis also enhanced the autonomy of the office of vice principal, as travel between the Durban and Pietermaritzburg campuses became more expensive and, accordingly, more decision-making powers were delegated to Deneys.[26]

In 1977, the economic consequences of the post-Soweto instability, as well as the fuel crisis, triggered a financial crisis that impacted severely on the universities. In only his second year as vice principal, Deneys was forced to order the freezing of posts – an unpopular move, but according to decisions of the council and the senate.[27] Deneys may have been taking and enforcing unpopular decisions, but he retained the respect of both staff and students because of his innate sense of fairness and his sense of humour. According to John Benyon, the head of the joint department of history and political science, a head of department could take any problem to Deneys, who would take the time to grasp it thoroughly before giving advice 'that was always sound'.[28]

Of greater significance was Deneys's support for efforts to form a social sciences student council, motivated by Douglas Irvine of the political science department (which was in the throes of a divorce from the history department).[29] The social sciences were firmly based on the Durban campus and Professor Lawrence Schlemmer was a leading figure in the Durban department. He was an important participant in the constitutional change conference Deneys organised in 1978 and later headed the Inkatha Institute, which provided the secretariat for the Buthelezi Commission. The Durban academics did not have much interest in the establishment of a fully blown social sciences faculty in Pietermaritzburg, but the numbers of students interested in the social sciences was increasing on the inland campus.

In 1986, Douglas Irvine was appointed acting dean of social science in Pietermaritzburg and assigned the task of putting together a credible list of courses from those available in the arts and commerce faculties. Despite the fact Deneys's daughter Jennifer was studying social sciences in Cape Town, he always professed not to know the difference between social sciences, sociology and social work, claiming that they were all simply about 'being nice to people'. Irvine was quite likely to have been the victim of his 'counter-suggestible' nature. Nevertheless, Deneys gave the fledgling faculty his full support.[30] Another research facility of great importance to the university, the Alan Paton Centre, only came to fruition after Deneys had retired, but Deneys and former history professor Mark Prestwich, both encouraged Paton to donate his papers to the University of Natal, which his widow Anne Paton did after her husband's death.[31]

This was but one of the wide range of issues dealt with by the vice principal. Deneys also dealt with issues ranging from English language development, conservation research and practical work in the Drakensberg (in co-operation with the Natal Parks Board), the acquisition of artworks for a university art gallery, the approval of the College Lecture lunch menus, the formation of a group to foster the teaching of mathematics and sciences and the ongoing problems with the campus grounds, buildings and infrastructure, and the proverbial 'drains' he passed on to Colin Webb.[32]

Deneys was able to take an early step to reduce gender-based residential discrimination. In 1983 the changing admissions policy resulted in more women first-year students than men. Deneys arranged for twelve women to take up residence in William O'Brien, the hallowed home of male chauvinism on campus and the largest male-only residence of any university in South Africa.

Deneys saw this as a way to 'civilise' William O'Brien, a year or two after he had disciplined the students who filled the swimming pools with beer cans. It was also a move towards the full residential integration that he had observed in Europe.[33]

One of Deneys's strongest policies was to improve relations between town and gown – the city and the university. He had consistently refused to join the Victoria Club because of its discriminatory policies – not only against black people and women, but also against Jews. One of his close friends, local attorney Leslie Weinberg, had been refused membership, 'blackballed', as the term was in those days. Nevertheless, as vice principal, Deneys was occasionally obliged to use the club for official entertaining.[34] However, he made much greater and more enjoyable use of the Pietermaritzburg Golf Club, playing every weekend and sometimes during the week. These games were key to his building connections with local business people, in those days, almost exclusively white men. His strategy was broadly focused: firstly, the business community could provide bursaries; donations could be sought for books, equipment and infrastructure and job opportunities could be made available to students and new graduates; secondly, Deneys's business contacts proved extremely valuable in setting up the constitutional change conference and in the workings of the Buthelezi Commission.

From early on in his term as vice principal, Deneys pushed for the use of computers in as many fields as possible in the university. At his retirement ceremony in 1987 he made specific mention of this, saying: 'The little place we came to has grown fourfold and has started to believe in computers.'[35] This belief was carefully fostered by Deneys, who was able to use his management position and his experience on the Research Committee to align both administrative and academic thinking around the need for the new technology. He was also active in soliciting outside funding for the acquisition of computers, through Project Ulwazi/Project Knowledge, lobbying both local MP Mike Tarr and the KwaZulu homeland government for their support.[36]

Deneys also focused closely on people problems. Obviously, many of these centred around student conduct and misconduct, especially drunkenness, which peaked during Rag festivities.[37] The influx of demobilised ex-Rhodesian students in 1980, as Zimbabwe achieved independence, also provided its challenges. Many suffered from post-traumatic stress, psychological and physical health challenges. Leaving the stress of war and the restrictions of military discipline for the freedom of student life led to many excesses.

One such incident occurred when a gang of young 'Rhodies' went 'bossies'.[38] They got blind drunk, collected every bottle and beer can to be found on the campus (particularly near the University Club in Golf Road) and threw them into the swimming pool. They were identified and apprehended by campus security and paraded in front of the vice principal. The security staff presented their evidence. Deneys asked the students for their version and they remained silent. Deneys then called in the university proctor, Professor James Lund, from the law faculty and they had a consultation. The sheepish and hungover young men awaited their fate, but the vice principal and the proctor had decided to handle the matter unofficially. Deneys told the students that he too had endured the stresses of military service and understood what was going on in their heads. He advised them to go back to bed and sleep it off, but if they ever misbehaved again, they would be suspended. But first, Deneys ordered, they were to strip down to their underpants and clean out the swimming pool.[39]

As vice principal, Deneys was in a position to gently nudge the university so that its resources were utilised in support of those working and learning outside the formal curriculum. He supported the Non-Academic Staff Association and the Extra-mural Studies and Extension Unit, headed by his formerly banned friend and neighbour, John Aitchison.[40] This was one of the outreach programmes of the university that provided evening enrichment lectures not only for students, but also for members of the public. Another university project that gained his full support was known as Bridging the Gap. This was focused on supporting and coaching new students who struggled with the transition between school and university. Deneys, who had struggled when he first went to Cambridge, had every sympathy with new students in a strange environment. He fired off memoranda to wardens of residences, the heads of the language laboratory and the library, campus security and anybody who could smooth the path for students and people needing to study and learn, pledging the full support of the university to such programmes.[41]

The Centre for Adult Education grew out of the Extramural Studies Unit, with Deneys's hearty support. An office was established on the Pietermaritzburg campus in 1979, headed by Robin Mackie. He was succeeded by John Aitchison, who developed it into perhaps the most important outreach arm of the university. Deneys was involved in the early establishment phase and kept an affectionate and watchful eye on its development. During the years of violence that began in 1987, the centre set up an Unrest Monitoring Project and gathered data on casualties, the location of incidents of violence and as much general information as possible, despite all the legal obstacles thrown in its way. The project developed an international reputation and disseminated reliable information as widely as possible. More than 40 foreign delegations and observers visited the university to consult the database and interview the staff.[42]

While the arts faculty enjoyed Deneys's full support – he was an enthusiastic and knowledgeable collector of works of art and a supporter of the performing arts – he did not forget his scientific and disciplinary roots. Such was his reputation as a committed scientist that the science and agriculture faculties inaugurated the Deneys Schreiner lecture series in his honour. These lectures were presented by the holders of prestigious Foundation for Research Development grants.[43] Deneys was active in the work of the Urban Foundation, a think tank established with the moral and material support of Harry Oppenheimer in 1977, in the wake of the Soweto Uprising. The foundation was tasked with developing projects and policies that could ameliorate the devastating impact of apartheid, especially on the educational prospects of black South Africans. Deneys was the most senior university academic involved in the foundation's mathematics and science discussion group and developed the report that was submitted to the Human Sciences Research Council in 1981.[44]

As the political situation in South Africa became increasingly tense in the early and mid-1980s, it became clear that despite the increasing government repression, the system of apartheid was collapsing rapidly. As vice principal, Deneys was adept at finding room to manoeuvre within the maze of contradictory edicts and regulations coming from Pretoria. In the 1980s black students were trickling into the university and one of the major problems was finding them suitable accommodation. Dr Gunther Wittenberg, of the religious studies department, was determined to establish a Bachelor of Theology degree that would be open to all races. Agnostic Deneys fully supported this initiative, but accommodation for the students became a hot issue. The government got involved when white residents in Scottsville began objecting to black students living in the suburb.

The Department of Community Development decreed that black students could not live in off-campus accommodation in Golf Road, but must be accommodated in Denison Residence. However, the Department of National Education had just ordered the eviction of some black students who were already living quietly in Denison with Deneys's permission. His reaction to this government confusion was unbridled mirth and, for him, it was a clear indication that the apartheid system was collapsing.[45] Deneys handled the matter with subtlety. He carefully researched the matter and drew on work done by the South African Institute of Race Relations on the benefits for black students of living in university residences before reaching his conclusions.[46] A new university policy for admission to residences was determined, in flat defiance of the law, as Deneys told Else.[47] Finally, in a manner reminiscent of his advice to Pat Stilwell some years earlier, on how to handle the demands of Owen Horwood, he decided to do as little as possible publicly. Polite and soothing letters were addressed to residents and officials, but no black students were removed and their presence was soon accepted as normal.

On the family front, the highly organised and ambitious Oliver, after receiving a first-class law degree, had been awarded an Elsie Ballot Scholarship to Cambridge.[48] He was not only intelligent, but also extremely hard-working and planned his daily and weekly activities with military precision. The family focused on his ambitions and his achievements and the daily routine at Highwood, including mealtimes, was adjusted to fit his schedule. Oliver was seen as more than just a rising star, he was the Schreiner who would fulfil dynastic ambitions and become the chief justice his grandfather had never been. However, he had some of his father's traits, such as worrying over tests and exams. The university saw Oliver as potentially a fine ambassador and he did not disappoint. He went to Cambridge in 1975 to further his legal studies.

He had been engaged for a year before he married his South African fiancée in a traditional church ceremony in Trinity College Chapel in 1976. A daughter was born of the marriage nearly two years later and Oliver was delighted with the new baby.[49] A few weeks later, on 8 March 1978, Oliver was cycling to college early in the morning and was killed in an apparent hit-and-run accident. There were no witnesses and the vehicle and its driver disappeared. His tutor, Dr Seal, described him as 'brilliant' and expressed his bafflement at the strange accident.[50] Despite official investigations, the mystery of the accident was never solved; certainly in the late 1970s, forensic technology was not as advanced as it is in the twenty-first century, nor were surveillance cameras a ubiquitous presence in streets in the United Kingdom and elsewhere.

For Deneys, his eldest son's death was a devastating blow. His daughter Barbara declared that it was the first time that she had ever seen her father cry. Barbara, a drama student, was performing in the musical *Oliver* in the Hexagon Theatre and was called out of a dress rehearsal to learn of her brother's death. She had to perform a few nights later.[51] Deneys flew to Britain to support Oliver's widow, meet his first grandchild under the most distressing circumstances imaginable, attend to all the legal formalities and make all the necessary arrangements with Cambridge University and the British civil authorities.

The Schreiners carried on as best they could. Oliver had been seen as the hope of the next generation. He had a brilliant academic record and was to have been named the first Harry Holland Law Fellow at Trinity College.[52] Oliver clearly saw himself as the Schreiner who would get to the top of the greasy pole. Fellow law students in Pietermaritzburg talked of him as a future chief justice.

Observers on the campus saw a more withdrawn and distracted Deneys for many months after the tragedy. However, despite his grief, he continued doing his job as vice principal and focused his energies on what had long been one of his interests: contributing to constitutional debate in South Africa. Using the authority of his university office, Deneys organised a conference on the Pietermaritzburg campus to examine possible constitutional options for South Africa.

Notes

1. University of KwaZulu-Natal (UKZN) Archives: S236/1/1, BIO, Draft Press Release.
2. Personal conversation with Deneys Schreiner.
3. Professor MacMillan had represented the Union of South Africa at both the Commonwealth and the Olympic Games in the 1930s and been named Springbok Athlete of the Year in 1937. See Bill Guest, *Stella Aurorae: The History of a South African University, Volume 2, the University of Natal (1949–1976)* (Pietermaritzburg: Natal Society Foundation, 2017), p.106. Deneys Schreiner's athletic career did not reach such dizzy heights, but he probably related better to sportsmen and women than his predecessor had.
4. Guest, *Stella Aurorae, Vol. 2*, p.404.
5. Else Schreiner, Reminiscences, 2016.
6. Guest, *Stella Aurorae, Vol. 2*, pp.405–9, 414–15.
7. Stuart Saunders, *Vice-Chancellor on a Tightrope: A Personal Account of Climactic Years in South Africa* (Cape Town: David Philip, 2000).
8. John Benyon, Reminiscences, email of 11 January 2018. See also Bill Guest, *Stella Aurorae: The History of a South African University, Volume*

3, *The University of Natal (1976–2003)* (Pietermaritzburg: Natal Society Foundation, 2018), pp.5–6.
9. ADM Walker, 'Noel Desmond Clarence (1921–1995)', *Natalia* 25 (1995), pp.84–6.
10. 'Pmb Prof Labelled "Fascist" by UK Demos', *Natal Witness*, 8 January 1976.
11. Andrew Marr, *A History of Modern Britain* (London: Macmillan, 2007), pp.250–1. See also Robert Anderson, *British Universities: Past and Present* (London: Hambledon Continuum, 2006), p.151.
12. Marr, *History of Modern Britain*, pp.340–2.
13. Anderson, *British Universities*, pp.136–7.
14. UKZN Archives: BIO – S236/1/1, 'Report on Visits to British Universities', GDL Schreiner, 16 March 1976.
15. UKZN Archives: SP25/1/1/1, Schreiner, GDL (Prof & Vice Principal UNP), 1976–1987 (Newspaper Cuttings), *Natal Witness*, 26 May 1980.
16. HW van der Merwe and David Welsh, eds, *The Future of the University in Southern Africa* (Cape Town: David Philip, 1977).
17. GR Bozzoli, 'The Role of English Universities in South Africa', in *The Future of the University in Southern Africa*, edited by HW van der Merwe and David Welsh (Cape Town: David Philip, 1977), pp.188–95.
18. Comments of Colleen Vietzen, former Pietermaritzburg campus university librarian. Conversation with the author at the Alan Paton Centre, February 2017.
19. UKZN Archives: SP 25/1/1/1 BIO – S236/1/1, University Parking Policy Memo, 1 March 1977.
20. UKZN Archives: SP25/8/30–46, Schreiner, GDL, see, for example, Schreiner letter to Mrs ES Theunissen of Golf Road, 15 May 1985.
21. Francis Antonie is currently the director of the Helen Suzman Foundation.
22. Douglas Irvine, Reminisences, 15 January 2018.
23. UKZN Archives: SP 25/1/1/1, Schreiner, GDL (Prof & Vice Principal UNP), 1976–1987, letter from Macintyre-Reed to GDL Schreiner, 25 March 1976.
24. UKZN Archives: SP 25/1/1/1, Schreiner, GDL (Prof & Vice Principal UNP), 1976–1987, letter from GDL Schreiner to Macintyre-Reed, 25 March 1976.
25. UKZN Archives: SP25/8/30–46, Schreiner, GDL, Memo, 22 October 1976, Impact of petrol restrictions on student field trips and field research.
26. Douglas Irvine, Reminiscences, 15 January 2018.
27. UKZN Archives: SP25/8/30–46, Schreiner, GDL, Memo re freezing of post.

28. John Benyon, Reminiscences, email of 11 January 2018.
29. UKZN Archives: SP25/5/1–17, Schreiner, GDL, administration files, letter from Douglas Irvine, 29 August 1983.
30. Douglas Irvine, Reminiscences, 15 January 2018.
31. Guest, *Stella Aurorae, Vol. 3*, p.40.
32. UKZN Archives: SP25/4/1–15, Schreiner, GDL, documents.
33. Guest, *Stella Aurorae, Vol. 3*, p.184.
34. Douglas Irvine, Reminiscences, 15 January 2018.
35. UKZN Archives: SP25/1/1/1, Schreiner, GDL, Retirement Speech 1987. See also SP25/4/9, Audio-visual and electronic services on computers (1974–1982).
36. UKZN Archives: SP25/5/1–17, Schreiner, GDL, administration files, correspondence, Project Ulwazi/Project Knowledge.
37. UKZN Archives: SP25/8/30–46, Schreiner, GDL, various correspondence dealing with student drunkenness.
38. 'Bossies' is derived from the Afrikaans expletive *bosbefok*, loosely and politely translated as 'mad in the head as a result of prolonged exposure to bush conditions'.
39. Reminiscences, Jennifer Verbeek, email of 15 October 2017.
40. UKZN Archives: SP25/4/1–15, Schreiner, GDL, documents, SP25/4/6, Extra-mural studies and extension unit, letter from John Aitchison, 20 August 1982.
41. UKZN Archives: SP 25/4/1–15, Schreiner, GDL, documents. There are numerous letters and memoranda in the Schreiner Papers indicating this support.
42. John Aitchison, Reminiscences, email of 2 June 2019.
43. Guest, *Stella Aurorae, Vol. 3*, p.108. The Foundation for Research Development is now the National Research Foundation.
44. UKZN Archives: SP25/8/12–29, Schreiner, GDL: Memo, 10 February 1981.
45. Address by Professor Colin Gardner, eulogy, Deneys Schreiner memorial service, Tembaletu, 2007
46. UKZN Archives: SP25/4/1–15, Schreiner, GDL, documents, 22 July 1985, SAIRR research paper.
47. GDL Schreiner, private correspondence, letter to Else, 18 June 1985.
48. Guest, *Stella Aurorae, Vol. 2*, p.302.
49. Owing to the emotionally harrowing nature of the event, Oliver's widow and daughter have requested that their names are not mentioned in this work.
50. *Daily News*, 9 March 1978. The article incorrectly gives Dr Seal's initial as 'U'. Deneys correctly refers to him as 'Anil Seal'.

51. Barbara Schreiner, Reminiscences with David Robbins, 2016.
52. GDL Schreiner, private correspondence, letter to Else, undated, *circa* March 1978.

10

Vice Principal
Protests and Political Engagement (1976–80)

As vice principal, Deneys occupied a leadership position that gave him more scope to wield political influence than he had as a discipline-based academic in the chemistry department.[1] Political awareness was hard-wired into his genes, as was evident from his astute comments on national and global affairs in the letters sent to his father during the Second World War and during his Cambridge years. He was conscious of the family's liberal legacy, even if he refused to make himself available as a candidate for Parliament or any other public office. As vice principal Deneys was always seeking ways to undermine the effects of apartheid and to posit democratic alternatives.

South Africa had been shaken to its core by the Soweto Uprising, beginning on 16 June 1976. Prime Minister John Vorster ordered maximum repression and the security forces set to work, assisted by the entire apparatus of a repressive state: brutal crowd control methods, detention without trial, widespread spying and heavy censorship. While the province of Natal and the homeland of KwaZulu were less affected by the youth-driven unrest than urban areas in the Transvaal and the Cape, tension on university campuses mounted. At the University of Zululand at KwaDlangezwa, near Empangeni, students burned down the library and the administration buildings.[2]

Tensions between activist students and the police on the campuses in Durban, Pietermaritzburg and at the Medical School in Wentworth mounted.³ Protests and demonstrations were organised and police spies infiltrated the Pietermaritzburg campus. Anne Murphy was an administrative officer in the Students' Representative Council (SRC) offices when the police swooped on a picket line of student demonstrators and raided the SRC offices. Dozens of students were taken to the Loop Street police station. Anne spent hours collecting and cross-checking the names of all those who had been arrested and went to Deneys's office to report. He was keeping late hours and she was able to see him. She read through the names and paused, just before the end: 'And?' Deneys prompted.

Anne sighed. 'Nodi Murphy' (her sister), she said.

'I was waiting for that,' said Deneys, 'And?'

'Barbara Schreiner,' concluded Anne.

'I was waiting for that one too,' said Deneys and rummaged in a safe in his office from which he extracted a wad of money. 'Those two deserve to stay where they are and learn a lesson, but I suppose I had better go and bail them all out,' he said.⁴

Pat Stilwell, then the university's attorney, remembers a late call from Deneys asking to meet at the local magistrate's court. Pat was able to arrange an emergency late-night hearing and Deneys arrived with a bank bag full of cash, from which he proceeded to extract enough money to bail out all the students in the dock. Pat did not know whether the cash came from a university slush fund or out of Deneys's own pocket.⁵

Deneys did more than simply bail students out of insalubrious police cells. His attitude to government attacks on liberty and university autonomy differed entirely from the distant stand-offish approach of Francis Stock. In 1979, the government appointed the Rabie Commission to rationalise and sharpen the draconian but poorly co-ordinated security legislation. Professor Anthony Mathews, the James Scott Wylie Professor of Law in Pietermaritzburg, asserted: 'The rule of law does not constitute the whole of freedom but it is certainly a basic part of it.'⁶ Mathews then quoted OD Schreiner's comment that 'a complaint that the rule of law has been infringed is a political and not a legal complaint'. Mathews went further and claimed that the Rabie Commission used OD's remark to 'discard the rule of law as a helpful guide in framing a new security policy'.

The report of the Rabie Commission was tabled in Parliament in 1982 and resulted in the drafting of an omnibus security bill, which became law as the Internal Security Act (No. 74 of 1982). It has been described as

> the last word in security legislation, a monument to over 30 years of experience in drafting statutes which could defend apartheid security against its many opponents; a monument to the way in which loopholes and avenues of expression could be closed down one by one, until space for legitimate political opposition vanished altogether.[7]

Furious at the Rabie Commission's distortion of his father's words, Deneys planned and co-ordinated the official but futile university response. Lawrence Baxter and Julian Riekert from the law faculty drafted a position paper for Deneys's consideration and Tony Mathews submitted a scathing memorandum. Deneys added a section charging the state with the explicit responsibility for protecting academic freedom, so that the university could 'fulfil its obligations to the State and the Community'.[8] The reaction of the Pretoria securocrats in PW Botha's regime can only be imagined.

Deneys's contributions to defending university autonomy and student rights had been recognised by the National Union of South African Students (NUSAS) when it held its annual conference in November 1977 on the Pietermaritzburg campus. It was opened by Deneys, who stated that he had been a member of NUSAS 37 years earlier and that the current conference was still discussing the same issues that were discussed then. He called for more unity between student organisations in the interests of building a just South Africa. Deneys was invited to serve as an honorary vice president of NUSAS for the following two years, 1978 and 1979.[9]

The Soweto Uprising prompted some tentative moves towards constitutional change or, at least, a repackaging of apartheid. Even the National Party realised that the exclusion of coloured and Indian people from any meaningful role in the body politic was a major logical flaw in the apartheid policy, although they refused to acknowledge that the entire policy was unjust, let alone logically flawed. As a result, the policy positions being discussed in government circles were merely tinkering with apartheid, as no National Party politician in the 1970s dared mention the unmentionable – one person, one vote, in a unitary state.

The government's favourite constitutional tinkerer was Professor Denis Worrall, an English-speaking political scientist who had taught at the universities of Natal and Rhodes. He was mooting models and flying kites for the *'verligte'* (enlightened) National Party members; constitutional contraptions that later took wings as the Tricameral Parliament. It would be an exaggeration to say that there was a ferment of constitutional ideas swirling around, but for the first time since the early 1960s, there was, at the very least, some flexibility in the sclerotic body politic. Deneys wanted to pre-empt any 'sticking-plaster' solution dreamed up behind closed doors by Broeders and bureaucrats.[10] He decided to set up a conference with the widest range of representative views, both academic and political, that were possible under the restrictive laws of the time.[11]

John Benyon, the new professor of historical and political science and Douglas Irvine, the principal political scientist in the department, were called into Deneys's office to discuss his ardent wish for the University of Natal to make a contribution to the developing national political debate. The timelines were short, as the government proposals were still being worked on, but appeared to be close to being finalised. However, Deneys believed that there was a brief window of opportunity for the university to make a creative intervention.

First, there was the question of funding. However, the originality of the conference's concept evoked a sympathetic response from big business in Johannesburg. Deneys and John Benyon flew to Johannesburg and went cap in hand to Anglo-American, where they received a warm reception and a large grant from the Chairman's Fund.[12] Other big business organisations, such as Standard Bank and the Stewarts and Lloyds Group, also lent their support. Think tanks such as the Africa Institute, the Institute of Plural Studies and the Foreign Affairs Association supported and helped to organise the conference. In the background was Deneys's father, OD Schreiner, then in his declining years, but still alert and, after all his constitutional battles, anxious to see serious moves made to end apartheid.[13] Strangely, the South African Institute of Race Relations (SAIRR), a stronghold of liberal thought with a close association with the Schreiner family, is not mentioned as one of the sponsoring organisations.

An illustrious steering committee, headed by Sir Richard Luyt, vice chancellor of the University of Cape Town, was assembled. It included three other vice chancellors, some of the country's leading social scientists, from both English and Afrikaans universities and academic traditions, but Deneys was firmly in the driving seat. The Natal University vice chancellor, Professor Desmond Clarence, acknowledged Deneys as the inspiration for the conference.[14] Deneys was ably assisted by Sheila Hindson (Meintjes) as organising secretary, with Benyon and Irvine from historical and political science and John Milton from the law faculty as academic support. Members of the Schreiner family were roped in to lend a hand. Barbara, at that time a speech and drama student, was tasked with arrangements for the sound system, an important job since the entire proceedings were being recorded. The conference was held in the Main Hall of the Old Arts Block (now the Colin Webb Hall) and Barbara positioned the sound-receiving equipment in the wings of the stage, so as to get the best audio results. Deneys urged all speakers to face the dish on the stage when speaking, not the other dish – as that one was his daughter.[15]

The significance of this conference is that it fitted both a pattern in Deneys's life and in the University of Natal's trajectory. Deneys had been interested in constitutional and human rights issues since the 1950s, when he lived in Johannesburg. He had been an organiser of the 1961 Natal Convention, shortly after moving to Pietermaritzburg, and fifteen or so years later, during another period of deepening political crisis, Deneys used his initiative to try again. The university had hosted the 1961 Natal Convention and Edgar Brookes, the polymath professor, had driven the earlier process. This time, instead of organising ashtrays, Deneys was driving the conference.

Natal was the single region of South Africa where persistent attention had been paid to constitutional issues. This was partly as a result of history, going back all the way to the National Convention in Durban in 1909, before the Union of South Africa was established. Deneys made this link in his foreword to the published proceedings of the conference.[16] It was also a reflection of political reality: the interwoven lives of Africans, coloureds, Indians and whites in the province gave the lie to the pretensions of separate development. No National Party sophistry and impressionistic map-making could disguise the fact that separate development was completely impractical and unworkable in South Africa, and nowhere more so than in the political patchwork quilt that was the province of Natal and the homeland of KwaZulu. This was obvious to all races and to influential white groups, such as the business community and farming community – especially the sugar farmers.

Irvine and Benyon took up Deneys's challenge with a will and the conference was pulled together in a matter of months and held in February 1978. It attracted a wide range of participants for the times. Its principal weakness, as with every internal discussion or consultation arranged before 1990, was the enforced absence of banned organisations and exiled or detained individuals, a fact emphasised in the conference proceedings. Many of the papers were hastily prepared, given the tight time frames of the conference, but nevertheless they represented a significant range of opinions and were 'thoughtful and constructive'.[17] Inevitably, the participants were predominantly white and, this time round, the successor to the United Party, the New Republic Party, did participate.

The minority of black participants were largely delegates from homeland governments, a few academics from black universities, a smattering of journalists and one or two community organisation representatives and religious leaders. The latter included the Right Reverend Alphaeus Zulu, the first black Anglican bishop of Zululand (recently retired). Zulu had been a member of the African National Congress (ANC) who later joined Inkatha (becoming a senior office-bearer), believing that its message was the promotion of peaceful change. He was a frequent guest at Highwood, as many religious figures were, and he and Deneys not only shared similar political views, but also shared a similar outlook on life.[18] They both fundamentally believed in human goodness and that this could lead to the peaceful resolution of conflicts. The bishop's connections in both ANC and Inkatha circles proved invaluable to Deneys as he set about encouraging people to participate in the conference on constitutional change, as well as a few years later when he set up the Buthelezi Commission.

Deneys's target participants were members of the provincial elites: businessmen, traditional leaders, academics, journalists and opinion-makers more generally. The wide range of people who had attended Sunday evening soireés at Highwood, as well as the movers and shakers he golfed with on Saturdays, formed an immensely useful pool of contacts for Deneys.

Inkatha, the Zulu cultural movement that preceded the Inkatha Freedom Party, was formed in 1975. It fostered the process of African 'elite formation' and brought together a modernising African intellectual class, an emerging African middle class and traditionalist Zulu elders and chiefs.[19] The conference on constitutional change attracted modernising intellectuals.

In his foreword to the published conference proceedings, Deneys wrote: 'In 1977 a new but urgent consensus had been reached amongst South Africans of all racial groups and of all political persuasions. This agreement was that those political powers which had previously been reserved for White South Africans must be extended to include other South Africans.'[20]

While the wording was cautious, Deneys's intent was radical: South Africa had to be governed in the interests of all of its peoples. It seems a truism now, but in the 1970s such a conclusion was still taboo because white politicians, of various political shades, were trying to avoid the obvious fact that black majority rule was inevitable. In 1977 north of the Limpopo, Ian Smith's white minority Rhodesian regime was still desperately fighting a bloody war to avoid facing that reality. Further west, South African troops, largely white conscripts, were fighting in Angola to the same end. Even John Vorster (aided and guided by the conservative Republican Secretary of State of the United States, Henry Kissinger), was pressuring Smith to give in. Deneys alluded to the constitutional discussions in both South West Africa (Namibia) and Rhodesia (Zimbabwe) as he developed his argument for the necessity for constitutional discussions in South Africa.

This argument rested on three clearly articulated points: First (and most important) was that in South Africa, 'discussion between White and Black South Africans is minimal'. Therefore, a fundamental precondition for debate, 'with its inherent adjustment of views', which would enable the building of consensus, 'simply was not taking place'. The second 'disturbing feature' was the adherence of each major political party to a different constitutional model, 'so that the examination of the merits of a particular new model was inextricably linked with the political power struggle'. The third issue was more complex. It related to a change in thinking about suitable systems of government in deeply divided societies. Political scientists had been developing a new language to express their thinking: 'Even amongst political scientists this new language retaining [sic] something of a Humpty Dumpty property: "When I use a word", Humpty Dumpty said in a rather scornful tone, "it means just what I chose it to mean – neither more nor less."'[21]

Deneys outlined the complicated vocabulary then coming into vogue: 'pluralism', 'consociational government' and 'confederation', to name just a few. These words, Deneys wrote, were often viewed with suspicion as methods of 'excluding from real political power those who were now theoretically to be newly admitted to such power'.[22] The purpose of the conference was to bring together experts who would discuss the implications of various constitutional models and the representatives of the groups of South Africans who would be affected by any new Constitution. This, Deneys hoped, would begin a national discussion and prompt further debate. Both Deneys and Vice Chancellor Desmond Clarence placed great emphasis on the need for further debate. In Deneys's words:

> If the publication of this book is followed by a return to the old 'no-debate' situation, it must be true that both the book and the Conference can be regarded as failing. If the atmosphere of the Conference – one of co-operative discovery of both common purpose and disagreements, of adjustment of views and attempted understanding between South Africans – extends now to a wider group of people, both this book and the Conference will have succeeded.[23]

Denis Worrall presented the latest thinking generated by the government and the National Party's think tanks, including, although not explicitly stated, the Broederbond. Broadly speaking, there were to be three houses of Parliament, for coloureds, Indians and whites, as well as frills such as an electoral college and a president's council in the place of the senate. The whites would dominate through numbers – in other words, the minority white population was to be turned into a constitutional majority among other minorities.[24] Much of this thinking crystallised into law a few years later as the Tricameral Constitution. None of this cogitation included or reflected any black views, a matter of considerable annoyance to the leader of KwaZulu, Chief Minister Mangosuthu Buthelezi.

Professor Deon Fourie, a political scientist from the University of South Africa (UNISA) and a reservist military officer, produced an incisive analysis of the absurdities of apartheid boundaries from a security perspective. His argument was that if a long regular border, such as South West Africa's northern border with Angola and Zambia, was difficult to patrol, patrolling the irregular patchwork borders of independent homelands would be costly in terms of funds, manpower and general military resources. Fourie issued a guarded call for comprehensive and inclusive political reform as being in the best interests of South Africa's security.[25] Frederik van Zyl Slabbert, a rising opposition politician, who became leader of the Progressive Federal Party the following year, pointed out that the tendency at the conference was either to analyse present circumstances, or to project solutions quite far into the future.[26]

The significance of the conference was that in a time of popular black revolutionary action and white political stagnation, the University of Natal, prodded by Deneys, was prepared to be innovative and proactive. The conference was a rare opportunity for academics, politicians and intellectuals of liberal opinion, to gather in a forum where they could share original ideas. Although representation from other race groups left much to be desired, the conference was a start on a very long road. In the short term, the conference was a failure since it did not open up the debate that Deneys had hoped, but there were some observers who took careful note of its existence, followed its progress and studied its findings. One of these was KwaZulu Chief Minister Buthelezi.

Notes
1. Douglas Irvine, Reminiscences, email of 29 December 2017.
2. Sibongile Eunice Biyela, 'The Historical Development of the University of Zululand Library with Particular Reference to Buildings, Staff, Collection and Computerization (1960–1987), Honours thesis, University of Zululand, 1988. Biyela, writing before the unbanning of the liberation movements in 1990, simply mentions the university library being 'closed' on 18 June 1976.
3. Bill Guest, *Stella Aurorae: The History of a South African University, Volume 2, the University of Natal (1949–1976)* (Pietermaritzburg: Natal Society Foundation, 2017), pp.396–7.
4. Anne Dominy (née Murphy), Reminiscences, 2018.
5. Pat Stilwell, Reminiscences, email of 3 October 2017.

6. Anthony S Mathews, *Freedom State Security and the Rule of Law: Dilemmas of the Apartheid Society* (Cape Town: Juta, 1986), pp.xxviii–xxix.
7. Ayodeji Perrin, 'Gay Marriage in South Africa: A Human Rights Legacy, an Anti-apartheid Legacy or Both?' https://www.academia.edu/5234647/Gay_Marriage_in_South_Africa_A_Human_Rights_Legacy_An_Anti-_Apartheid_Legacy_Or_Both, fn138.
8. University of KwaZulu-Natal (UKZN) Archives: SP25/8/27, Schreiner, GDL, Documents VP's Office, letter from GDL Schreiner to Lawrence Baxter and Julian Riekert, Law Faculty, 14 November 1979.
9. UKZN Archives: SP25/4/5, Schreiner, GDL, Documents, NUSAS 1975-1979.
10. 'Broeders' was the colloquial, sometimes derogatory term for members of the secretive Afrikaaner Broederbond, the powerful organisation behind the National Party, which gave it policy and political direction.
11. Unless otherwise indicated, most of the information in the following paragraphs is drawn from John Benyon, ed., *Constitutional Change in South Africa: Proceedings of a Conference on Constitutional Models and Constitutional Change in South Africa*, held at University of Natal, Pietermaritzburg, 14–16 February 1978 (Pietermaritzburg: University of Natal Press, 1978) and from discussions with Douglas Irvine in January 2018.
12. John Benyon, Reminiscences, email of 11 January 2018.
13. I am indebted to John Benyon for this opinion.
14. Benyon, *Constitutional Change*, p.x.
15. Barbara Schreiner, Reminiscences, 2017.
16. Benyon, *Constitutional Change*, pp.xii–xiii.
17. Benyon, Reminiscences.
18. Else Schreiner, Reminiscences, 2016. See also BB Burnett, 'Alphaeus Hamilton Zulu (1905-1988)', *Natalia* 18 (1988), pp.93–6.
19. Suzanne Francis, *Institutionalizing Elites: Political Elite Formation and Change in the KwaZulu-Natal Provincial Legislature* (Leiden: Brill, 2011), p.42.
20. Benyon, *Constitutional Change*, p.xi.
21. Benyon, *Constitutional Change*, p.xii.
22. Benyon, *Constitutional Change*, pp.xi–xii.
23. Benyon, *Constitutional Change*, p.xiii.
24. Benyon, *Constitutional Change*, pp.127–135.
25. Benyon, *Constitutional Change*, pp. 180–90.
26. Benyon, *Constitutional Change*, p.123.

11

'Toughest One Yet for Prof Schreiner'
The Buthelezi Commission (1980–2)

In April 1980, Prince Mangosuthu Gatsha Buthelezi, the chief minister of the KwaZulu Homeland Territorial Authority, arrived in the vice principal's office on the Pietermaritzburg campus with a surprising proposition: would Deneys chair a special commission tasked with developing a new Constitution for the joint KwaZulu and Natal region?

The role of the Buthelezi Commission has been underplayed in many post-1994 South African histories, although it is discussed in several pre-1994 works. It is understandable that Thula Simpson makes no mention of it in his detailed history of Umkhonto weSizwe, but Ben Temkin, in his detailed biography of Buthelezi, mentions Deneys and the commission just once, almost in passing. It is barely mentioned in three of the major modern general histories of South Africa, although there is a useful discussion in TRH Davenport and Christopher Saunders's history, published in the hopeful days after the first democratic national election in 1994.[1]

The significance of the Buthelezi Commission is that it was the first black South African-initiated move to break the apartheid constitutional logjam. Buthelezi had rejected independence for KwaZulu, so another route had to be found. The government's constitutional fiddling encompassed the three racial minorities only. Within the liberation movements, particularly the African National Congress (ANC), little thought, if any, had been given to constitutional or governmental issues. With Nelson Mandela and the internal leadership still in jail on Robben Island, the leadership-in-exile had not moved much beyond the rhetoric of the Freedom Charter. In August 1979 the National Executive Committee of the ANC in exile met in Morogoro, Tanzania, and considered a report of the Politico-Military Strategy Commission. This document, dubbed the 'Green Book', focused on revolutionary strategy and tactics, rather than on issues of state reconstruction, and was adopted as the basic guideline for the movement's struggle within South Africa.[2]

In October 1979, Buthelezi, accompanied by an Inkatha delegation, met several members of the ANC at a hotel near Heathrow Airport, outside London. The meeting was chaired by Bishop Alphaeus Zulu.[3] Buthelezi distanced himself from the armed struggle, claiming that it was 'emotionally and intellectually alien' to the masses of black South Africans. Instead, he proposed a multi-strategy approach, in which each movement was to fight the system in its own way. This was not in line with the ANC's recently adopted Green Book strategy and the outcome of the meeting was a split between the ANC and Inkatha. Buthelezi was hurt by the failure of the meeting and was reluctant to discuss what was said in the meeting for many years.

However, even in 1983, Buthelezi was still uttering veiled threats to whites who had supported the Tricameral Constitution in PW Botha's whites-only referendum that it might be possible for Inkatha to form a 'marriage of convenience' with the banned and exiled ANC and Pan Africanist Congress.[4] Shula Marks has characterised Buthelezi as an 'ambiguous' figure but, showing some sympathetic understanding, she describes him as being caught in the almost intolerable situation of apartheid in South Africa, fully aware of the 'futility of opposing the might of the South African state with slogans and stones, as in Soweto in 1976'.[5] However, particularly after the London meeting, Buthelezi became increasingly hostile to the radicalised ANC, partly because of his repudiation of the notion of armed struggle.[6] As time passed, however, Buthelezi showed few qualms at unleashing violence against his opponents on the left. Radical critics characterised Inkatha as being 'Zulu traditionalist', a 'major conservative force in black politics' and as having a 'penchant for vigilantism and traditionalism that operated along parochial, authoritarian lines'.[7] The breach between the two organisations widened and ultimately became a bloodstained chasm in the years leading up to 1994.[8]

The establishment of the commission in 1980 preceded the years of major violence and was one way out of Buthelezi's dilemma. In fact, he was not alone in seeking a constitutional route out of the problems of the Natal and KwaZulu conjoined region. The government's consolidation proposals for the KwaZulu homeland threatened the commercial security of the sugar industry and, pipping Buthelezi to the post, the Durban Chamber of Commerce and the South African Sugar Association set up a commission to propose alternative scenarios. It was headed by Professor JA Lombard, of the University of Pretoria, who had participated in Deneys's conference on constitutional change in 1978.[9]

Lombard's recommendations, in early 1980, were that the region should be collaboratively, or federally, governed with co-equal representation for largely rural 'white' Natal, for largely 'black' KwaZulu and for the economic heart, the Durban metropolitan area.[10] This consociational, business-focused but non-statutory proposal was ignored by the government. Buthelezi sought to build on this initiative and may have reasoned that it would be more difficult for the government to ignore proposals coming from a statutory institution, such as a homeland government, than from the commercial sector.

The question that must be asked is: why did Buthelezi select Deneys Schreiner to head his signature initiative? Arthur Konigkramer, a senior and very influential member of Inkatha and editor of the Zulu-language newspaper *Ilanga* for many years, has stated that it was because of Schreiner's 'impeccable liberal credentials. Something the Prince fully identified with.'[11] There was also Deneys's track record: the Natal Convention in 1961, the constitutional conference at the university in 1978 and, above all, his name, lineage and position in the liberal hierarchy in South Africa.

Deneys's appointment as chairman was described by the *Natal Witness* as the 'most challenging assignment of his career'.[12] The article quoted an unnamed colleague of Deneys's lauding his appointment, claiming that Deneys's deepest interest was in the law and that he had an intuitive judicial sense and a deep capacity for listening to and understanding widely differing points of view.[13] Over and above all this, there was something else: by selecting Deneys to head the commission, Buthelezi was placing his trust in the grandson of the man who had defended his maternal grandfather, Dinuzulu kaCetshwayo, against treason charges in 1907. This appealed to Buthelezi's strong sense of history.[14] He wanted the commission to be called the Schreiner Commission, but Deneys demurred. He insisted that, as it was Buthelezi's idea, it should be called the Buthelezi Commission. In fact, Deneys made his participation conditional upon its being called the Buthelezi Commission, so the chief minister agreed.[15]

In an interview to mark his retirement, Deneys said: 'When I was Chairman of the Buthelezi Commission I had a real conviction Buthelezi was a man of peace. I still believe he would prefer it. But I thought he would have been prepared to accept a loss of his own power.'[16]

Buthelezi is an ambiguous figure in South African politics; proud of his heritage, sensitive to slights on his dignity and resolutely opposed to taking so-called independence for KwaZulu on Pretoria's terms. By the late 1980s and the early 1990s, he was much hated by the left. However, in the late 1970s and early 1980s, the situation was different, certainly more nuanced, at least in white opposition politics. The way government perceptions about Buthelezi changed was highlighted by Gerhard Maré and Georgina Hamilton in 1986:

> Whereas ten years ago Buthelezi and the National Cultural Liberation Movement, Inkatha, were perceived to be part of the radical opposition to apartheid and his approaches for

participation were scorned, today the same overtures, in the context of recent events, have gained a level of acceptance by the state and even by business that would have been unthinkable in the mid-1970s.[17]

Buthelezi's claims to be a legitimate leader came from several sources. His paternal Buthelezi line included Mnyamana kaNgqengelele, Cetshwayo's 'prime minister' or chief adviser.[18] This was the basis of his claim to be hereditary 'prime minister' or leader of KwaZulu. His maternal line came from the Zulu royal house itself. His mother, Princess Magogo, was a daughter of Dinuzulu, a gifted musician, an expert in Zulu traditional music and culture who became a widely admired cultural leader.[19] Buthelezi's claim to be a prince, *unntwana*, is based partly on his maternal ancestry, but is reinforced by his being elevated to this status as prince of KwaPhindangene by King Goodwill Zwelithini.[20] However, Buthelezi was also a graduate of the University of Fort Hare and many of his fellow students played leading roles in the African liberation struggles, including Robert Mugabe, Nelson Mandela, Walter Sisulu and Govan Mbeki.[21] Therefore, Buthelezi also had links to African intellectual modernity. He was a member of the ANC and described the Inkatha Cultural Movement (the predecessor of the Inkatha Freedom Party) as the 'internal' wing of the ANC for many years. One critical feature in assessing Buthelezi is his sense of personal dignity and his sensitivity to criticism. He has been described as particularly thin-skinned.[22]

The National Party government was fumbling around for a constitutional model that would mask the inherent contradictions in apartheid. The process followed in drawing up the proposals was opaque and top-down and there was no real public participation. Africans were completely excluded and coloureds and Indians were consulted selectively. PW Botha established the President's Council to advise on a new Constitution. This nominated body had some coloured and Indian members (and one Chinese), but whites were in the majority and the representation of whites was manipulated to ensure that the National Party was in an overall majority. Alwyn Schlebusch, a favourite enemy of the English-language universities, presided over the new body.[23] Mike Tarr, the Progressive Freedom Party MP for Pietermaritzburg South, summed up the flaws in the composition of the President's Council by highlighting the exclusion of Africans and, as far as the coloured and Indian members were concerned, Tarr said: 'There is little doubt that many of these nominated members cannot claim to represent the communities they are purported to.'[24]

Inkatha submitted its proposals to Schlebusch and Buthelezi warned PW Botha that Africans had to be included in the project because violence could not be averted simply by 'marching to anti-communist drums'.[25] However, he was completely and rudely rebuffed. Angry, and with his sensitive ego humiliated, Buthelezi returned to KwaZulu, vowing to establish his own commission. However, this was not just a decision made in pique – a commission had been under discussion within Inkatha since 1979. It was foreshadowed by the establishment of the Inkatha Institute, which was also Buthelezi's brainchild.

The Inkatha Institute was a think tank established by the central committee of Inkatha in 1979. It became operational in 1980, when Professor Lawrence Schlemmer took a year's sabbatical from his post at the University of Natal in Durban to act as its first director. The goal was to help Inkatha become more relevant in planning for peace and in formulating a black response to critical issues of debate. The institute acknowledged receiving funding from the KwaZulu Chief Minister's office, the Urban Foundation and the political foundation of the conservative West German Christian Democratic Party, the Konrad Adenauer Stiftung.[26] Schlemmer served as the secretary to the Buthelezi Commission and the staff of the Inkatha Institute provided the critically needed support services. Schlemmer had worked with Deneys a few years earlier at the constitutional conference.

The KwaZulu Legislative Assembly endorsed Buthelezi's proposals and gave them legal status, rejecting any suggestion that the commission should be ethnically structured.²⁷ This was incongruous, but illustrates how the contradictions in the system of apartheid could be exploited. An ethnically defined institution, namely, a homeland legislature, was the only vehicle legally capable of creating the commission. Herein lay the liberal dilemma: working within the system meant using illiberal institutions. Nevertheless, because of Buthelezi's vision (and the reality of the socio-political situation), the commission had a non-racial, province-wide mandate and was able to claim national relevance. Deneys explained this by referring to the fact that the KwaZulu Legislative Assembly had been charged with responsibility to all persons defined by the national government as 'belonging to KwaZulu'. These people were spread throughout South Africa and in Natal were the majority group.²⁸

The national context within which the Buthelezi Commission was conceived and appointed was grim. Apartheid was on ideological autopilot, unrest was increasing and PW Botha was focusing increasingly on military means of repression. The concept of the 'total onslaught' and the 'total strategy' needed to counter it were being developed and Botha was articulating them at full volume and with wagging finger.²⁹ Part of the total strategy was constitutional adaptation, although the processes followed in drafting a new Constitution were secretive and exclusionary. Botha's response to the announcement of the Buthelezi Commission was 'swift and predictable'.³⁰ Speaking in Parliament in Cape Town, Botha said a categorical 'No' and stated that the government was 'unequivocal' in its opposition; no member of the National Party or government official would serve on the Buthelezi Commission.

The membership of the Buthelezi Commission was drawn from as wide a range of races, communities and views as possible. The membership of the commission was, 'carefully composed to give balanced representation of racial, economic, political and other interest groupings in Natal'.³¹ The members, however, were not drawn exclusively from KwaZulu and Natal, much of the academic expertise was drawn from universities in the Transvaal and the Cape provinces.

In soliciting support for the commission and in securing members, Deneys and Buthelezi used all their wide political, professional and social networks. Many of those who had participated in the conference on constitutional change also participated in the work of the Buthelezi Commission. However, Deneys sought to bring in influential people from outside academia and the party political arena and from across the country. Harry Oppenheimer, chairman of the Anglo-American Corporation, was perhaps the heaviest hitter from outside the province.

From civil society there were representatives of the Natal Law Society, the Natal Teachers' Society, the Natal Agricultural Union, the Natal Chamber of Industries, the South African Cane Growers' Association, the Durban Chamber of Commerce, the Natal African Teachers' Union, the Natal Sugar Industry, the South African Federated Chamber of Industries, the Institute of Bankers in South Africa and the Inyanda Chamber of Commerce (including the National African Federated Chamber of Commerce and Industries).

There were academics from the universities of Cape Town, Natal, South Africa, Stellenbosch and Zululand. The two overseas-based academics were Heribert Adam (Simon Fraser University, Vancouver, Canada) and Arend Lijphart (University of California, San Diego). Both of these political scientists were recognised experts on electoral systems. The churches were represented by the Roman Catholic Archbishop of Durban, the Most Reverend Denis Hurley, and Anglican Bishop Alphaeus Zulu. No representatives of the Buddhist, Hindu, Islamic or Jewish faiths seem to have participated.

Politicians from the Reform Party (Indian), the Labour Party (coloured), the Progressive Federal Party and the New Republic Party (white) attended. There were no black African political parties represented. In 1980, Inkatha Yenkululeko Yesizwe, to give its full name, was officially a 'cultural movement', not a political party, and all the other parties of any significance were proscribed. There were planners from the Natal Town and Regional Planning Commission and its KwaZulu equivalent. Educationalists and teachers, the head of the KwaZulu Nursing Services and a retired judge also participated.

The first session of the Buthelezi Commission was held on the Durban campus of the University of Natal on 30 October 1980 and its work continued for some eighteen months until its recommendations were made public in March 1982.[32] Most of the sessions were held in Durban and Pietermaritzburg and the bulk of the work was done by the subcommittees or working groups. There were no members of the commission from the University of the Witwatersrand. Does this talk to the parochialism of Natal or of the University of the Witwatersrand? Political figures, such as Colin Eglin of the Progressive Federal Party, who cut their constitution-writing teeth in the Buthelezi Commission, later played critical roles in the Convention for a Democratic South Africa (CODESA) talks that produced the Interim Constitution and the first South African democratic elections in 1994.

Bishop Zulu played a distinguished role and among the younger black members was Dr Oscar Dhlomo, the secretary general of Inkatha, who later broke with Buthelezi. Amichand Rajbansi, chairman of the South African Indian Council, took part. He became the head of the House of Delegates in the Tricameral Parliament, a position in which he provided much merriment to South Africans with his bad hairpiece and his off-the-cuff remarks. Two of the most famous of these were: 'Well, I will double-cross that bridge when I get there' and 'A tiger never changes its spots' (Rajbansi was known as the Bengal Tiger or the Tiger of Chatsworth).[33]

Given the tenor of the times, white males were in the majority on the commission and there were very few women members, the most influential being the University of Natal economist, Professor Jill Nattrass. However, the final report of the commission claimed that the 'concept of a widely representative Commission was broadly realised, although neither the National Party nor the banned Black South African political organisations were represented'.[34]

Deneys made sure that the work of the commission was well publicised and Richard Steyn, editor of the *Natal Witness*, allocated David Robbins, a reporter and feature writer, to cover the commission's activities. He had frequent briefings from Deneys and the contrast between the openness surrounding the Buthelezi Commission and the secrecy around the Constitutional Committee of the President's Council was very clear.[35]

There were eleven sections listed in the terms of reference. They encompassed constitutional, political, economic, educational, health and structural issues. The first and the last few terms are the most critical and, when taken with the sections of the report for which he was responsible, indicate the depth and breadth of Deneys's influence. The first point set out the overall context for the work of the commission:

> 1.a. In terms of the requirements of peace, stability, prosperity and equity, to consider fully and appreciate the present position of KwaZulu and Natal within a constitutional and political structure of South Africa.
> 1.b. To assist and evaluate the *rationality* [emphasis added], desirability and viability of the present constitutional, social and economic situation of KwaZulu and Natal in the light of historical development, and the current and emerging political reality of South and Southern Africa.
> 2. To enquire into and report and make recommendations on the constitutional future of the areas of KwaZulu and Natal within the context of South Africa and Southern Africa.
> 3. To relate the conclusions of 2. above to the issue of the constitutional future of South Africa as a whole.[36]

In other words, as Edgar Brookes had said in 1961 about the Natal Convention, the Buthelezi Commission was not a 'Natal Stand of the old type', but also had the purpose to ensure that 'we and our children after us shall share the future as friends and fellow-citizens'.[37] The ninth of the terms of reference, rather curiously, reads:

9. To identify any negative consequences of the present social, political and economic situation in KwaZulu and Natal which might indicate the desirability of changes in the system; such problems might include manifestations of marginality, alienation and apathy; and to ensure that changes eliminate groups which are not catered for by the standard of social practices and the operating institutions of society.[38]

This clumsy phrasing is not simply a sign of the baleful influence of the jargon of social scientists, but an example of the coded language that had to be used to work around the paranoia of Pretoria. The final clause reads: 'In all relevant matters referred to above, through research and the gathering of other evidence, to take full account of the preferences, needs and perceptions of the citizens of Kwazulu and Natal, as a basis for arriving at proposals of the broadest possible legitimacy.'[39]

One of the key processes undertaken by the commission and that distinguished it markedly from the constitutional tinkering of the government was the attitude surveys, overseen by Lawrence Schlemmer. This was critical because at the time the media was censored (although not as heavily as during the state of emergency in the later 1980s), the airwaves were totally monopolised by the government-controlled South African Broadcasting Corporation and mechanisms for consulting with the man or woman on the Umlazi bus were few and far between. The attitude surveys were important and were undertaken by professional companies, Inter-Continental Marketing Services South Africa and Mark-en-Meningsopnames.[40]

The surveys indicated a hardening of black attitudes and an impatience at the lack of progress, despite the rhetoric of reform. They also indicated that were was much suspicion of the government. The government was also distrusted by some right-wing whites. The commission was strongly convinced of a very high level of polarisation between the extremes and recognised the growing potential for direct violent confrontation among disaffected black youth.[41]

There was, however, widespread acceptance that the division of the region into separate KwaZulu and Natal areas and political structures 'had no advantages'.[42] Independence for KwaZulu along the lines of Bophuthatswana or the Transkei was rejected by at least seven out of ten people. On the other hand, the commission found that representation in South African 'central affairs' was 'pervasively felt to be a primary requirement of any political dispensation'.[43] This may seem obvious from the vantage point of the present day, but, given the silencing of most non-statutory black voices in early the 1980s, it was a point that needed to be made.

Deneys, as chairman, could attend the meetings of all the specialist working groups and did so, encouraging and advising the members. There were six groups: economic development; education; planning and administration; political and constitutional; social services and health; and the attitude surveys. Deneys drafted the introduction to the main report and either the chairmen or specialist drafters, such as the economist Jill Nattrass, drafted the reports of each working group. Deneys was most actively involved in the political and constitutional working group, headed by Professor Marinus Wiechers, an influential political scientist, who later became the rector and vice chancellor of the University of South Africa (UNISA).

In his introduction to the report, Deneys stressed the national significance of the Buthelezi Commission and characterised the commission as an attempt to avoid the consequences of armed struggle, which destroys the 'youth of both sides' and politically destroys 'those who are prepared to seek co-operative and peaceful solutions, and replaces them with extremists, again on both sides'.[44] He also stressed that the commission based its work on the 'hallowed' African principle of debating and seeking consensus over divisive issues, but reminded readers that the Buthelezi Commission may well be 'the last time in South African politics that a Black leadership group, with national and international credibility and significant following, reaches out to others with an invitation to explore the possibility of a creative and generally acceptable political compromise'.⁴⁵

The main political and constitutional principles accepted by the commission were: 'i. That every person has the right, through the political process, to influence those decisions which affect his or her life' and 'ii. That exclusion of any group, by law, from central governmental institutions violates democratic principles.'⁴⁶

In two short sentences the commission expressed the complete antithesis to the entire philosophy of apartheid and undermined all the fancy franchises and talk-shops being proposed by the National Party in the name of 'reform'. The commission warned that if these principles were not accepted, South Africa would soon find itself in a conflict situation, as disaffected youth grew more militant. Therefore, 'some form of power sharing is the only real alternative to continued instability and that refusal to reach some accommodation is directly beneficial to those internal and external forces which seek to use violence to bring about change'.⁴⁷

The report strongly emphasised that the commission received no official evidence on the government policy, described as 'separate development', and therefore inferences had to be drawn from statements by ministers and National Party leaders. This, of course, was the result of the refusal of the government and the National Party to participate. Although the commission accepted the principle of full universal franchise, it backed away from the political implications of the system and recommended 'consociationalism', namely, group-defined democracy, including the principle of minority veto.⁴⁸ Judging by comments Deneys made a few years later, he did not personally agree with this conclusion, as it ran contrary to his liberal beliefs.⁴⁹

In summary the Buthelezi Commission findings and recommendations were:
- There was negligible support among the surveyed citizens and established political and business leaders for independence for KwaZulu and its separation from Natal (this excluded

the members of the National Party prepared to speak to the commission and the opinions of National Party supporters recorded in the attitude surveys);
- growing material inequality in the region could not be combated by a divided administrative and political dispensation;
- separation could only increase alienation between blacks and whites, which would lead to violence;
- considering the distorting effect of great inequality, it was surprising that 'so slight a basic ideological cleavage exists between blacks and whites', the majority supporting a free market economy, law and order, constitutional democratic principles and even the need to protect minority rights;
- within the KwaZulu/Natal region there should be a regional structure of government, with mutually agreed subdivisions based on community interests;
- the limited powers of the Natal provincial administration should be increased so that they match those of the KwaZulu government;
- there should be an executive initially selected on a 'consociational' basis, with initial equality between whites and blacks and with representation for Indians and coloureds as well;
- the legislative assembly would be elected by universal adult suffrage within each community of interest's regional area on a proportional representation basis.

As an interim measure, the commission advised that there should be a combined executive committee under the co-chairmanship of the administrator of Natal and the chief minister of KwaZulu. The commission also foresaw that developments in Natal and KwaZulu should move forward independently of developments in the rest of the country, but that the models developed in the region could be applied in the rest of the country.[50]

Of the 43 commissioners, 39 signed the final report without reservation. Two (representing civil society organisations without political mandates) signed with reservations and two (both New

Republic Party politicians) refused to sign it at all. This David Welsh described as a 'quaint reminder of [the] politically antediluvian nature' of the New Republic Party.[51]

Buthelezi made the report public and a copy was sent post-haste to Pretoria. It was immediately rejected. Ministers, 'hardly giving the ink time to dry before tossing it on a top shelf to gather dust', spurned the report. Contemptuously referring to the document as the 'Schreiner Report', the minister designated to deliver the repudiation was none other than Owen Horwood, Natal leader of the National Party and minister of finance. He described the constitutional and political sections as 'unacceptable', although he was forced to acknowledge that the socio-economic research underpinning the commission's recommendations was worthwhile. However, as the commission recommended that Natal and KwaZulu should be a single political entity and this was counter to government policy, no further comment was necessary.[52] To call this a reductionist argument is an understatement.

The left was critical of the commission's links with business and capital, but this was challenged by two thinkers within the business world, Peter Berger and Bobby Godsell (who sat on the commission as an alternate to Harry Oppenheimer):

> Despite an obvious desire to accommodate the KwaZulu leadership in order to draw it into constitutional negotiations at central level, and despite strong business backing and participation, the government has responded more negatively than positively to the Buthelezi Commission and the KwaZulu-Natal Indaba proposals, to the extent that analysts in a Marxist tradition such as [Roger] Southall were perplexed by the government's rejection of a well organised 'capitalist' campaign.[53]

Deneys put the matter in a broader perspective in a speech a few years later, after the whites-only referendum on the adoption of the Tricameral Constitution:

The rebuff that had been given to the Black initiative by the rejection of the Buthelezi Commission report which occurred within a few hours of it reaching the South African government, and therefore occurred before it could even have been considered, was insignificant when compared with the effect of the result of the referendum.[54]

Deneys's fears of the violent consequences of the government rejection of peaceful overtures were to become painfully apparent in the later 1980s and early 1990s. Even Nelson Mandela was appalled. Shortly before he was released from Victor Verster Prison on 2 February 1990, he wrote to Dr Chota Motala: 'Pietermaritzburg has featured so much recently that one may be tempted to think that it is the only city in the country and the breeding ground for all the sins of the world.'[55]

Notes
The phrase quoted in the title of this chapter is from the *Natal Witness*, 26 May 1980.
1. Thula Simpson, *Umkhonto we Sizwe: The ANC's Armed Struggle* (Cape Town: Penguin Random House, 2016); Ben Temkin, *Buthelezi: A Biography* (London: Frank Cass, 2003), pp.212, 285; William Beinart, *Twentieth-Century South Africa* (Oxford: Oxford University Press, 2001); Nancy Clark and William Worger, *South Africa: The Rise and Fall of Apartheid* (New York: Longman, 2004); Nigel Worden, *The Making of Modern South Africa* (Cape Town: Juta, 1994); TRH Davenport and Christopher Saunders, *South Africa: A Modern History* (London: Macmillan, 2000), pp.463–5.
2. Simpson, *Umkhonto we Sizwe*, pp.251–2.
3. Jack Shepherd Smith, *Buthelezi: The Biography* (Johannesburg: Hans Strydom Publishers, 1988), p.114.
4. Shula Marks, *The Ambiguities of Dependence in South Africa: Class, Nationalism and the State in Twentieth-Century Natal* (Johannesburg: Ravan Press, 1986), p.121.
5. Marks, *Ambiguities of Dependence*, p.119.
6. Colleen McCaul, 'The Wild Card: Inkatha and Contemporary Black Politics', in *State, Resistance and Change in South Africa*, edited by Philip

Frankel, Noam Pines and Mark Swilling (London: Croom Helm, 1988), p.165.
7. Christopher Merrett, 'A Small Civil War: Political Conflict in the Pietermaritzburg Region in the 1980s and Early 1990s', *Natalia* 43 (2013), pp.19-36.
8. Gerhard Maré and Georgina Hamilton, *An Appetite for Power: Buthelezi's Inkatha and the Politics of 'Loyal Resistance'* (Johannesburg: Ravan Press, 1987), p.139. See also Simpson, *Umkhonto we Sizwe*, p.253.
9. John Benyon, ed., *Constitutional Change in South Africa: Proceedings of a Conference on Constitutional Models and Constitutional Change in South Africa*, held at University of Natal, Pietermaritzburg, 14-16 February 1978 (Pietermaritzburg: University of Natal Press, 1978), p.295.
10. Suzanne Francis, *Institutionalizing Elites: Political Elite Formation and Change in the KwaZulu-Natal Provincial Legislature* (Leiden: Brill, 2011), p.50. See also Marina Ottaway, *South Africa: The Struggle for a New Order* (Washington, DC: Brookings Institution, 1993), p.95.
11. Arthur Konigkramer, email of 2 May 2017.
12. *Natal Witness*, 26 May 1980.
13. *Natal Witness*, 26 May 1980.
14. Arthur Konigkramer, Interview, email of 1 February 2018.
15. Else Schreiner, Reminiscences, 2016; confirmed by Arthur Konigkramer, Interview, email of 1 February 2018.
16. Interview with Georgina Hamilton, *Sunday Tribune*, 12 December 1987.
17. Maré and Hamilton, *Appetite for Power*, p.5.
18. John Laband, *Kingdom in Crisis: The Zulu Response to the British Invasion of 1879* (Pietermaritzburg: University of Natal Press, 1992), p.26.
19. 'Magogo kaDinuzulu', *Wikipedia*, https://en.wikipedia.org/wiki/Magogo_kaDinuzulu.
20. Information provided by John Laband, email of 2 February 2018.
21. Marks, *Ambiguities of Dependence*, p.116.
22. Maré and Hamilton, *Appetite for Power*, pp.93-5.
23. Christopher Hill, *Change in South Africa: Blind Alleys or New Directions?* (London: Rex Collings, 1983), pp.157, 165.
24. MA Tarr, 'Those Whom the Gods Wish to Destroy: A Few Comments on the Current Political Scene', *Reality* 14, 5 (1982), pp.12-14.
25. Maré and Hamilton, *Appetite for Power*, pp.164-5. See also Hermann Giliomee and Bernard Mbenga, *New History of South Africa* (Cape Town: Tafelberg, 2007), pp.374-5.
26. The Urban Foundation was an organisation set up largely by big business to support projects that promoted political, economic and social stability, very much within the broad status quo. See Robin Lee, 'The Urban

Foundation: Another Perspective', *Reality* 14, 3 (1982), pp.15–17; see also Maré and Hamilton, *Appetite for Power*, pp.176–7.
27. *The Buthelezi Commission: The Main Report*, Vol. I (Durban: H+H Publications, 1982).
28. *Buthelezi Commission Report*, Vol. I, p.29.
29. James Selfe, 'Adaptions to the Security-Intelligence Decision-Making Structures under PW Botha's Administration', Master's thesis, University of Cape Town, 1987, p.3.
30. Smith, *Buthelezi*, p.162.
31. David Welsh, 'Review of the Buthelezi Commission', *Reality* 14, 4 (1982), pp.6–7.
32. Smith, *Buthelezi*, p.162.
33. https://www.iol.co.za/news/politics/best-of-the-bengal-tiger-1206123.
34. *Buthelezi Commission Report*, Vol. I, p.15.
35. David Robbins, personal communication, February 2018.
36. *Buthelezi Commission Report*, Vol. I, p.34.
37. Randolph Vigne, *Liberals against Apartheid: A History of the Liberal Party of South Africa, 1953–68* (London: Macmillan, 1997), pp.145–6.
38. *Buthelezi Commission Report*, Vol. I, p.36.
39. *Buthelezi Commission Report*, Vol. I, p.36.
40. *The Buthelezi Commission: The Main Report*, Vol. II (Durban: H+H Publications, 1982), p.17.
41. *Buthelezi Commission Report*, Vol. I, p.100–1.
42. *Buthelezi Commission Report*, Vol. I, p.102.
43. *Buthelezi Commission Report*, Vol. I, p.102.
44. *Buthelezi Commission Report*, Vol. I, p.32.
45. *Buthelezi Commission Report*, Vol. I, pp.32–3.
46. *Buthelezi Commission Report*, Vol. I, p.104.
47. *Buthelezi Commission Report*, Vol. I, p.104.
48. Welsh, 'Review of the Buthelezi Commission', p.6. See also Arend Lijphart, 'Power-Sharing in South Africa', Policy Papers in International Affairs, No. 24, Berkeley, University of California, Institute of International Studies, 1985, pp.48, 78–80.
49. See Chapter 12.
50. This summary is based on *Buthelezi Commission Report*, Vol. I, pp.124–9; Tarr, 'Those Whom the Gods Wish to Destroy', pp.12–14; and Welsh, 'Review of the Buthelezi Commission', pp.6–7.
51. Welsh, 'Review of the Buthelezi Commission', p.7. One member had died before the signing of the report.
52. Smith, *Buthelezi*, pp.174–5.

53. Peter L Berger and Bobby Godsell, *A Future South Africa: Visions, Strategies and Realities* (Cape Town: Human & Rousseau/Tafelberg, 1988), p.21.
54. University of KwaZulu-Natal (UKZN) Archives: SP25/1/1/1, Schreiner, GDL (Prof & Vice Principal UNP) 1975-1987, *Natal Witness*, 27 September 1985.
55. Letter from Nelson Mandela to Chota Motala, 10 January 1990. Quoted by Goolam Vahed, *Chota Motala: A Biography of Political Activism in the KwaZulu-Natal Midlands* (Pietermaritzburg: University of KwaZulu-Natal Press, 2017).

12

Aftermath of the Buthelezi Commission Report
Deneys's Predictions Fulfilled (1982–7)

The report of the Buthelezi Commission received mixed reviews. There was the outright rejection by the government from the right, while, from the left, Gerhard Maré and Georgina Hamilton criticised the commission for lacking a democratic mandate and for its lack of accountability.[1] Roger Southall, writing from a measured, but radical perspective, claimed that the common objective of consociational strategy was to 'recruit subordinate racial élites to [a] front that is deliberately counter-revolutionary'.[2] Bernard Magubane was less measured; in flamboyant language, he blasted the idea of 'social pluralism' that underpinned consociational government as being 'reactionary and dangerous'. He continued: 'The thrust of the pluralist paradigm was counter-revolutionary. It involved the manipulation of ethnic, cultural and racial interests in maintaining the status quo. Its advocates were white ruling class intellectuals whose position was threatened by the Marxist paradigm that they first caricatured and then dismissed.'[3]

Magubane continued his polemic with an accusation that the social scientists who participated in the Buthelezi Commission were 'concoct[ing] concepts, categories and relationships that had a vested interest in the existing social order. This constitutes the essence of counter-revolutionary theory – that is, theory which is deliberately proposed to stall or scuttle revolutionary or social change.'[4]

Magubane dismissed consociational democracy as a 'most moronic concept'.[5] Despite the caustic language, Magubane's basic point was tacitly admitted by Deneys (undoubtedly a member of the ruling-class intellectuals so roundly condemned by Magubane). In his introduction to the commission's report, Deneys wrote: 'The Buthelezi Commission represents an attempt, by the route of agreed co-operation, to avoid the armed struggle.'[6] In essence, this is evolutionary, rather than revolutionary.

A more measured analysis was given by Laurence Boulle of the law faculty on the Durban campus. He pointed out that the President's Council report and the Buthelezi Commission report both came out during the first half of 1982 and, while the former overshadowed the latter in public and academic minds, the 'proximate timing' invited a 'juxtaposition and comparative analysis'. He also made it clear that 'each report is the issue of a different lineage in South Africa's constitutional history'. The Buthelezi Commission report drew on many of the principles of consociationalism and liberal constitutionalism.[7] The President's Council report bore the dents of apartheid-lite panel-beating.

Mike Tarr stressed a fundamental point of importance in the Buthelezi Commission report: it 'started from the standpoint of full and equal citizenship rights for all South Africans'.[8] This is a critical issue distinguishing the Buthelezi Commission report from the President's Council report, which ignored the position of black South Africans completely. There is another distinction, pointed out by David Welsh: 'The Buthelezi Commission's work is of high intellectual calibre, and stands in dramatic contrast to the pedestrian superficialities offered by the Constitutional Committee of the President's Council.'[9]

The question to be asked of left-wing critics is how, under the political circumstances of the early 1980s, it would have been possible to obtain a democratic mandate for the Buthelezi Commission. There was press censorship, detention without trial and intimidation of citizens by the security forces. The agency that gave the commission its legal status, the KwaZulu Legislative

Assembly, had its own deficiencies. It was not fully elected and included a large number of nominated traditional leaders in its membership and what passed for elections in KwaZulu had been held under the oppressive conditions of apartheid.

Deneys characterised the work of the Buthelezi Commission as being 'essentially an approach designed to avoid preconceived ideologies – to allow the facts to define the proposals for the future'.[10] He pointed out in an interview with David Robbins that the Reef (now the heart of the province of Gauteng) was at the heart of South African political thinking, where the vast majority of the urban black population lived outside the homelands. East of the Drakensberg Mountains, 'KwaZulu is an integral part of all Natal's major urban conurbations'.[11] Therefore, Deneys's reasoning went, different solutions were needed in Natal to those for the Transvaal.

While the commission was far from a perfect vehicle for political change, it did what was practically possible in the circumstances and it did it well, certainly better than the President's Council's constitutional committee. Nevertheless, this was not good enough in the face of government intransigence. Oscar Dhlomo bravely declared that government rejection did not matter, as a liberation movement did not lose credibility when the oppressor rejected the demands for the liberation of the masses.[12] But it did matter, for two main reasons: the political and material conditions in South Africa, and particularly in KwaZulu and Natal, did not change and, secondly, despite all the publicity around the commission, Inkatha was not able to deliver significant improvements on the ground.

Deneys returned to his university duties to face a last attempt by the government in 1983 to impose more effective segregation on the universities in terms of the Universities Amendment Bill, known as the Quota Bill. In terms of this piece of legislation, the government would set a quota of black students who could attend the English-language universities and the universities would then have to implement the system. This was intended to replace the permit system whereby the minister issued permits to black students on an individual basis. The proposed change prompted widespread protests in the English-language universities, as they objected to being forced to do the government's dirty work and insisted that academic merit should be the sole criterion for admitting students. Deneys wrote a memorandum to Desmond Clarence, the vice chancellor, stressing that the university should not become 'the Government's "agent" in enforcing the quota system' and that the University of Natal still desired to be an open university, able to 'admit suitably qualified students without reference to their racial origins'.[13]

The Quota Bill sparked one of the few legally permitted protest marches of the 1980s. Deneys had to obtain a permit from the chief magistrate of Pietermaritzburg to allow the march to take place as it would be multiracial and a Group Areas Act permit was required.[14] The march to the City Hall took place on 2 June 1983 and 2 000 students and academics were led by the vice chancellor, Desmond Clarence, the Durban vice principal, Piet Booysen (1977–83), Alan Paton and Deneys, all in their academic robes. When they reached the City Hall, Paton told the gathering that the main reason for the draconian change was that it would save the minister and the civil service a lot of work.[15] Else described the sight of Deneys at the head of the march in his mortar board and academic robes, white beard flaring, his expression implacable: 'It was an astonishing sight, he seemed unstoppable. In fact, he looked quite terrifying. I knew it was difficult, nearly impossible, to stand in the way of what he believed to be right.'[16]

However, some of the marchers carried placards, which had not been authorised and Deneys had made a public call for members of the public to join the march, which also prompted official displeasure. Deneys was forced to write an apology to Mr Liebenberg, the chief magistrate.[17] The Quota Bill became law, but it was never fully implemented.

Buthelezi's personal sensitivities became more acute as student militancy increased (as Deneys had warned that it would). Students receiving bursaries from the KwaZulu government were required to sign pledges that they would not denigrate or vilify (as Buthelezi was wont to say) Inkatha or the chief minister. Deneys and the new vice chancellor, Professor Piet Booysen (1984–91), travelled to Ulundi to persuade Mangosuthu Buthelezi of the need to respect the principles of academic freedom and also of the practical need not to prohibit medical students from working in KwaZulu clinics.[18]

The Buthelezi Commission report still remained relevant in the absence of any other positive political new directions. In 1985 Deneys referred to it at some length when he opened a conference of the South African Political Science Association, with the theme 'Democratisation in South Africa'. He challenged the gathering to provide leadership in seeking a way out of the country's constitutional impasse and offered to lock the political scientists in a room until they could come up with a compromise plan.[19] The Tricameral Constitution had taken effect in 1984 and the Natal Provincial Council had been abolished. The New Republic Party, bereft of its last source of patronage, died with barely a whimper.

The end of the provincial council system meant that KwaZulu lacked an equivalent negotiating partner and this caused some anger in Ulundi. However, Buthelezi persevered in his efforts to have some form of joint administration established and the KwaZulu Cabinet White Paper on the Buthelezi Commission report stated that it had made an 'extremely convincing case' for the integrated planning and administration of KwaZulu and Natal as a single region.[20] This eventually led to the formation of the KwaZulu-Natal Indaba, which was aimed at establishing a form of joint rule in the region. The Buthelezi Commission report was used as the basis for the proposals, but on this occasion, Desmond Clarence, rather than Deneys, presided. Initially, the Indaba report was rejected by PW Botha, as the Buthelezi Commission report had been, but some of its recommendations were later implemented in a watered-down form.[21]

Else was in the United Kingdom in June 1985 and Deneys wrote to her describing his hectic activities in her absence:

What I am at the moment is a peculiar mixture of an overworked university administrator, a journalist, a political advisor and an anti-pollution and poison expert. All of a mad suddenness things are piling up in a most peculiar way while I sit and wait for a 'phone call from your end. The Buthelezi Commission is really becoming a thing of the foreground. You get references to it on T.V. and [Frederik van Zyl] Slabbert has been to Ulundi to launch the P.F.P.'s multiracial membership policy. He was three days late. I went last Friday and am now in the throws [sic] of writing an up date 'white paper' in terms of the constitutional changes that have already taken place.[22]

Deneys was critical of the process, pointing out that 'the indaba suffers from the disadvantage that despite talk of devolving power, there is in fact a tremendous concentration of power'.[23]

The Indaba led to the establishment of a joint executive authority between KwaZulu and the Natal provincial administration, as had been recommended as an interim step by the Buthelezi Commission.[24] There was a joint executive committee, co-chaired by Buthelezi as KwaZulu chief minister and by the administrator of Natal, Radclyffe Cadman, and various joint planning and project committees reported to their political principals.[25] Oversight and public accountability mechanisms were cumbersome and the entire system was opaque.

As the network of the securocratic state expanded, more or less as a shadow government parallel to the standard structures, a myriad of joint liaison committees and joint project committees began developing under the umbrella of the joint executive authority. These provided ideal cover for the co-ordination and operation of the security forces under the joint management committees that operated during the state of emergency, for example during the notorious Trust Feed massacre.[26] The 1988 Trust Feed massacre in KwaZulu-Natal, in which eleven people were shot dead, was significant in that it was one of the first cases of violence in which the involvement of senior police officers was proved. Truth and Reconciliation commissioner Richard Lyster said it was clear the massacre was not a random incident, but was orchestrated by the police to ensure the dominance of Inkatha in the area. Local police station commander Brian Mitchell had been involved in a conspiracy with Inkatha to break the United Democratic Front (UDF)-aligned Trust Feed Crisis Committee.[27] That this type of combined operational structure could flourish was unquestionably the worst of the unintended consequences of the Buthelezi Commission.

The proclamation of a state of emergency in June 1986, shortly before the tenth anniversary of the Soweto Uprising, provoked anger and despondency at the University of Natal. As the protests mounted, and students became more militant, the police took stronger and more blatant action on the campus. On one occasion, the police entered the Students Union building and began intimidating students in the hall. Deneys was alerted and carefully put on his academic robes before marching down to confront the arrogant officer in charge. 'Get off my campus,' he ordered. 'You do not have my permission to be here, now go!' And the police sullenly complied: the gown and the beard and Deneys's innate dignity had a satisfactory effect.[28] A small, albeit temporary victory had been won.

When a state of emergency was imposed in 1986, a mass protest meeting was held in the Students Union and Deneys addressed the gathering and committed the university to continuing to support the work that the banned organisations had been doing. This critical statement was omitted from the press coverage of the meeting, but John Aitchison took it as permission for the Centre for Adult Education to carry on with its activist work. The centre even provided a venue for the regional executive of the newly banned UDF to hold its clandestine meetings.[29]

Once more rallies were held and the English-language universities protested, calling upon the government to lift the state of emergency and declaring that 'universities must be forums for free, critical thought'.[30] By this stage Deneys was the most recognisable face of the university and the leader of the official protests. He chaired the meetings that planned the protests and drafted the resolutions and documents. The university senate passed a Deneys-backed resolution on 7 May 1987, expressing concern at the position of universities, 'in a society in which essential freedoms are so restricted and repressed by violent means that confrontation leading to further violence becomes endemic'. The senate demonstrated its commitment to democracy by closing the university on Friday 8 May, as a demonstration of support for its resolution.[31]

However, by this time the student body was deeply divided and agents of the state had infiltrated student organisations and undermined what had passed for a liberal consensus. Right-wing students, claiming to speak in the name of academic freedom, protested to Deneys at the closure of the university and demanded an apology from him.[32] The South African Students Federation, a right-wing, though allegedly non-political, organisation that was suspected of being funded by the government, called for disaffiliation from the National Union of South African Students (NUSAS) and false and defamatory pamphlets began to circulate on the campus.[33]

The circulation of a hoax pamphlet naming two students and two staff members enabled Deneys take official action. He went to the police and threatened to lay charges against persons unknown. The police were forced to start an investigation, but they used it as a cover to interview campus radicals on the whereabouts of Martin Wittenberg, a young postgraduate student who was joint secretary of the Pietermaritzburg UDF. Colin Gardner (from the English department) and Christopher Merrett (from the university library) were interviewed by Major Smit of the Security Police. However, as a result of Deneys's intervention, the major was forced to conduct the interview in the vice principal's office. Deneys showed 'great aplomb and nerve in dealing with these shady and powerful characters'.[34]

Martin Wittenberg was in hiding and the Schreiners were one of the families that sheltered him.[35] Many academics, including Merrett, feared arrest and detention without trial and Deneys counselled them as best he could. He advised Merrett to flee to Lesotho until things quietened down.[36] The conflict that the Buthelezi Commission had foreseen was developing ferociously. The Schreiners also sheltered the Reverend Simon Gqubule, the principal of the Federal Theological Seminary in Imbali and his wife, Miriam, after Inkatha vigilantes attacked the institution.

Meanwhile, Jennifer travelled to Britain to stay with her brother Deneys (Neys), his wife Heather and their two small children, Deneys (Neysie) and their daughter Lyndall. They were living in Hounslow, to the west of London. While she was there, Jennifer disappeared for many weeks without an explanation.

Notes

1. Gerhard Maré and Georgina Hamilton, *An Appetite for Power: Buthelezi's Inkatha and the Politics of 'Loyal Resistance'* (Johannesburg: Ravan Press, 1987), p.167.
2. Roger J. Southall, 'Consocialisation in South Africa: The Buthelezi Commission and Beyond', *Journal of Modern African Studies* 21, 1 (March 1983), pp.77–112.
3. Bernard M Magubane, *My Life & Times* (Pietermaritzburg: University of KwaZulu-Natal Press, 2010), pp.287–9.
4. Magubane, *My Life & Times*, p.290.
5. Magubane, *My Life & Times*, p.291.
6. GDL Schreiner, 'Introduction', *The Buthelezi Commission: The Main Report*, Vol. I (Durban: H+H Publications, 1982), p.32.
7. Laurence Boulle, 'The Constitutional Law Implications of the Buthelezi Commission Report', *Comparative and International Law Journal of Southern Africa* 15, 3 (1982): pp.257–305.
8. MA Tarr, 'Those Whom the Gods Wish to Destroy: A Few Comments on the Current Political Scene', *Reality* 14, 5 (1982), p.12.
9. David Welsh, 'Review of the Buthelezi Commission', *Reality* 14, 4 (1982), p.7.
10. GDL Schreiner, *Political Ecology in a Checker-Board Region: George Campbell Lecture* (Pietermaritzburg: University of Natal Press, 1981), pp.4–5.

11. David Robbins, 'Natal/KwaZulu: The Road Ahead', *Reality* 16, 6 (November 1984), pp.4–11.
12. Maré and Hamilton, *Appetite for Power*, pp.166–7.
13. University of KwaZulu-Natal (UKZN) Archives: SP25/4/4, GDL Schreiner Documents, documentation on Universities Amendment Bill, 1983.
14. UKZN Archives: SP25/4/4, GDL Schreiner Documents, memo of 30 May 1983.
15. *Natal Witness*, 3 June 1983.
16. Else Schreiner, Reminisences to David Robbins, 2016.
17. UKZN Archives: SP25/4/4, GDL Schreiner Documents, documentation on Universities Amendment Bill, 1983, letter of 7 June 1983.
18. GDL Schreiner Letters, Letter from Else to family, 25 January 1984.
19. *Natal Witness*, 27 September 1985, article by David Robbins.
20. 'White Paper on Buthelezi Commission: KwaZulu Cabinet', *Clarion Call* 1, 11 (June 1984), pp.4–5.
21. 'The KwaZulu/Natal Indaba', *Clarion Call* 2 (1987), p.12–13.
22. GDL Schreiner Letters, letter to Else, 18 June 1985. Frederick van Zyl Slabbert was the leader of the Progressive Federal Party (PFP) at the time. The earlier draft of the KwaZulu Cabinet White Paper had appeared in *Clarion Call* 1, 11 in June 1984.
23. *Sunday Tribune*, 12 December 1987.
24. *Buthelezi Commission Report*, Vol. I, pp.112–16.
25. Peter Miller, 'Radclyffe Macbeth Cadman' [obituary], *Natalia* 42 (2012), pp.108–10.
26. Fred Kockott, 'Uncovering the Truth behind the Trust Feed Massacre', *Daily News*, 5 April 2012. https://www.iol.co.za/dailynews/opinion/uncovering-the-truth-behind-the-trust-feed-massacre-1283657.
27. See http://www.justice.gov.za/trc/media/1996/9607/s960725k.htm.
28. Else Schreiner, Reminiscences, 2017.
29. John Aitchison, Reminiscences, email of 3 June 2019.
30. *Natal Witness*, 16 August 1986.
31. UKZN Archives: SP25/3/1, Schreiner, GDL, Politicization Disruption.
32. UKZN Archives: SP25/3/1, Schreiner, GDL: Politicization Disruption, 11 May 1987. See also *Natal Witness*, 9 May 1987.
33. UKZN Archives: SP25/3/1, Schreiner, GDL: Politicization Disruption, 27 June 1986. See also Lou Levine, ed., *Hope beyond Apartheid: The Peter Kerchhoff Years of PACSA, 1979–1999* (Pietermaritzburg: Pietermaritzburg Agency for Community Social Action, 2002), pp.32–5.
34. Christopher Merrett, 'Under the State's Emergency: Memories of Pietermaritzburg, 1986', *Natalia* 46 (2016), pp.63–79. See also Else Schreiner,

Condolence Folders, 2008, letter from Christopher Merrett to Else Schreiner, 2 May 2008.
35. Information from Monika Wittenberg, Martin's mother, Reminiscences, 2017. My wife and I also sheltered Martin during this time.
36. Merrett, 'Under the State's Emergency', p.68.

13

Jennifer's Trial and Retirement Years (1987–2008)

On Thursday 17 September 1987, Deneys was chairing a meeting of the university Co-ordination and Liaison Committee when he received a message that left him visibly upset. Quickly excusing himself, he handed over the chair to somebody else and left the meeting. Douglas Irvine, the dean of social sciences and a close friend, was worried by this uncharacteristic behaviour. As soon as the meeting ended, Irvine went to the vice principal's office to find out what had happened. Lois Cross, the long-serving personal assistant in the vice principal's office, told him that Deneys's daughter Jennifer had been detained by the security police and that Deneys had gone home.[1]

Else described her feelings on receiving the news: 'That morning when that appalling voice on the phone said "Mrs Schreiner we are phoning to tell you that we have detained your daughter Jennifer, under Section 29". That was almost an unhandlable shock. Section 29 is solitary confinement for the purposes of interrogation.'[2]

Jenny had been detained at her flat in Marie Court in Wynberg in Cape Town. During the raid a weapons cache and 'subversive' literature were found. The story of Jenny's arrest and trial, from a mother's point of view, has been told by Else in her moving account, *Time Stretching Fear*.[3] This chapter will not repeat many of the details to be found there, as its focus is on Deneys and the effect that these events had on him.

Douglas Irvine hastened to Highwood. Else was not available to visitors, but Deneys and Douglas sat together in the garden and Deneys unburdened himself. He was, understandably, emotional and angry at Jenny's actions. What possessed her to keep weapons in her flat? The Schreiner tradition was non-violent protest and Jenny had violated these principles. How could she have been so stupid, so careless? Who had betrayed her? When did she desert her liberal principles? Why had she betrayed the family? The questions poured out of him. Douglas tried to calm him and suggested that perhaps Jenny's commitment to communist principles was carrying the family traditions forward in a new way.[4] As *Time Stretching Fear* is Else's book, there is no mention of Deneys's initial anger at his daughter in it.

Ironically, in the Buthelezi Commission report, Deneys had predicted that angry youths would turn to violence, although he could not have predicted that one of them would be his own daughter. It later transpired that when Jenny took the protracted absence from Deneys and Heather's home in London, she had gone to Zambia for military training with Umkhonto weSizwe (MK).

Jenny and Tony Yengeni began working together in the MK Western Cape structures in late 1986, while she was completing her Master's degree in social science. According to Thula Simpson's history of MK, on 20 July 1987, Jenny and Tony detonated a car bomb outside an apartment block called Castle Court in central Cape Town, which was used as married quarters by the military. The following evening they met again and Jenny was told that the next target would be DF Malan Airport, now Cape Town International Airport. Jenny placed a bomb in the women's toilet, set to detonate at midnight when there was least chance of causing casualties. The bomb was discovered, but before it could be disarmed, it exploded, causing extensive damage to the building. Jenny's next mission was to transport Mzwandile Vena, the new MK Western Cape commander, from Botswana to Cape Town in August. A few weeks later, on 16 September, Tony Yengeni was arrested. At 3.40 am the following morning, Jenny was arrested in her flat at 5 Marie Court, Wellington Avenue, Wynberg.[5] She was detained in terms of Section 29 of the notorious Internal Security Act, which allowed for indefinite detention and was used to isolate and intimidate the state's victims, as they had no recourse to family, courts or lawyers.

Douglas stayed in close touch with Deneys and found that he quickly shook off his shock and anger and focused his all energy on Jenny. He still had three months to go before his retirement at the end of 1987 and there were the usual official commitments plus the rounds of farewell functions to be endured, despite the family trauma. Deneys and Else went to Cape Town whenever they could and made every effort to see Jenny, but political detainees were held incommunicado. Jenny had managed to persuade the security police to inform her mother that she was being detained and that was that.

The Schreiners consulted lawyers and also Richard Steyn, the editor of the *Natal Witness*. While the media were not allowed to report on Section 29 detainees, there was a loophole. Jenny's parents could put out a statement that the media could print. The Schreiners' statement appeared in the *Natal Witness* and Steyn had made sure that it went out on the wire services, so that the national press, and particularly the press in Cape Town would pick it up. This served as a warning to Jenny's friends and comrades. The newspapers went to town over her 'illustrious' background: daughter of the vice principal of Natal University, granddaughter of Judge OD Schreiner, great-granddaughter of Cape Premier WP Schreiner and great grand-niece of Olive Schreiner. Else's work on the National Council of Women and her term as its national president was also examined. The life of the Schreiners became public property.

Amidst all this upheaval, Deneys had to complete his time as vice principal. His retirement party, on Wednesday 25 November, was held in the Margaret Kirwood Room. The vice chancellor, Piet Booysen (1984–91), gave a eulogy and the major groupings on campus all thanked him for his work and support. Ray Hawksworth, the estates manager, presented him with a table that he had specially crafted from scrap wood, including a top made from the old teak laboratory table where Deneys used to work.[6] Deneys spoke of his years on the campus and his term as vice principal. He thanked the three women in his life: Else, Lois Cross and Dulcie Somers Vine.[7] He said that he and Else had raised a family of young people of whom they were very proud and family life had been good practice for his career on university committees: 'I learned how to be in a minority of one.' More seriously, he spoke of the university's progress to racial integration and complimented Piet Booysen on his commitment to change. While many were demanding rapid change in education, Deneys had a word of caution: this was not possible because education was a long process that began with the very young.[8]

Then, instead of a holiday, or a trip overseas, the Schreiners rushed to Cape Town to support Jenny. The University of Cape Town offered its full support and Deneys and Else were able to stay with the vice chancellor, Professor Stuart Saunders, and his wife Anita, until they were able to make their own arrangements. Else confronted the Security Police who refused to answer any questions, although she and Deneys were able to access Jenny's flat in Marie Court, as the landlady wished to rent it out to another tenant and Jenny's belongings needed to be removed. The police assured Else that Jenny was being well looked after and the Schreiners were able to give her a Bible, the Catholic Jerusalem Bible, as religious friends thought Jenny might find it more interesting than the Gideon or King James Bible that she had been allowed. She was not allowed to see a lawyer, but Deneys and Else began working their connections. Helen Suzman warned Adriaan Vlok, the minister of police, that Jenny suffered from hypoglycaemia and that special care needed to be taken with her diet. This elicited the information that there was no prospect of early release and that the police were aware of her health and dietary needs. Suzman told Deneys and Else that Vlok's 'beady eyes' would be watching the police.[9]

While no lawyer or family member could visit a detainee, the law permitted visits by a magistrate or a judge. The judge president of Natal, Judge Alexander Milne, spoke to Deneys and offered to contact the judge president of the Cape and ask him to visit Jenny. Judge George Munnik duly complied and got word back that he had seen Jenny and that she appeared to be well. In December 1987, Jenny was allowed to write to her parents and siblings. The most important point she made was to talk of her motivations and upbringing:

> Never in my life have I done anything in an ill-considered or an adventurist way – and that is thanks to you and the way I was brought up to act responsibly and to take life seriously. The reality of our land its a harsh one, and so harsh decisions have got to be taken. You brought me up to act on my beliefs, and to oppose injustice, and that has been my guide throughout. I am aware that the paths of action that each of you and I would choose would differ in a variety of ways, and some of you are in for a big surprise. My experience over the last couple of months has done nothing to change my commitment, and were I to be out tomorrow, I would continue with the same work.[10]

As soon as he had retired, Deneys and Else moved to Cape Town to support Jenny throughout the long Schreiner/Yengeni trial. It outlasted apartheid and the release of Nelson Mandela on 11 February 1990. Jenny and her co-trialists were only granted bail on 9 November 1990 and indemnified in 1991. Jenny and her co-accused selected Advocate Dawid de Villiers SC, a disillusioned former National Party supporter and leading member of the Broederbond and a top trial lawyer, to head the defence team. Other members of the defence team included Advocate Pius Langa (later chief justice of South Africa and chancellor of the University of Natal), Mike Donen (who became a firm friend) and Johnny de Lange (who later sat on the African National Congress [ANC] benches in the democratic parliament with Jenny). The leading prosecutor was Advocate Hendrik Klem SC, described by Else as 'the man we grew to hate'.[11]

The presiding judge, Selwyn Selikowitz, was relatively young and had ruled in a recent case in favour of the End Conscription Campaign. The families of the fourteen defendants organised support groups and co-operated with catering and logistics. Deneys and Else were on lunch-collection duty, so they were not able to participate in one of the last, pre-1990, major freedom marches headed by Archbishop Desmond Tutu. They joined the Yengeni Trialists Support Group in 1988 and set about fundraising, not only for legal costs, but also to support the families of the other detainees. In January 1989, Deneys and Else were back in Pietermaritzburg, where they celebrated their ruby wedding anniversary with their son Deneys, Heather and their grandchildren Neysie and Lyndall. The youngsters organised a breakfast with ruby table decorations, ruby milk and ruby-coloured scrambled eggs.[12]

Jenny's attempted suicide shook Deneys and Else and exacerbated their feelings of helplessness.[13] They visited her in hospital and learned of the physical and psychological abuse she had suffered at the hands of the security police and the false confession that had been extorted from her. Jenny is a very private person and does not talk openly about her ordeal, but Ruth First, Joe Slovo's wife endured similar abuse at the hands of the security police in the early 1960s and was also driven to attempt to take her own life. She took sleeping pills, but not enough to kill her. As she recovered, she asked her doctor if she was heading for a breakdown. His response was, 'You've already had one.'[14] Jenny's emotional condition must have been very similar to that of Ruth First.

The Schreiners tried to destress with breaks on the Cape West coast and even managed a visit to Deneys and Heather in London. They were in London in February 1990 when President FW de Klerk announced the release of Nelson Mandela and the unbanning of the ANC and other liberation organisations. Alas, while other detainees were released quickly, including some of Jenny's co-defendants, Jenny's trial dragged on into 1991. Else and Deneys attended every session and kept careful notes of police evidence, of state prevarication and of potential lies and abuse. Deneys also released some of his stress practising his woodworking skills, albeit in rather cramped conditions.

In October 1990 Jenny was taken to a secret meeting in Pollsmoor Prison with unnamed 'top officials', only to discover that they were Nelson Mandela, Jacob Zuma and Alfred Nzo, who assured her and the other detainees that their ordeal was nearly over and that they would be released soon, but they needed to be patient.[15] Meanwhile, the trial ground on. On 30 October, Jenny was called to give evidence and described how she endured solitary confinement, the abuse of the interrogators and the psychological humiliation. Deneys and Else sat and listened to their daughter recounting her experiences from the witness box, on her birthday. Fortunately, the ghastly ordeal was nearly over because on Friday 10 November 1990, Jenny was granted bail of R40 000.

Deneys had to rush around the banks, late on a Friday afternoon, trying to find a branch with enough cash to give him. Eventually he succeeded and at 4 pm, desperately late for South African bureaucracy, Deneys and the lawyers appeared before Judge Selikowitz, who granted Jenny bail. However, the judge wondered why Jenny was not permitted to attend meetings of the ANC, the South African Communist Party (SACP), the United Democratic Front (UDF) and other such organisations, since they had all become legal. He wished Jenny a good weekend. The case was adjourned over the December recess and Jenny was granted permission to go back to Pietermaritzburg with her parents for Christmas. In March 1991 the trialists were finally indemnified in terms of the agreements between the government and the ANC. Life for all the Schreiners could begin again.

Jenny moved to Johannesburg where she worked at the ANC's headquarters, then known as Shell House, on Nelson Mandela's staff. She was involved in the constitutional negotiations known as CODESA (Convention for a Democratic South Africa). The report of the Buthelezi Commission served as source material in some of the CODESA committees, but times had changed and consociationalism was no longer in vogue. Of far greater importance was that the tectonic plates of politics had shifted so far since 1982 that full universal franchise and proportional representation in Parliament, plus a Bill of Rights, were embedded into the foundations of the new democracy.

On 27 April 1994, immensely long queues of South Africans of all races formed at voting stations throughout the land to cast their ballots in the first democratic, universal franchise elections in the history of the country. The main voting centre in Pietermaritzburg was the City Hall, where Deneys and Else cast their ballots in a peaceful, joyous occasion. A few days later, Heather, Deneys's daughter-in-law, was standing in a queue at the post office in Longmarket Street when she noticed an elderly man making faces at her. She did not recognise him and grew more and more irritated at his inappropriate behaviour until the penny dropped: it was Deneys without his beard. They both burst out laughing. The great protest beard had been shaved off with the dawn of democracy.[16] However, the clean pink skin did not stay exposed for very long, as Deneys promptly set about regrowing his beard.

As the gloss wore off the new South Africa, Deneys expressed his exasperation and disappointment with the inefficiencies and stumbles of the democratic rulers, but never gave vent to anger or hostility. The clumsy amalgamation of the University of Natal and the University of Durban-Westville and the autocratic rule of Professor Malegapuru William Makgoba as vice chancellor of the new institution affected him more deeply in a personal way. This is understandable since he had spent the greater part of his career at the University of Natal and his son Deneys (Neys) was an academic on the Durban campus.

Deneys was able to do his woodworking in his workshop at Highwood, rather than in the cramped quarters in Cape Town where they stayed during Jenny's long trial. Fishing and golfing proved even more relaxing. He and Else were able to fulfil a long-held ambition and visited China. Deneys was also active on the governing body of NAPAC (the Natal Performing Arts Council), which became the Playhouse Company as government subsidies were cut and the cultural structures of apartheid were reshaped.[17]

However, his major project, in conjunction with Else and interested community members, was the establishment of the Tembaletu Educational Trust.[18] This began in 1989 and was focused on building a community-driven vocational education and training facility for the marginalised communities around Pietermaritzburg. It was a logical extension of his interest in academic support and adult education at the university. It was also a very practical and very typical response from Deneys to the violence and dislocation in the townships and peri-urban areas around Pietermaritzburg.

When the Girls' Collegiate School and the Wykeham School amalgamated to form the Wykeham Collegiate, the Victorian buildings of the former in Burger Street became available. Deneys and Else acted swiftly, before developers and demolishers could swoop on the site and destroy the historic buildings, and acquired them for the trust. It took some astute negotiations with the school boards, the city and provincial authorities (as the property abutted on their properties around the Old Grey's Hospital complex). But, with a home that could be renovated by the very people the Tembaletu project was training, the trust could begin its work. Deneys chaired the Tembaletu board of trustees between 1993 and 2003.

Programmes were offered in computer literacy, basic adult literacy, school syllabus enrichment and support, HIV and health classes, cooking, sewing and gardening. The project devised its programmes according to needs identified in the community and Deneys and Else, together with the committee, arranged trainers and badgered donors for funding. It was an opportune time to start such a project, as apartheid was crumbling and foreign donors were anxious to find worthwhile projects that would facilitate the transformation of the country. The Australian and Canadian embassies, the European Economic Community (now the European Union) and the United States Agency for International Development all made substantial donations. One of the most successful spin-off projects was the newspaper supplement, *Learn with Echo*.[19] For over twenty years, Tembaletu lived up to its name, which in isiZulu means 'Our Hope'.

Deneys and Else also indulged in their passion for art and supported many rising, but underprivileged young artists. Their particular focus was on African art and they bequeathed their extensive collection to the Tatham Art Gallery. They fostered and patronised the work of Vuminkosi Zulu and the artist-teachers associated with the Ndaleni Art Teachers Training College. Their daughter-in-law, Heather, played a major part in the curation of the collection and in the staging of a major exhibition. She also wrote a Master's dissertation on their collection and described it as reflecting the distinctiveness of the region of KwaZulu-Natal.[20] As a tribute to their dedication to the arts, one of the galleries at the Tatham was named the Schreiner Gallery.

While Jenny and Barbara pursued their careers in government, Deneys (or Neys) the engineer, taught in the faculty of engineering on the Durban campus of the university. He also committed himself to addressing management issues and served as dean of the faculty for some years. His relationship with Vice Chancellor Makgoba was tense and contributed to his decision eventually to return to the United Kingdom.[21] But at the time he and Heather lived in Pietermaritzburg and Neys rode to Durban every morning on his motor cycle. Their children, Neysie and Lyndall, were collected every afternoon after school by Deneys and spent the time with their grandparents at Highwood until their parents came home. The youngest Deneys (Neysie) remembers how devotedly his grandfather watched him play cricket and rugby, even though he was not very good at the sports.

Else and Deneys visited Pretoria frequently to stay with Jenny, her partner, musician Anthony Stevens, and their sons, Nikita and Raul (named after Soviet leader Nikita Krushchev and Cuban leader Raul Castro respectively) and Barbara, her son Monde, and her partner Kathy Eales. Traditional family holidays to the Kruger National Park continued and Oliver's widow and daughter came out from England and joined them on occasion.

The Alan Paton Centre began an oral history project recording the memories of leading South African and Natal liberals and struggle veterans and Deneys was interviewed by Randolph Vigne, the author of *Liberals against Apartheid*. Regrettably, the interview is not particularly useful for a biographer of Deneys Schreiner, as Vigne did most of the talking. Deneys was barely able to get a word in edgeways.[22]

Deneys's health began failing in the early 2000s and his powers of speech were affected. Although he could clearly follow conversations, friends and family could see how frustrated he was at not being able to participate in them. He was still able to plant a commemorative tree at Tembaletu in 2007 and was described in the trust's annual report as the project's founder, but this was to be his last public function.[23] Less than a year later, Deneys fell and broke his hip while out shopping with Else and refused hospitalisation and extensive surgery. He died, with Else and the children around him, peacefully in his bed on 27 April 2008, Freedom Day, the day commemorating the arrival of the democracy for which, Deneys, in his quiet way, had fought so hard to achieve.

Among the tributes that poured in to Highwood was a formal communiqué from the vice chancellor of the University of KwaZulu-Natal, Professor Makgoba,[24] and a warmer letter from the deputy vice chancellor and head of the college of agriculture, engineering and science, Professor PJK Zacharias, who described Deneys as a 'legend in his lifetime' and said that his passing on Freedom Day was a fitting coincidence.[25]

Sue Rosenberg wrote from London that Deneys was 'a man I so admired in many ways – for his social conscience, political views, academic standing and leadership, intellect, deep love of his country, and on a more personal level for his warmth, humour and kindness'.[26]

Richard Rangiah, the director of the Tembaletu Trust, described both the Schreiners as having a 'visionary idea of an educational park, Tembaletu has contributed to changing the lives of literally thousands of otherwise marginalised people across the province, sometimes in little ways and every so often in life-altering ways too'. He concluded on behalf of his staff: 'We shall all remember him strolling through the passageways of Tembaletu, popping into offices for a quick chat and joke with the staff.'²⁷

In addition to the remembrances at the university, a memorial service was held at Tembaletu and many tributes were paid, with his old friend, colleague and compatriot Colin Gardner playing the leading role. His son, Deneys (Neys), and grandson Deneys (Neysie), also spoke. The Reverend Simon Gqubule, former rector of the Federal Theological Seminary, who, with his wife Miriam, had stayed with the Schreiners when they were evicted from Imbali by anti-democratic vigilantes, told of how Deneys's sense of tolerance extended to encouraging him saying grace at the Schreiner table.²⁸

Notes

1. Douglas Irvine, Reminiscences, email of 15 January 2018.
2. Mary Kleinenberg and Christopher Merrett, *Standing on Street Corners: A History of the Natal Midlands Region of the Black Sash* (Pietermaritzburg: Natal Society Foundation, 2015), p.109.
3. Else Schreiner, *Time Stretching Fear: The Detention and Solitary Confinement of 14 Anti-apartheid Trialists 1987-1991* (Cape Town: Robben Island Museum, 2000).
4. Douglas Irvine, Reminiscences, email of 15 January 2018.
5. Thula Simpson, *Umkhonto we Sizwe: The ANC's Armed Struggle* (Cape Town: Penguin Random House, 2016), pp.393, 409, 411-12.
6. University of KwaZulu-Natal (UKZN) Archives: SP25/1/1/1, GDL Schreiner (Prof & Vice Principal UNP), 1976-1987, memo from Nancy Knowler (Public Relations) to Vice Chancellor Piet Booysen.
7. Dulcie Somers Vine (1916-91) was secretary and registrar's representative on the Pietermaritzburg campus (1953-77). GDL Schreiner, 'Dulcie May Somers Vine (1916-1991)', *Natalia* 22 (1992), pp.68-70.
8. UKZN Archives: SP25/1/1/1 GDL Schreiner (Prof & Vice Principal UNP), 1976-1987, Retirement Speech, 1987.
9. Else Schreiner, Reminiscences, May 2016.
10. Quoted in Schreiner, *Time Stretching Fear*, pp.12-13.
11. Schreiner, *Time Stretching Fear*, p.72.
12. Schreiner, *Time Stretching Fear*, p.81.
13. Schreiner, *Time Stretching Fear*, pp.25-32.

14. Donald Pinnock, *Writing Left: The Radical Journalism of Ruth First* (Pretoria: UNISA Press, 2007), pp.234–5.
15. Schreiner, *Time Stretching Fear*, p.204.
16. Heather Schreiner, Reminiscences, 2017. See also Rob Haswell, 'Tribute to a Man Who Stood up for What he Believed in', *The Mirror*, 16 July 2008.
17. Else Schreiner, Reminiscences, 2017.
18. The spelling 'Tembaletu' does not conform to modern Zulu orthography, but, according to Else, a simplified form was selected to facilitate fundraising from foreign organisations and white big business.
19. Tembaletu Community Education Centre, *Annual Review 1992*.
20. Heather Schreiner, 'Contextualising the South African Art Collection of Else and Deneys Schreiner', Master's thesis, University of KwaZulu-Natal, 2009), p.24.
21. Makgoba was the last vice chancellor of the University of Natal and the first of the University of KwaZulu-Natal.
22. Alan Paton Centre: 95APB16, KwaZulu-Natal Oral History Project Prof Denys [*sic*] Schreiner, interviewed by Randolph Vigne, 12 April 1995.
23. Tembaletu Community Education Centre, *Annual Report 2007*.
24. Else Schreiner, Condolence Folders, 2008, 'Notice to the University Communique: Professor Deneys Schreiner – 1923–2008'.
25. Else Schreiner, Condolence Folders, 2008, letter from Professor Zacharias to Else Schreiner, 15 May 2008.
26. Else Schreiner, Condolence Folders, 2008, Letter from Sue Rosenberg to Else and family, 26 May 2008.
27. Else Schreiner, Condolence Folders, 2008, 'Tribute to Deneys Schreiner', Colin Gardner, 1 June 2008.
28. Else Schreiner, Condolence Folders, 2008, 'Tribute to Deneys Schreiner', Colin Gardner, 1 June 2008.

Conclusion

Drawing the Strands Together

Assessing Deneys Schreiner's life requires us to look at influences going back to the nineteenth century: at Olive, a great-aunt who set the literary world alight and at WP, a grandfather who stood by his principles at the expense of his political career. Then there was OD, Deneys's father, whose stand on the integrity of the Constitution unquestionably blighted his chances of career advancement and was ultimately unsuccessful. However, OD's judicial stance made legal history in South Africa and inspired young lawyers of future generations.

Deneys was always conscious of the Schreiner family lineage and traditions, but he consciously avoided using the Schreiner name and reputation to his own advantage and inculcated into his children that, if the name meant anything, it did not mean privilege, but service. His life was defined by his principles, his character and by the service he gave to others. In conducting research for this biography, hardly any informants made any negative remarks about his character. One informant thought he took official parsimony to the point of meanness at the university, but that has been the only black mark against his name, if it can be regarded as such.

This study of Deneys's life provides an opportunity to look at the strengths and weaknesses of liberalism in South Africa. One important strength is the determination and commitment that people like Deneys and Else showed in keeping the liberal flame alive during the apartheid years. This suggests the type of continued commitment necessary to nurture liberal values in practical and political ways in the democratic South Africa. The creation of the country's new Constitution in the mid-1990s is the crowning achievement for liberal thinkers in South Africa. The roots of this achievement can be traced back to the Natal Convention in 1961 and to the conference on constitutional change that Deneys organised in 1978. One weakness of liberalism is that it is often seen as, and liberals sometimes practise it as, an elite philosophy that does not connect with people on the ground. In the case of Deneys, although he came from an elite background, through his lived values and targeted activities, he did make such connections – one of the best examples being Tembaletu.

Looking at his university career, it is perhaps instructive to contrast the University of Natal with a university such as Rhodes, which was of comparable size to the Pietermaritzburg campus. This Eastern Cape campus, also one of the 'liberal' English-speaking universities, was less infused with liberal practices than the University of Natal. Students at Rhodes were treated more paternalistically than they were in Natal and denunciations of government crackdowns on students were fiercer in Natal than in the Eastern Cape. The vice chancellors of Rhodes whose terms of office overlapped with Deneys's active years, professors Hyslop and Henderson, were authoritarians. Hyslop even refused to allow black students to stay in 'white' residences during a conference of the National Union of South African Students (NUSAS).[1] One of the affected students was Steve Biko, a student at Natal's medical school. The crass and insensitive treatment he experienced at Rhodes contributed to his determination to break from NUSAS and establish the South African Students Organisation (SASO) and the Black Consciousness Movement.[2] This conservatism at Rhodes is in stark contrast to Deneys's decision to allow black students to stay in University of Natal residences, regardless of the letter of the crumbling apartheid laws, and his open-hearted efforts to make them feel welcome.

Deneys played a significant role in developing a liberal ethos at his university at a time when the personalities of those in power, such as Owen Horwood and Francis Stock, were decidedly illiberal. Nithaya Chetty and Christopher Merrett have described Deneys as, 'one of the staunch champions of freedom in the university and society as a whole'. They remark on the parochialism of the University of Natal, but approvingly quote South African Communist Party leader and Cabinet minister Blade Nzimande, who praised Deneys as a father figure because of his passionate commitment to transformation and the hard work he put into making young black students feel accepted.³

The University of Natal played an important role in setting down early markers on the road to a transformed South Africa through the constitutional debate it fostered at various critical stages from the 1960s, through the 1970s and into the 1980s. The other three English-language universities did not offer their leadership with such a specific constitutional focus. The University of Natal's role was a result of the province's particular history and the efforts of people such as Deneys who repeatedly guided, nudged and directed the process. He summed up the role of the university in a modest contribution he wrote in a major commemorative history of Pietermaritzburg, published the year after he retired:

> Throughout the period of increasing tensions in the country and the growth of restrictive legislation, the University has successfully carried out its annual and long term educational function. It has attempted to protect its own position as a member of the international university community and, also, the rights of each of its constituent parts. It has had varied succcess but it will not weaken in its continuous endeavours.⁴

It is important to explore the multiple strands of South Africa's modern history. The liberation struggle was not a linear series of events leading from Rivonia, or from the Freedom Charter nearly a decade earlier, through the Soweto Uprising to the formation of the United Democratic Front and eventually to the unbanning of the African National Congress and the glorious days of April 1994. There were other parties, factions and intellects working away at subverting the system, including Inkatha, at least until the mid-1980s. Deneys was part of those processes and his daughter, Jenny, was a very important participant in activities that are part of what is currently the dominant narrative. All the Schreiners of Highwood played their roles in the liberation struggle in its broadest sense.

Deneys was a good man, a fine scholar and a clever thinker who made a difference at many levels in the lives of thousands: colleagues, students, the marginalised and the hopeful. All this was framed by his beard. If this study has managed to get behind the beard and reveal the character of the man behind the beard, it will have succeeded in its mission.

Notes

1. The Rhodes University administration held dogmatically to this attitude for many years and even in my personal experience NUSAS members attending conferences at Rhodes were accommodated in school hostels rather than in the residences of the university.
2. Information supplied by Professor Jeff Peires, email, 3 June 2019. See also Paul Maylam, *Rhodes University 1904–2016: An Intellectual, Political and Cultural History* (Grahamstown: Institute of Social and Economic Research, Rhodes University, 2017).
3. Nithaya Chetty and Christopher Merrett, *The Struggle for the Soul of a South African University: The University of KwaZulu-Natal; Academic Freedom, Corporatisation and Transformation* (Pietermaritzburg: Natal Society Foundation, 2014), p.17.
4. Deneys Schreiner, 'The University and Political Protest', in *Pietermaritzburg 1838–1988: A New Portrait of an African City*, edited by John Laband and Rob Haswell (Pietermaritzburg: University of Natal Press, 1988), p.212.

Select Bibliography

Reminiscences and interviews
Note: Many discussions were held with Else Schreiner, her children and grandchildren, too many to be specifically mentioned. In this list a broadbrush distinction is drawn between structured interviews and less formal talks and reminiscences. Where the information was conveyed by email, this is indicated.

Aitchison, John, Reminiscences, emails, 2 June 2019; 3 June 2019.
Benyon, John, Reminiscences, email, 11 January 2018.
Dominy (née Murphy), Anne, Reminiscences, 2018.
Drewes, Siegfried, Reminiscences, email, 10 June 2017.
Forsyth, Christopher, Reminiscences, email, 12 September 2017.
Guest, Bill, interview, 27 October 2016.
Irvine, Colleen, Reminiscences, 15 January 2018.
Irvine, Douglas, Reminiscences, emails, 29 December 2017; 15 January 2018.
Konigkramer, Arthur, Interview, email, 2 May 2017; 1 February 2018.
Laband, John, 'Some Reminiscences of Deneys Schreiner', email, 14 October 2016.
Laband, John, Reminiscences, email, 2 February 2018.
Morewood, Chris, Reminiscences, email, 1 October 2017.
Peires, Jeff, Interview, email, 3 June 2019.
Riekert, Julian, Reminiscences, email, 9 April 2017.
Robbins, David, Interviews, conversations and emails, 2016–18.
Schreiner, Barbara, Reminiscences and interviews, 2016–17.
Schreiner, Deneys (Neys), Reminiscences, 2017.
Schreiner, Else, Reminiscences and interviews, 2016–17.

Schreiner, Heather and Lyndall, Reminiscences, 2017.
Schreiner, Jennifer, Reminiscences and interviews, 2016–17.
Stilwell, Pat, Reminiscences, email, 3 October 2017.
Verbeek, Jennifer, Reminiscences, email, 6 September 2017; 15 October 2017.
Verbeek, Jennifer, Interview and reminiscences, 2017.
Vietzen, Colleen, Interview, 28 October 2016.
Weber, Meredith, Interview, email, 11 December 2016.
Wittenberg, Monika, Reminiscences, 2017.

Books and chapters in books
Ancer, Jonathan. *Betrayal: The Secret Lives of Apartheid Spies*. Cape Town: Tafelberg, 2019.
Alexander, Peter F. *Alan Paton: A Biography*. Oxford: Oxford University Press, 1994.
Anderson, Robert. *British Universities: Past and Present*. London: Hambledon Continuum, 2006.
Barzun, Jacques. *The American University: How it Runs, Where it is Going*. London: Oxford University Press, 1969.
Beinart, William. *Twentieth-Century South Africa*. Oxford: Oxford University Press, 2001.
Benyon, John, ed. *Constitutional Change in South Africa: Proceedings of a Conference on Constitutional Models and Constitutional Change in South Africa*. Held at University of Natal, Pietermaritzburg, 14–16 February 1978. Pietermaritzburg: University of Natal Press, 1978.
Berger, Peter L. and Bobby Godsell. *A Future South Africa: Visions, Strategies and Realities*. Cape Town: Human & Rousseau/Tafelberg, 1988.
Bizos, George. *Odyssey to Freedom*. Cape Town: Random House Struik, 2007.
Bozzoli, GR. 'The Role of English Universities in South Africa'. In *The Future of the University in Southern Africa*, edited by HW van der Merwe and David Welsh, 188–95. Cape Town: David Philip, 1977.
Brooke, Christopher NL. *A History of the University of Cambridge 1870–1990*, Vol. IV. Cambridge: Cambridge University Press, 1993.
Brookes, Edgar. *A South African Pilgrimage*. Johannesburg: Ravan Press, 1977.

Cardo, Michael. *Opening Men's Eyes: Peter Brown & the Liberal Struggle for South Africa*. Johannesburg: Jonathan Ball, 2010.

Chetty, Nithaya and Christopher Merrett. *The Struggle for the Soul of a South African University: The University of KwaZulu-Natal; Academic Freedom, Corporatisation and Transformation*. Pietermaritzburg: Natal Society Foundation, 2014.

Clark, Nancy and William Worger. *South Africa: The Rise and Fall of Apartheid*. New York: Longman, 2004.

Clark, Ronald W. *The Huxleys*. London: Heinemann, 1968.

Clingman, Stephen. *Bram Fischer: Afrikaner Revolutionary*. Cape Town: David Philip, 1998.

Dart, Raymond (with Dennis Craig). *Adventures with the Missing Link*. London: Hamish Hamilton, 1959.

Davenport, TRH and Christopher Saunders. *South Africa: A Modern History*. London: Macmillan, 2000.

De Villiers, René. 'Afrikaner Nationalism'. In *The Oxford History of South Africa, Vol. II: South Africa 1870–1966*, edited by Monica Wilson and Leonard Thompson, 405–6. Oxford: Clarendon Press, 1975.

Emery, Frank. *The Red Soldier: Letters from the Zulu War, 1879*. London: Hodder & Stoughton, 1977.

Francis, Suzanne. *Institutionalizing Elites: Political Elite Formation and Change in the KwaZulu-Natal Provincial Legislature*. Leiden: Brill, 2011.

Gilbert, Martin. *Never Despair: Winston S Churchill 1945–1965*. London: Heinemann, 1988.

Giliomee, Hermann and Bernard Mbenga. *New History of South Africa*. Cape Town: Tafelberg, 2007.

Gregg, Lyndall. *Memories of Olive Schreiner*. London: W & R Chambers, 1957.

Guest, Bill. *Stella Aurorae: The History of a South African University, Volume 1, Natal University College (1909–1949)*. Pietermaritzburg: Natal Society Foundation, 2015.

———. *Stella Aurorae: The History of a South African University, Volume 2, the University of Natal (1949–1976)*. Pietermaritzburg: Natal Society Foundation, 2017.

———. *Stella Aurorae: The History of a South African University, Volume 3, the University of Natal (1976–2003)*. Pietermaritzburg: Natal Society Foundation, 2018.

Haydon, Anthony P. *Sir Matthew Nathan: British Colonial Governor and Civil Servant*. St Lucia: University of Queensland Press, 1976.

Hill, Christopher. *Change in South Africa: Blind Alleys or New Directions?* London: Rex Collings, 1983.

———. *The World Turned Upside Down: Radical Ideas during the English Revolution*. London: Penguin, 1991.

Kahn, Ellison, ed. *Fiat Iustitia: Essays in Memory of Oliver Deneys Schreiner*. Cape Town: Juta, 1983.

Kenny, Henry. *Architect of Apartheid: HF Verwoerd; An Appraisal*. Johannesburg: Jonathan Ball, 1980.

Kennedy, Ludovic. *On my Way to the Club*. Glasgow: Fontana, 1990.

Kgware, WM. 'The Role of Black Universities in South Africa'. In *The Future of the University in Southern Africa*, edited by HW van der Merwe and David Walsh, 225–36. Cape Town: David Philip, 1977.

Kleinenberg, Mary and Christopher Merrett. *Standing on Street Corners: A History of the Natal Midlands Region of the Black Sash*. Pietermaritzburg: Natal Society Foundation, 2015.

Kros, Jack. *War in Italy: With the South Africans from Taranto to the Alps*. Johannesburg: Ashanti Publishing, 1992.

Laban, John. *Kingdom in Crisis: The Zulu Response to the British Invasion of 1879*. Pietermaritzburg: University of Natal Press, 1992.

Lambert, Michael. *The Classics and South African Identities*. London: Bloomsbury Academic, 2011.

Lawson, KC. *Venture of Faith: The Story of St John's College, Johannesburg, 1898–1968*. Johannesburg: Council of St John's College, 1968.

Levine, Lou, ed. *Hope beyond Apartheid: The Peter Kerchhoff Years of PACSA, 1979–1999*. Pietermaritzburg: Pietermaritzburg Agency for Community Social Action (PACSA), 2002.

Magubane, Bernard M. *My Life & Times*. Pietermaritzburg: University of KwaZulu-Natal Press. 2010.

Maré, Gerhard and Georgina Hamilton. *An Appetite for Power: Buthelezi's Inkatha and the Politics of 'Loyal Resistance'*. Johannesburg: Ravan Press, 1987.

Marks, Shula. *The Ambiguities of Dependence in South Africa: Class, Nationalism and the State in Twentieth-Century Natal*. Johannesburg: Ravan Press, 1986.

Marks, Shula, ed. *Not Either an Experimental Doll: The Separate Worlds of Three South African Women; Correspondence of Lily Moya, Mabel Palmer and Sibusisiwe Makhanya*. Pietermaritzburg: University of Natal Press and Killie Campbell Africana Library, 1987.

Marr, Andrew. *A History of Modern Britain*. London: Macmillan, 2007.
Mathews, Anthony S. *Freedom, State Security and the Rule of Law: Dilemmas of the Apartheid Society*. Cape Town: Juta, 1986.
Maylam, Paul. *Rhodes University 1904–2016: An Intellectual, Political and Cultural History*. Grahamstown: Institute of Social and Economic Research, Rhodes University, 2017.
McCaul, Colleen. 'The Wild Card: Inkatha and Contemporary Black Politics'. In *State, Resistance and Change in South Africa*, edited by Philip Frankel, Noam Pines and Mark Swilling, 146–73. London: Croom Helm, 1988.
Meer, Fatima, ed. *The South African Gandhi: An Abstract of the Speeches and Writings of MK Gandhi, 1893–1914*. Durban: Madiba Publishers, 1995.
Meintjes, Sheila. 'Farmers to Townspeople: Market to Labour Reserve'. In *Pietermaritzburg 1838–1988: A New Portrait of an African City*, edited by John Laband and Rob Haswell, 66–9. Pietermaritzburg: University of Natal Press, 1988.
Merrett, Christopher. *A Culture of Censorship: Secrecy and Intellectual Repression in South Africa*. Pietermaritzburg: University of Natal Press, 1995.
Orpen, Neil. *Victory in Italy: South African Forces in World War II*, Vol. V. Cape Town: Purnell, 1975.
Ottaway, Marina. *South Africa: The Struggle for a New Order*. Washington, DC: Brookings Institution, 1993.
Paton, Alan. *Hofmeyr*. Cape Town: Oxford University Press, 1964.
Pinnock, Donald. *Writing Left: The Radical Journalism of Ruth First*. Pretoria: UNISA Press, 2007.
Saunders, Stuart. *Vice-Chancellor on a Tightrope: A Personal Account of Climactic Years in South Africa*. Cape Town: David Philip, 2000.
Schreiner, Deneys. 'The University and Political Protest'. In *Pietermaritzburg 1838–1988: A New Portrait of an African City*, edited by John Laband and Rob Haswell, 213. Pietermaritzburg: University of Natal Press, 1988.
Schreiner, Else. *Time Stretching Fear: The Detention and Solitary Confinement of 14 Anti-apartheid Trialists 1987–1991*. Cape Town: Robben Island Museum, 2000.
Schoeman, Karel. *Olive Schreiner: 'n Lewe in Suid-Afrika 1855–1881*. Cape Town: Human & Rousseau, 1989.
Schoeman, Karel, ed. *The Missionary Letters of Gottlob Schreiner 1837–1846*. Cape Town: Human & Rousseau, 1991.

Sharpe, Tom. *Riotous Assembly*. London: Secker & Warburg, 1971.

Simpson, Thula. *Umkhonto we Sizwe: The ANC's Armed Struggle*. Cape Town: Penguin Random House, 2016.

Slovo, Joe. *Slovo: The Unfinished Autobiography*. Johannesburg: Ravan Press, 1995.

Smith, Jack Shepherd. *Buthelezi: The Biography*. Johannesburg: Hans Strydom Publishers, 1988.

Spiers, Edward M. *The Late Victorian Army: 1868–1902*. Manchester: Manchester University Press, 1992.

Steyn, Richard. *Jan Smuts: Unafraid of Greatness*. Johannesburg: Jonathan Ball, 2015.

Suzman, Helen. *In No Uncertain Terms: Memoirs*. Johannesburg: Jonathan Ball, 1993.

Temkin, Ben. *Buthelezi: A Biography*. London: Frank Cass, 2003.

Thompson, Paul. *Natalians First: Separatism in South Africa, 1909–1961*. Johannesburg: Southern Book Publishers, 1990.

Three-Peace: Poems by Lisa Combrinck, Frank Meintjies & Barbara Schreiner. Pretoria: Ralph Irons Publishers, 2016.

Tobias, Phillip. *Into the Past: A Memoir*. Johannesburg: Wits University Press, 2005.

Vahed, Goolam. *Chota Motala: A Biography of Political Activism in the KwaZulu-Natal Midlands*. Pietermaritzburg: University of KwaZulu-Natal Press, 2017.

Van Der Merwe, HW and David Welsh, eds. *The Future of the University in Southern Africa*. Cape Town: David Philip, 1977.

Vigne, Randolph. *Liberals against Apartheid: A History of the Liberal Party of South Africa, 1953–68*. London: Macmillan, 1997.

Walker, Eric A. *WP Schreiner: A South African*. Oxford: Oxford University Press, 1969.

Wilson, Harold. *A Prime Minister on Prime Ministers*. London: Book Club Associates, 1977.

Wilson, Monica and Leonard Thompson, eds. *The Oxford History of South Africa, Vol. II: South Africa 1870–1966*. Oxford: Clarendon Press, 1975.

Worden, Nigel. *The Making of Modern South Africa*. Cape Town: Juta, 1994.

Journals and periodicals

Austin, BA. 'On the Development of Radar in South Africa and Its Use in the Second World War'. *URSI Radio Science Bulletin* 358 (September 2016): 69–81.

Barkham, John. 'Dockside Diva'. *Life*, 13 March 1944.
Boulle, Laurence. 'The Constitutional Law Implications of the Buthelezi Commission Report'. *Comparative and International Law Journal of Southern Africa* 15, 3 (1982): 257-305.
Bozas, Achilles. 'The Natal Provincial Council, 1910-1986'. *Natalia* 16 (1986): 45-50.
Burnett, BB. 'Alphaeus Hamilton Zulu (1905-1988)'. *Natalia* 18 (1988): 93-6.
Coghlan, Mark. 'The Horticulturalists, Freedom Radio and the Erase Erasmus Society: Pietermaritzburg-Based Protest against the Nationalist Government in the 1950s and Early 1960s'. *Natalia* 25 (1995): 54-64.
Dominy, Graham. '"On the Side of the Angels": Helen Suzman and the 1966 Robert Kennedy Tour'. *Helen Suzman Foundation Brief*, 2016. https://www.politicsweb.co.za/comment/on-the-side-of-the-angels.
Gardner, Colin. 'George Deneys Lyndall Schreiner (1923-2008)' [obituary]. *Natalia* 38 (2008): 83-5.
Haasbroek, J. 'Die Britse Koningsbesoek aan Bloemfontein, Maart 1947'. *Navorsinge van die Nasionale Museum Bloemfontein* 16, 8 (2000): 213-59.
Hollister, Lincoln S. 'Memorial of David Robert Waldbaum: March 22, 1937-April 11, 1974'. *American Mineralogist* 60 (1975): 514-17.
Jamieson RT, GDL Schreiner and B Schonland. 'Age Measurements on a Pegmatite Mica from the Rhodesian Shield'. *Nature* 175 (1955): 464.
Jöns, Heike. 'The University of Cambridge, Academic Expertise and the British Empire, 1885-1962'. *Environment and Planning A* 48 (2016): 94-114.
Kahn, Ellison. 'Oliver Deneys Schreiner: The Man and His Judicial World'. *South African Law Journal* 97 (1980): 566-615.
———. 'The Wits Faculty of Law, 1922-1989: A Story with a Personal Touch'. *Consultus* (October 1989): 103-12.
'The KwaZulu/Natal Indaba'. *Clarion Call* 2 (1987): 12-13.
Lee, Robin. 'The Urban Foundation: Another Perspective'. *Reality* 14, 3 (1982): 15-17.
Merrett, Christopher. 'A Small Civil War: Political Conflict in the Pietermaritzburg Region in the 1980s and Early 1990s'. *Natalia* 43 (2013): 19-36.
———. 'Under the State's Emergency: Memories of Pietermaritzburg, 1986'. *Natalia* 46 (2016): 63-79.

Miller, Peter. 'Radclyffe Macbeth Cadman' [obituary]. *Natalia* 42 (2012): 108–10.

Natal Witness. 'Leslie Weinberg' [obituary]. Reproduced in *Natalia* 40 (2010): 158–9.

Robbins, David. 'Natal/KwaZulu: The Road Ahead'. *Reality* 16,6 (November 1984): 4–12.

Schreiner, GDL. 'Dulcie May Somers Vine (1916–1991)'. *Natalia* 22 (1992): 68–70.

Selvan, RL. 'Early Days at the Johannesburg Bar'. *Consultus* (October 1994): 115–27.

Southall, Roger J. 'Consocialisation in South Africa: The Buthelezi Commission and Beyond'. *Journal of Modern African Studies* 21, 1 (March 1983); 77–112.

Stewart, Andrew. '"The Klopper Affair": Anglo-South African Relations and the Surrender of the Tobruk Garrison'. *Twentieth Century British History* 17, 4 (2006): 516–44.

Tarr, MA. 'Those Whom the Gods Wish to Destroy: A Few Comments on the Current Political Scene'. *Reality* 14, 5 (1982): 12–14.

Walker, ADM. 'Noel Desmond Clarence (1921–1995)'. *Natalia* 25 (1995): 84–6.

Welsh, David. 'Review of the Buthelezi Commission'. *Reality* 14, 4 (1982): 6–7.

'White Paper on Buthelezi Commission: KwaZulu Cabinet'. *Clarion Call* 1, 11 (June 1984): 4–5.

Whyte, William. 'The Intellectual Aristocracy Revisited'. *Journal of Victorian Culture* 10, 1 (2005): 15–45.

Theses, dissertations, lectures and reports

Biyela, Sibongile Eunice. 'The Historical Development of the University of Zululand Library with Particular Reference to Buildings, Staff, Collection and Computerization (1960–1987)'. Honours thesis, University of Zululand, 1988.

Bourhill, James Fraser. '"Red Tabs": Life and Death in the 6th South African Armoured Division, 1943–1945'. PhD thesis, University of Pretoria, 2014.

The Buthelezi Commission: The Main Report, Vol. I. Durban: H+H Publications, 1982.

The Buthelezi Commission: The Main Report, Vol. II. Durban: H+H Publications, 1982.

Education Beyond Apartheid. Report of the Education Commission of the Study Project on Christianity in Apartheid Society (SPRO-CAS). Johannesburg: Christian Institute, 1971. https://disa.ukzn.ac.za/sites/default/files/pdf_files/rep19710000.037.052.005.pdf.

Lijphart, Arend. 'Power-Sharing in South Africa'. Policy Papers in International Affairs, No. 24. Berkeley, University of California, Institute of International Studies, 1985.

Meintjes, Sheila. 'Edendale 1850–1906: A Case Study of Rural Transformation and Class Formation in an African Mission in Natal'. PhD thesis, University of London, 1988.

Moseneke, Dikgang. 'Separation of Powers, Democratic Ethos and Judicial Function'. Lecture delivered at the University of the Witwatersrand on 23 October 2008. https://www.sahistory.org.za/archive/separation-powers-democratic-ethos-and-judicial-function-oliver-schreiner-memorial-lecture.

Murray, Bruce. 'World War II and Wits Student Politics'. Seminar paper, African Studies Institute, University of the Witwatersrand, 1993.

Randall, Peter, ed. *Anatomy of Apartheid*. SPROCAS Occasional Publication No. 1. Johannesburg: Christian Institute, 1970.

Schreiner, GDL. *Political Ecology in a Checker-Board Region: George Campbell Lecture*. Pietermaritzburg: University of Natal Press, 1981.

Schreiner, Heather. 'Contextualising the South African Art Collection of Else and Deneys Schreiner'. Master's thesis, University of KwaZulu-Natal, 2009.

Selfe, James. 'Adaptions to the Security-Intelligence Decision-Making Structures under PW Botha's Administration'. Master's thesis, University of Cape Town, 1987.

Tembaletu Community Education Centre. *Annual Review 1992*.

Tembaletu Community Education Centre. *Annual Report 2007*.

Internet sources

Frescura, Franco. 'National or Nationalist? A Critique of the National Monuments Council, 1936–1989. http://www.sahistory.org.za/franco/historical-conservation-nationalist.html.

Perrin, Ayodeji. 'Gay Marriage in South Africa: A Human Rights Legacy, an Anti-apartheid Legacy or Both?' https://www.academia.edu/5234647/Gay_Marriage_in_South_Africa_A_Human_Rights_Legacy_An_Anti-_Apartheid_Legacy_Or_Both.

Shrecker, Ellen. 'Political Tests for Professors: Academic Freedom during the McCarthy Years'. The University Loyalty Oath: 50th Anniversary Retrospective Symposium, 7–8 October 1999, University of California, Berkeley. http://www.lib.berkeley.edu/uchistory/archives_exhibits/loyaltyoath/symposium/schrecker.html.

Public archives
Alan Paton Centre, University of KwaZulu-Natal, Pietermaritzburg.
Department of Defence, Documentation Centre, Pretoria.
National Archives of South Africa, Pretoria.
University of KwaZulu-Natal Archives, Pietermaritzburg.
University of South Africa, Special Collections, Pretoria.

Private archives
Schreiner, Else. Condolence Folders, 2008 (including newspaper cuttings).
Schreiner, GDL. Private Correspondence Folder, 1946–c.1985.
Schreiner, OD. Private Correspondence, 1925–1979 (27 vols).

Index

African National Congress (ANC) 153–4
    constitutional issues 153
    breach with Inkatha 154, 155
Aitchison, John 113, 134, 135, 178
Alan Paton Centre 132, 192
Antonie, Francis 129
Aston, John 68

Baxter, Lawrence 144
Benyon, John 126, 145, 146, 147
Berger, Peter 167
Bernard Price Institute (University of the Witwatersrand) 3, 31, 73, 76–7, 111
Black Sash 78, 83, 97
Booysen, Piet 175, 176, 185
Botha, PW 4, 157, 158, 159, 176
Boulle, Laurence 173
Bozzoli, George 128
Broederbond 145, 187
Brookes, Edgar 111, 115
Brown, Peter 100, 113, 115
Burnett (ghost) 90
Buthelezi, Mangosuthu Gatsha
    break with ANC 154–5
    Chief Minister 4, 150, 153, 156–7, 158, 175–6, 177
    claim to be a legitimate leader 157
    meeting with ANC in Britain 154
    see also Buthelezi Commission
Buthelezi Commission (1980–2) 4, 110, 132, 148
    aftermath 174, 177, 178
    attitude surveys conducted for 163–4
    chair 155–6, 164
    findings and recommendations 165–7
    KwaZulu Legislative Assembly 158–9
    mandate 159
    members 159–60, 161
    opposition by PW Botha and government 159, 167, 168
    origins and significance 153, 158, 164
    political and constitutional principles 165
    publicity given to 161–2
    representation 161
    response to 167, 168, 172–3
    underplayed in historical accounts 153
    specialist working groups 164

terms of reference 162
timespan 161
title 156

Cambridge
   conditions post-Second World War 52
censorship in SA 125, 128, 142, 163, 173, 185
kaCetshwayo, Dinuzulu 12, 157
   trial 2, 16, 156
Chetty, AS 99, 100
Chetty, Nithaya 198
Christian Institute 115
Clarence, Desmond 126, 146, 176
Colenbrander, Hilde 100
Colenbrander, Peter 100
constitutional alternatives (Natal and KwaZulu) (JA Lombard commission, 1980) 155
constitutional reform conference, University of Natal (1978) 145-51, 155
   funding 146
   organisation 146
   participants 148, 150, 151
   purpose 149-50, 151
   see also Buthelezi Commission; Natal Convention (1961)
constitutional reform (government) *see* President's Council
Costello, George 91
Cronwright, Samuel 14
Cross, Lois 183, 186

Dainton, Dr 58
Deneys Schreiner lecture series 135
Dhlomo, Oscar 161, 174
Ditchburn, Hilda 130
Dominy, Graham xv
Drewes, Siegfried 91
Dunne, Tim 103
Durban Chamber of Commerce commission on constitutional reform 155

Eales, Kathy 192
Eckhart, Ecky (JCPP) 100
Edendale x, xiv, 10
Eisenhower, Milton Stover 68
Ensor, Paula 116
Extension of University Education Act (1959) 80, 82

Forsyth, Christopher 89-90
Fourie, Professor Deon 151-2
Freedom Radio 111

Gardner, Colin 114, 115, 179, 194
Gerdener, Theo 120
Godsell, Bobby 167
Gqubule, Miriam 180
Gqubule, Simon 180, 194
Gumede, Archibald Jacob (Archie) x, 10

Hamilton, Georgina 156, 172
Harpur, FJ 36, 44
Hawksworth, Ray 186
Hawksworth, Winton 118
High Court of Parliament Act 1952 73
Hindson, Sheila 146
The Horticulturalists 110-11
Horwood, Owen 102, 198
Huxley family 2-3

Inkatha xiv, 4, 10, 148, 154–5, 156, 157, 158, 160, 161, 174, 178, 180, 199
Inkatha Institute 131, 158
Inter-Continental Marketing Services South Africa 163
Internal Security Act (No. 74 of 1982) 144
Irvine, Colleen 101
Irvine, Douglas 131, 132, 145, 146, 147, 183

Jabavu, John Tengo 15
Jameson Raid 1, 15

Kemball, Dr 58
King, Terry 100
Kipling, Rudyard 14
Koornhof, Piet 119
Kops, Else *see* Schreiner, Else
KwaZulu homeland consolidation 155
KwaZulu-Natal Indaba 176–7
KwaZulu Legislative Assembly 159, 173

Laband, John 76, 79, 80
Leibbrandt, Robey 18
Learn with Echo 191
liberal organisations, attack on *see* Schlebusch Commission; Liberal Party of South Africa
Liberal Party of South Africa 4, 82, 83, 113, 114
liberalism in South Africa 196–7 *see also* Liberal Party of South Africa
Lombard, JA 155

Lund, James 134
Luyt, Richard 125, 146
Lyndall, Rebecca 12 *see also* Schreiner, Rebecca
Lyster, Richard 178

Macintyre-Reed, Malcolm 130
Mackie, Robin 135
MacMillan, Ronnie 103
Magubane, Bernard 172–3
Makgoba, Malegapuru 192, 193
Malherbe, EG 88
Maré, Gerhard 156, 172
Mark-en-Meningsopnames 163
Marks, Shula 154
Martin, Frank 120
Mathews, Tony (Anthony) 115, 143–4
Meester, Waldo 103–4
Meintjes, Sheila *see* Hindson, Sheila
Memorable Order of Tin Hats (MOTHS) 47
Merrett, Christopher 179, 180, 198
Millin, Philip 18
Milner Alfred 15
Milton, John 146
Mkhize, Evelyn 97
Morewood, Chris 90, 91
Motala, Chota 84, 99, 100
Motala, Rabia 84, 100
Msimang, Henry Selby x, 10
Murphy, Anne 143
Murphy, Nodi 143

Natal Convention (1961) 4, 111–112, 147, 155, 162, 197
Natal and resistance to the establishment of a republic 110

Natal and KwaZulu, administration as a single region 147, 155, 162–3, 164, 165, 166, 167, 176, 177
Natal University College *see* University of Natal
national convention (over Union) (1909) 16, 82, 147
National Union of South African Students (NUSAS) 144, 179, 197
Nattrass, Jill 161, 164
Ndaleni Art Teachers Training College 192
Nichols, Geoff 36
Mkhambathi 94 102
Nuffield Geochronological Unit *see* Bernard Price Institute
NUSAS *see* National Union of South African Students
Nzimande, Bonginkosi (Blade) ix–x, xiii, xiv, 100, 198

Oppenheimer, Harry 135, 160, 167

pass curfew 24–5
pass law protests 16, 83
Paton, Alan 17, 60, 82, 115, 132, 175
Paton, Anne 132
Pennsylvania State College 62, 65, 68, 69
Pietermaritzburg cultural institutions 1950s 9
Pietermaritzburg and Group Areas Act 10 *see also* Edendale
Pietermaritzburg Golf Club 133
Pietermaritzburg Parliamentary Debating Society 99

President's Council 157–8
Prestwich, Mark 132
Pretorius, Paul 116
Progressive Party 82, 114, 120
Prohibition of Political Interference Act 114

Quota Bill 174–5

Rabie Commission 143–4
Rajbansi, Amichand 161
Randall, Peter 115
Rangiah, Richard 193
Reitz, Francis Hester 15
Republic, South African and the opposition to in Natal 110
  see also [The] Horticulturalists; Freedom Radio
Rhodes and Schreiner family 1, 14, 15, 17
Rhodes University as a liberal institution 197
Riekert, Julian 94, 99, 100, 144
Robbins, Dave xv, 161
Robinson, Mike 94, 101
Rosenberg, Sue 193
royal family visit to South Africa 54–5

Saunders, Stuart 186
Schlebusch, Alwyn 158
Schlebusch Commission 115–16, 121
Schlemmer, Lawrence 115, 131–2, 158
Schonland, Basil 76–7
Schreiner, Barbara Gay (DS's daughter) 30, 96, 98–9, 137, 143, 146, 192

birth 84
education 5, 93, 121
son 192
Schreiner, Bill (William) (DS's
    brother) 17, 23, 24, 35, 36, 38,
    41, 51, 52, 55, 56, 57, 61
Schreiner, Buchan Deneys Jeremy
    (DS's grandson) *see* Schreiner,
    Neysie
Schreiner, Hilson Deneys (DS's son)
    see Schreiner, Neys
Schreiner, Deneys (OD's son)
    Early life
      birth and childhood 17, 23–5
      schooling 25–9
    University education
      University of the Witwatersrand
        30–1
      University of Cambridge 45–6,
        50–2, 53, 54, 55, 56, 58, 59, 62
    Second World War 29
      4/22 Field Regiment 36, 43–44
      6th Armoured Division 36, 37,
        42, 46
      army training 31, 35–6, 38
      Cairo (on leave) 41–2
      censorship 46
      demobilisation 50
      Egypt 38–9, 41–2
      health 41, 42, 43
      Italy 42–7
      Pietermaritzburg 36
      Potchefstroom 35
      signing up 34–5
      'up north' 36–7, 38–9, 41–2
    Family life
      birth of daughter Barbara 84
      birth of daughter Jenny 84
      birth of son Hilson Deneys 72
      birth of son Oliver Conrad 62
      discussion in family 98–9
      as children's storyteller 92–3
      death of son, Oliver 137–8
      early relationship with Else 53–4
      engagement to Else 58–9
      Verwoerd incident 93–4
      as grandfather 96, 192
      holidays in South Africa 93–5, 192
      marriage to Else 60–1, 97
      return to South Africa from
        USA 73
      wedding anniversary (ruby) 188
    Researcher, Bernard Price Institute
      for Geophysical Research,
      University of the Witwatersrand
      73, 76, 77, 85
    Researcher, Pennsylvania State
      College 62, 65–70, 73
      academic and research experience
        69–70, 73
      cricket team 71
      signing oath of loyalty to US
        69–70
      social life 71, 72
    Professor, Inorganic and Analytical
      Chemistry, University of Natal
      (Pietermaritzburg) 85, 89–92,
      101, 103–4
      building a mass spectrometer 90–2
      deputy dean and dean of science
        105
      role on committees and
        associations of the University
        103–105, 128
      Van Wyk de Vries Commission
        104–5

INDEX 215

Vice principal, University of Natal (Pietermaritzburg) 105, 121, 124–37, 199
   academic freedom 143, 144, 175, 176, 178–9
   accommodation for black students 136–7
   accommodation for women students 132
   and banned organisations 178
   computerisation 134
   National Union of South African Students 144
   opposition to censorship 128
   response to Rabie Commission 144
   retirement events 185–6
   sheltering of activists 180
   Sportsman of the Year Award banquet 118–19
   support for social sciences 132
   and students 102, 128, 132, 134, 135, 136–7, 198
   support to those working and learning outside curriculum 134–35
   town and gown 133
   visit to British universities 126–7
   Universities Amendment Bill (1983) 174

Political activities and views
   academic freedom 65, 66, 69, 81, 143, 144, 174–6, 178–9
   beard as form of protest 20–1, 79–80, 190
   Buthelezi Commission 4, 110, 133, 153, 155–156, 160, 161–2, 164–5, 167–8,174
   on censorship 103,128
   concerns about prospects in SA post-1948 election 56
   conference on constitutional change (1970s) 145–51
   counselling activist academics 180
   liberal views xii, xiii, xvi, 4, 40, 53, 63, 72, 82–83, 114, 117–18, 142, 148, 155–6, 165, 180, 188, 190, 194, 196
   Liberal Party of South Africa 4, 82, 83, 113, 114
   Natal Convention (1960) 4, 111
   National Union of South African Students (NUSAS) 144
   protest marches at Wits against Separate Universities Bill 81
   protests in 1970s 117, 143
   protests in 1980s 175, 178–9
   sheltering of activists 180
   support to Else as Progressive Party candidate 120
   South African Institute of Race Relations (SAIRR) (Pietermaritzburg) 114
   Treason Trial 84
   Urban Foundation 135–6
   views on Smuts in 1949 61–2

General
   the arts 192
   beard 20–1, 79–80, 90, 104, 117, 175, 178, 190
   characteristics xvi, 3–4, 11, 25–6, 27, 54, 56, 63, 85, 96, 97, 98–9, 113, 118, 127, 131, 136–7,179, 190, 194, 196
   death 193
   debate, enjoyment of 98–9

faith 57, 101
fishing 102
health 41, 42, 43, 193
immediate response to Jenny's detention 183–4, 185
influences on his broader intellectual development 65, 74
interest in geology and geomorphology 92
and libraries 28, 103, 104, 128
as mentor 102, 119
oral history interview 192–3
overview of life 3–6
retirement 190–1
science training for girls 98
soirees at Highwood 99–100, 148
sport 26, 29, 53, 71, 133
Tembaletu Educational Trust 191, 193
tributes after his death 193
trip to Italy during Cambridge years 55, 56, 57–8
Victoria Club 111, 133
Schreiner, Edna (OD's wife) (DS's mother) 17, 23–4, 36
Schreiner, Else (neé Kops) (DS's wife) xii, xiv, xviii, 4, 31, 53
and *Cry, the Beloved Country* 60
dedication to the arts 192
early married life 61, 62, 69, 70, 71, 72, 73
early relationship with Deneys 53–4
education 53
engagement to Deneys 58–9
experience of American academic life 71, 73
Kupugani office manager 97
National Council of Women 97
political involvement xii, 4–5, 78, 79, 83, 97, 109, 120
research position at Department of Scientific and Industrial Research 58, 60
response to Jenny's detention 183, 184
support of Deneys 97
Tembaletu Educational Trust 191
wedding 60–1
Schreiner, George Deneys Lyndall *see* Schreiner, Deneys (OD's son)
Schreiner, Gottlob (WP and Olive's father)
world view xi
marriage 12
missionary training and work 11, 12–13
Schreiner, Heather (Hilson Deneys's wife) 192
Schreiner, Jeanie (DS's sister) 17, 23, 24, 72
Schreiner, Jennifer Ann (Jenny) (DS's daughter) xvii, 5, 180, 199
attempted suicide 188
bail and indemnification 189
birth 84
career 189, 192
Convention for a Democratic South Africa (CODESA) 189
detention 2, 5, 6, 121, 183, 184–5, 186
education 93, 121
motivation for actions 187
permitted visits in detention 186–7
secret meeting in Pollsmoor Prison 189
sons 192

support by parents 185, 186–7, 188, 189
trial 183, 187–8, 189
Umkhonto weSizwe xii, 184–5
Schreiner, Lyndall (DS's granddaughter) 192
Schreiner, Monde (DS's grandson) 34
Schreiner, Neys (Hilson Deneys) (DS's son) xvii, 5, 76, 84, 93, 121, 121, 180, 190, 192, 194
Schreiner, Neysie (Buchan Deneys Jeremy) (DS's grandson) xvii, 96, 192, 194
Schreiner, Olive (Gottlob's daughter) 1, 12, 13–14
Schreiner, Oliver (DS's son) 5, 71, 76, 84, 121, 137
　daughter 137, 192
　death 121, 137
　education 84, 89, 93, 121, 137, 138
　marriage 137
　widow 192
Schreiner, OD (Oliver Deneys) (DS's father) xvii, 16–18, 19–20, 146
　Appellate Division 18, 19–20, 54–5, 72, 73
　South African Institute of Race Relations (SAIRR) 114
　views of 2, 19, 20
　Transvaal bench 18
Schreiner, Oliver Deneys *see* Schreiner, OD (DS's father)
Schreiner, Rebecca (Gottlob's wife) 13
Schreiner, Theo (Gottlob's son) 13, 16
Schreiner, WP (William Philip) (Gottlob's son) 1–2, 13, 14–16, 52
　world view xi

Schreiner, William Philip *see* Schreiner, WP
Schreiner family
　choice of names xvi–xvii
　domestic worker 97
　history (prior to birth of Deneys) 11–21, 57
　home (Highwood) 8, 96, 97, 137, 192 (see also under Schreiner, Deneys – *General* – soirées)
　home (Lyndall) 25, 84
　standing 3, 196
　see also under individual names
Schreiner Gallery 192
Separate Representation of Voters Bill 19, 72 (*see also* voters roll, removal of coloured voters)
Sikonje, Enoch 90
Smit, Major 179
Smith, Bob 60–1
Smuts, Jan
　installation as Chancellor of Cambridge University 57
　visit to Cambridge 61–2
Somers Vine, Dulcie 186
South African Institute of Race Relations (SAIRR) 114–5, 136, 146
South African Students Federation 179
South African Sugar Association commission on constitutional reform 155
Southall, Roger 167, 172
Springbok Legion 40
SPRO-CAS *see* Study Project on Christianity in Apartheid Society

St John's Diocesan College 25-6, 27-8
state of emergency 178
Stevens, Anthony 192
Stock, Francis 125-6, 143, 198
Stock, Gwen 125
Stilwell, Patrick 101-102, 114, 143
Study Project on Christianity in Apartheid Society (SPROCAS) 115
Sutton, Bill 116-17
Suzman, Helen 116, 120, 186

Tatham Art Gallery 192
Tarr, Mike 133, 158, 173
Tembeletu Educational Trust 6, 191, 193-4
Tobias, Phillip 3, 30, 77, 81
Trevelyan, GM 61
Tricameral Constitution 150, 167, 176
Trust Feed massacre 177
Trust Feed Crisis Committee 178
Turner, Rick 115, 116

United Democratic Front (UDF) 178, 179, 189
University of Cambridge 50, 51
University of Natal 6, 88, 89
   accommodation of departments on Pietermaritzburg campus 129-30
   Alan Paton Centre 132
   black students at xiii, 89, 136, 174
   Bridging the Gap 134-5
   Centre for Adult Education 135, 178
   computerisation 133
   conference on constitutional issues 145-51
   constitutional debate leadership provided 198
   divisions in student body 179
   Extra-mural Studies and Extension Unit 134
   financial crisis 131
   fuel crisis impact 130-1
   gender-based residential discrimination reduced 132
   as a liberal institution 197-8
   merger with University of Durban-Westville 190
   Non-Academic Staff Association 134
   parking on campus 129
   Project Ulwazi/Project Knowledge 133
   relationship between town and gown 133
   ex-Rhodesian student behaviour 134
   role of vice principle 124-132
   social sciences on Pietermaritzburg campus 131
   Sportsman of the Year Award banquet 118-19
   student protests in 1970s 117-18
   student protests in 1980s 178-9
   William O'Brien hall of residence 118, 119-20, 132-3
University of the Witwatersrand
   Bernard Price Institute 30
   student politics in Second World War 30-31
universities (SA)
   segregation 81-2

universities (USA) post-Second World War 67
Universities Amendment Bill 174
Unrest Monitoring Project 135
Urban Foundation 135-6, 158

Van Zyl Slabbert, Frederik 151
Verbeek, Alistair 91, 94, 95
Victoria Club 133
Vietzen, Colleen 103
Vigne, Randolph 193
Vlok, Adriaan 186
Voters roll, removal of coloured voters from 19, 20-21, 78
   OD's resistance to 19, 20
   Deneys's actions in relation to 20-21

Waldbaum, David 92
Webb, Colin 117, 124
Weinberg, Leslie 100, 133
Weinberg, Pessa 100
Welsh, David 173
Wiechers, Marinus 164
Wits *see* University of the Witwatersrand
Wittenberg, Gunther 136
Wittenberg, Martin 179, 180
Women's Defence of the Constitution League 78, 79 *see also* Black Sash
Wood, Cecil 103
World War II
   South African English and Afrikaans approach to 37
   Tobruk 37
Worrall, Denis 145, 150

Zacharias, PJK 193
Zulu, Alphaeus 148, 154, 161
Zulu, Vuminkosi 192